Tattooed Memories

Under the Canopy of the Vietnam War

Roger Allan Byer

Clunis Publishing

Clunis Publishing

ISBN 13: 978-1492774372
ISBN 10: 1492774375

Copyright © 2014 by Roger Allan Byer. All rights reserved. No part of this publication may be reproduced, stored in a retrieval system, or transmitted, in any form or by any means, electronic, mechanical, photocopying, recording or otherwise, without the prior permission of the author.

A desire to join the military is fulfilled when Roger Byer signs up with the US Army in 1968 during the height of the Vietnam conflict.

This decision takes the young Grenadian from the sun-soaked beaches of his island home to the jungles of wartime Vietnam and Cambodia.

Then, a decade later, after his military service is completed, fate reconnects Roger with his past, when on the morning of October 25 1983 the US Armed Forces invades his country, Grenada.

*

Reader Reviews

A coming of age story that grips the reader by the scruff of the neck as a Caribbean island boy's youthful idealism is confronted by the realities of life and sudden death in the jungles of Vietnam in 1970…..I read the story at one sitting, transported back in time by Roger's evocative style and vivid descriptions of action, boredom, and ultimately the totally unexpected encounter with his former unit in Grenada in 1983. Great stuff!

Allan Bierzynski F.C.C.A
Managing Director – Jonas Browne & Hubbard

"I call myself an eco-psychologist. I practice and teach martial arts and I've sat in meditation for hours in the icy rapids of the rivers of Chiang Mai in North-western Thailand. So I was anxious to read *Tattooed Memories*. I imagined it might provide some wilderness-type empowerment exercises I could share with my clients later.

By page ten I was completely broken, and I was only lying in bed reading. Though told with humour; though authored by a genuinely affable Caribbean soul, this story stops your heart with the unbearable savagery of war. Roger weaves military manoeuvre, social satire, whoredom and the mystical fragrance of ocean and jungle into an almost accidental philosophy of masculine evolution.

His heroism is as real as it is innocent, and Roger's storytelling skills are potent and clever. For anyone interested in the rigorous psychological transformation that is demanded of the shift from boyhood to manhood, especially in such extraordinarily challenging times as he faced, this book is a must read. It is one of the best works of contemporary Caribbean literature, by far."

Hazel Da Breo, PhD
Psychotherapist

Acknowledgements

My admiration and respect goes out to all of the "Skytroopers" of Charlie Company of the First Battalion of the Fifth Cavalry Regiment of the First Air Cavalry Division (Airmobile) of the United States Army, with whom I served in the III Corps area in the Republic of Vietnam from 1969 to 1970.

My fondest memories are reserved for Chief, F/O, Captain Vowell, Thanh, and Steve, the individuals closest to me during my tour of duty in that distant country. I hold them in special regard.

Colonel US Army (Ret) William Vowell, my Company Commander, and Lieutenant Dan Barlow, Charlie CO 3rd platoon leader in Vietnam, provided me with some vital reminders for the publication, information that only people who were there could adequately assist with.

My thanks and appreciation to Allan Bierzynski, John Albanie and Hazel Da Breo for their insight and advice. They, along with my niece Andrea Frederick read the manuscript in draft form. They were the first to read Tattooed Memories completely, and encouraged me not to let them be the last to do so.

Robert Sandiford edited this work initially. His technical guidance was important.

Angus Martin introduced me to the final route to publish, and kindly allowed me to use two of his photos of Grenada. Liam Martin was responsible for the advanced trimming and formatting of the manuscript. Liam was in fact, the final, final editor of *Tattooed Memories*.

*

DEDICATION

This book is dedicated to Mum, Bernard, Yvonne, Nigel, Aunty Olga and Uncle Len.

The writing of this book was inspired primarily by my wife, Ermine.

This book is for my daughters, Amanda and Stacey.

Tattoo: An evening drum or bugle signal calling soldiers to quarters.
  To mark the skin with an indelible pattern, by puncturing and inserting pigment.

The Oxford Reference Dictionary.

Preface

Roger, I remember you as a fine soldier and a marvelous human being. Over the years of my military service, I have told officers from a number of armies…Hungary, Finland, Chile and Argentina… about the young men of Charlie company, who always came through, who always carried out their duties to the best of their abilities, in times which were less than perfect. I admired all of you back then, and I still do today.

I have never served with soldiers who were your equals, and I mean that. Throughout twenty six (26) years of service in the US Army, Charlie company never appeared again. And that is the way I choose to remember all of you. You, Roger, and the men of that unit were very special, and I say this after two and a half decades of serving with soldiers everywhere.

I was privileged to command a total of five (5) companies. None of them were comparable to C/1-5th Cavalry. All of you have every right to be proud of your honorable and steadfast service.

Colonel William. O. Vowell US Army (Ret)
Former Company Commander
C/1-5th Cav, 1st Air Cavalry Div
Republic of Vietnam 1969-70

*

Introduction

The memories of my Vietnam War experience linger. Resonant and bittersweet, my recollections of those chapters in my life remain firmly embedded and very much alive in my consciousness today.

Persistent encouragement from my wife, Ermine, eventually persuaded me to record these experiences, mainly for my two daughters Amanda and Stacey. But I also wrote *Tattooed Memories* for the benefit of a few other people, friends and acquaintances of the period who may find the story of some interest to them.

This story unfolds late in that decade to challenge all decades, the 60's - a brief span in the greater scheme of time that introduced the world to incomparable people and events like The Beatles, Cassius Clay, Martin Luther King Jr., the Kennedys, Fidel Castro, the bay of pigs and the Cuban missile crises, the first moon landing, the first successful human heart transplant, Woodstock, and of course the Vietnam War.

The last was a conflict that succeeded in dividing the country over which it was fought, with devastating effects, while ultimately traumatizing and psychologically partitioning the mighty power that had sponsored the campaign for a democratic Vietnam in the first place, the United States of America.

This story is a true one, and the events are told as I remember them happening, blemishes and all (though the names of a few individuals have been changed to protect their identity). I was fortunate to have survived my journey from civilian to soldier, from a world of peace to a battle zone and back. Even as I write these words here, I can still see the small villages in Tay Ninh Province. I can smell the caustic odour of the cosmoline protective grease that we used to coat our M-16 rifles with to keep them from rusting in the sodden jungle.

And it is impossible for me not to still hear the gut-wrenching bark of my drill sergeant's voice, shouting us out of warm bunks at 0300 hours on a brooding winter's day during basic training at Fort Jackson in South Carolina, to partake in a nice five-mile run, with rifle and full battle kit, before breakfast.

Other sounds are more chilling: the whispered "*We have movement*" that signaled the enemy was out there, close, very close, was a warning from our point man through the gloom of a damp misty evening, as we rested, weary, on the side of a steep mountain trail somewhere deep inside of a triple canopied jungle, during a routine reconnaissance patrol.

These were trying times for me, to say the least, but they were also occasions for great hilarity and human bonding. As traumatic as life had a tendency to be, back then, I would not have wanted to be anywhere else than where it took me, for any reason whatsoever.

As I transferred my soldier's story from brain to paper, I often paused to smile at some precious gem of a recollection that came hurtling back at me out of my re-addressed past. I would then shake my head, sigh deeply, smile yet again, wipe my eyes and then write some more.

I invite you, readers, to travel back with me through the mists of time, on a somewhat bizarre journey, and let me reveal to you what happened to one young Caribbean man, who perhaps strayed a little too far from home one day.

TABLE OF CONTENTS

1. CONTACT 1
2. THIS IS WHAT I WANT TO DO, UNCLE LEN 12
3. FORT JACKSON RECEPTION CENTRE 19
4. BASIC COMBAT TRAINING 24
5. ADVANCED INDIVIDUAL TRAINING 55
6. MATERNAL INSTINCT AND THE LEATHER TALISMAN 63
7. I SMELL ASIA 66
8. BYER, GET YOUR SHIT TOGETHER – YOU'RE GOING OUT 70
9. LET ME TELL YOU ABOUT QUAN-LOI 75
10. POP SMOKE 84
11. A TYPICAL FORCE INSERTION 98
12. INCOMING 108
13. A BUNKER IN BINH LONG PROVINCE 110
14. XMAS DAY 1969 112
15. FIELD EXTRACTION 114
16. THE COMPANY COMMANDER AND THE MEDIC 117
17. MAD MINUTE 123
18. NIGHT AMBUSH 130
19. SERGEANT GRUMBLER AND THE WILD PIGS .. 141

- * PHOTOGRAPHS 145
- 20. SNAKE IN THE HOLE 181
- 21. MECHANICAL DINOSAURS 188
- 22. INTO THE TREES 191
- 23. I'M SORRY, THANH 194
- 24. BEING SHORT.. 198
- 25. POP FRAG 200
- 26. THE BLACK PANTHER... 205
- 27. VILLAGE OF THE DEAD 210
- 28. SICK CALL 213
- 29. FIRE SUPPORT BASE DAVID 217
- 30. THE OLD LADY AND THE BRACELET 242
- 31. THE JUNGLE- DON'T EVER TRUST HER............ 245
- **32. DOC, GET YOUR SHIT TOGETHER – YOU'RE GOING IN ... 247**
- 33. LOW QUARTER: UNDER THE FLOORBOARDS . 255
- 34. ARVN AND GENERAL GIAP 275
- 35. LOOKING FORWARD AT MYSELF......................... 279
- 36. LEAVING ON A JET PLANE 281
- 37. FORT DEVENS: DI DI MAU – TIME TO GO HOME 291
- 38. FULL CIRCLE: OPERATION URGENT FURY (1983) 308
- POSTSCRIPT 321
- GLOSSARY.. 323
- ABOUT THE AUTHOR 327

Chapter 1

Contact

I woke up on the morning of January 8, 1970 to a bright and deceptively peaceful morning. Birds were singing sweetly, and crickets were chirping their morning song. My unit, Charlie company of the First Battalion 5th Cav of the first Air Cavalry Division, had bivouacked overnight at the base of a nondescript hill in Tay Ninh province. This was our area of operations.

Our Company Commander, Captain Vowell, had received a radio message earlier from Battalion headquarters affecting our mission for the day. Our orders were to climb the hill to search for enemy ammunition caches and underground storage supply bunkers reported sited higher up on its unrevealing slopes.

That morning, while carrying out our ablutions, one of the troopers in our unit, a soldier by the name of Simon Plunkett tripped over his rifle which he had carelessly left lying on the ground. The safety lever was off, a display of gross clumsiness.

A discharged round echoed loudly across the valley floor and, more forebodingly, high up into the grey hillside overlooking our bivouac area like a brooding old man. The same hill that we were now preparing to climb to search for enemy munitions.

The damnable sound of that spent bullet took a long time to diminish. It was about 0630 hours. Plunkett was severely reprimanded by his platoon leader for his actions. Not that he had ever earned any stripes that could be lost to him. A guy who was never admired in the past for his soldiering techniques or general demeanour, he was, in military parlance a screw up. Never a team player, he had now evolved into a reckless threat.

We began ascending the hill at about 0700 hours and stopped for a break three-quarters of the way up, around 1000 hours. I was sitting beside a massive bomb crater. These craters, now water-filled mini lakes, had been created by massive assaults by B-52 strato-fortress heavy bombers from the U.S. Air Force's Strategic Air Command.

Their tremendous payloads of 1000-lb. bombs made the earth tremble, buckle and groan for miles around the actual impact areas. These bombing runs were called Arc-lights. They transformed a large part of the Vietnamese countryside into lake districts.

I was sitting with my back to a crater lake, my pack still on, wisecracking with F/O Lt Cleve Bridgman our Artillery Officer. His job description in the unit was that of a forward artillery observer. He was simply referred to as F/O.

A big, teddy-bear shaped, red faced and genial man, F/O liked to eat, chuckle and eat. He had just solicited a candy bar from me. "Come on, Doc, you owe it to yourself to share with old F/O ," he said. "Be a good lad and pass me a slab." He liked to rhyme too. He had already shared his own ration with himself earlier on, no doubt. Before I could answer F/O, somebody yelled out "Contaaacccct….!"

An indescribably loud wall of noise descended to smack me flush in the face, like an avenging wind. *We were being hit by the enemy*. Of the entire unimaginable experience that followed, if I had to single out the most unnerving factor of the following eight or so hell-orchestrated minutes of chaos and sheer mayhem, it would be the *noise* that was created by the unfolding battle. The noise of it!

While most of us were still resting on break, our lead platoon had moved out. The company stretched for about 100 meters from point to rear. By the time the whole unit got going, the front element would already have been moving for a while until we all caught up.

The lead platoon, the Third, had walked into a fortified bunker complex replete with machine guns. Mike Vickery, walking point, and John Rice, another trooper, were cut down immediately, both fatally wounded on the spot where they fell.

We later estimated that about sixteen North Vietnamese Army (NVA) soldiers had been waiting on the hilltop to ambush us. They were well concealed and securely dug in behind logs and sand-bagged emplacements; expertly camouflaged and almost impossible to observe from our approach up to their position.

They held the high ground while we had to come up to them in the open, unawares. And they had been tipped off almost four hours before, when our moron in uniform sent them a clear and irrefutable "here we come" signal by accidentally firing that fatal round from his rifle at the base of the hill. All they had to do was wait for us to spring their trap, which they did to great effect.

There is no way to aptly describe the feeling of being shot at, unless you could provide an actual practical demonstration to the uninitiated. Since this is more or less unlikely to happen, especially in times of peace, it is always difficult to convey with the desired accuracy or believability one of the most traumatizing events in a soldier's experience. This exposure to sudden death is nothing like the depictions found in most Hollywood action films of one sort or another. The average director's closest contact with a battleground may have been only the lifeless sets created in their own movie studios for the day's shoot.

But up here, on this ordinary hill…on this ordinary morning Time froze, or so it seemed. As we took the first hit, my world simply stopped turning. "Christ."

"What the fuck— We're hit!" The time it took me to get from my sitting position to flat on my chest was infinitesimal. This is the average human being's response to an assault from barking and viciously spitting AK-47 automatic rifles and RPG 40 rocket propelled grenade launchers, with crew served machine guns as a backup, hitting you suddenly and simultaneously with savage death delivering intent.

Harrowing firepower split the air with screaming lead and shrapnel. My pulse was racing, I was numb, I couldn't feel my face or fingertips, I couldn't catch my breath. I felt as though I was floating through the air in slow motion, like a giant balloon with a large red circle painted on my chest, advertising here I am—shoot me down.

Blinded by sweat and tears, everything was a blurring never-ending, kaleidoscopic nightmare. "I'm going to die" someone blurted out hysterically. Probably, I thought.

Tree limbs, flesh and bone, steel and metal, all succumb to this withering hail of hot lead. Grazing fire scythed down the hillside . And the noise of it, the noise. There was smoke and scattered debris everywhere. Everyone is yelling now -- the wounded, the frightened, the confused -- all of us up there on that hill.

"Bring up the fucking crew-served machine guns now," a platoon leader shouted to his men. These were the heavy belt-fed machine guns operated by a two-man crew.

Tattooed Memories

"Oh God! Fuck…I'm hit," said a radio operator.

"Second squad, return fire on line." Good, I thought, my senses still scrambled. It sounded like our Company Commander's voice directing our response. "We need an LAW up here now!" A light anti-tank weapon, that is. He was talking to the group of men who were pinned down further back down the hill. "First platoon, flank around to the right, try to breach them from over there."

Someone yelled the chilling words, "We have line ones…we have line ones." This meant some of our men were already dead. All radio operators were shouting various streams of frenzied requests and information. One Medevac helicopter was on station, another was inbound. Coordinates were being given for artillery fire support aimed at obliterating the offending hilltop and its defenders.

"No time for bracketing range-finding smoke rounds," our battle frenzied F/O urged the artillery battery. These were artillery shells fired by the artillery battery as range finders for our spotter F/O to pinpoint for them exactly where we needed their sustained fire power to be placed.

"What?" F/O continued. "Fuck you, too… Yes, now, not by fucking Xmas! Just fire for effect… give us everything you've got, man… people are dying up here… Yes, bring the rounds in on top of us… Yes, I authorize that." Our harried F/O was now shouting into his radio. "We're in heavy contact up here man, give us the goods… No, I'm not mad. If you have to, yes, but …for fuck's sake, do it!"

Another radio frequency squawked. A flight of navy F-4 Phantom jets, airborne from an offshore patrolling aircraft carrier, was on station overhead. "They want to know where we wanted them to put it." Welcome to the party, guys. We would let them make their target run-ins just as soon as we could manage to pull back down the hillside.

"MEDIC!" I was wrenched out of my stupor. Adrenalin and repetitive training started to overcome choking fear. Something audibly snapped in my brain. I grabbed my aid bag and my rifle, shucked my pack and began running up the hill, crouching low to the ground. Those guys up there were depending on me, they needed me, I reminded myself. Up the hill and into the flying shit that's what combat medics do, I had been told. I was finding out first-hand the veracity of this claim to fame at last.

Our company, dazed, down but not yet out, began to rally. Heavy return fire from our platoon hammered the bunker complex. Any tree, shrub, bush, or moving object between us and the bunker was soon cut to shreds, utterly vaporized.

Captain Vowell was suddenly everywhere, darting about like a demented soul, encouraging the men to get up and fight back. He looked like a snarling Viking warrior. Gut instinct would have already told this twenty-five-year-old combat veteran that he had already lost some of his men up here on this hill today.

And that noise! I couldn't hear myself think through the noisy uproar of the assault mixed with our deafening response. All I knew was that I was up and running. The other responding medics and I were in a frenzied state, trying to provide both immediate, stopgap trauma work, and trying to get people back down to relative safety where we could attend to them better.

Frequent, panicked yells of "MEDIC!" erupted now from everywhere across the battle-torn mountainside. "Oh God, I'm hit, Jesus, dear God." "MEDIC!" Then from another part of the hill, and another, I dart off to assist wherever I could, at the same time trying desperately to keep my head down and permanently attached to my neck.

Our Fire mission was on the way at last from Fire Support base Nancy. The artillery shells were already screeching overhead like runaway trains, hitting somewhere nearby, hopefully the enemy bunkers. They were falling a bit close to us, though. We would have to pull back down the hill real soon.

Two Blue Max Cobra helicopter gunships circled overhead. They wanted to know what side to engage from. We had to get off the hill to allow everybody on station to pulverize it into paper-making pulp. We gathered the dead and the wounded, and in a desperate, frenetic fashion, scrambled back down the hill away from the merciless firestorm.

"We need that Medevac chopper, right now!" someone shouted against a deafening wall of rage and fury as we retreated.

When we eventually made our way up to the bunkers, our dead were waiting for us. Mike Vickery's eyes had that vacant look, and his body lay spread-eagled like a deflated rag doll. This told me that he had died instantly, on the spot. As the point man for the lead platoon, he took the brunt of the first burst of enemy fire, sustaining chest and head wounds beyond anything any medic or surgeon would have been able to heal. I thank God that he would not have known what hit him.

John Rice, on the other hand, died in my arms. I tried feverishly to resuscitate him, working with a vigour that eventually slid into helplessness, because I could not save him. Half his jaw on the left side of his face had been shot away. He died of massive blood loss and the resultant shock. I cradled John's battered head in my lap, watching his brown eyes stare up at me as the light in them dimmed and then went out. The awful gurgling and rattling sounds from his throat eventually ceased, too, and there was a deafening silence. "MEDIC!".

I shook the fog from my head. I had to harness my grief. We had eight other guys who were wounded and in various stages of battlefield trauma, every one of them yelling "MEDIC!" at the same time. This included two of the five medics who were senior to me in the field. So I went back to work.

We worked on the wounded rapidly and professionally, to counter excessive bleeding and to try to prevent the critical onset of the effects of shock.

As we stumbled back down the hill yet again, the artillery shells from the fire mission that we had called up earlier were now raining down rounds on the hillside with an urgent and steady determination. We pulled back and gave them the necessary space to do their work.

My ears were ringing something awful, and everybody else was also half deaf from the explosive munitions' concussive blasts.

Well before we had completely pulled back off the hill, the F-4 phantom jets came screaming in with a vengeance. They tore across the skies making their long, sweeping target runs and dropping 500-lb napalm bombs. The mountainside reverberated with the awesome shock of this high-powered aerial bludgeoning.

The Cobra helicopter gunships circled patiently, awaiting their turn to unleash their rockets and gun-fire on the hill. They had the time because of their rotary turbine engine's fuel efficiency that allowed them to linger longer than the fixed wing Phantom jockeys could. The jets burnt fuel rapidly and could only remain in contact for a short while. The artillery fire mission's shells continued to pound the bunker complex with their customary dependability, and would continue to do so all night long.

Back at our morning's base camp, I had the gruesome task of supervising the loading and airlifting out of two body bags on the re-supply helicopter. I had filled out the appropriate forms and tagged the bags containing my comrade's bodies. I gave Captain Vowell their dog tags for safekeeping. He had the more burdensome responsibility ahead of him- to personally write home to their families.

Later that evening, as I lay on my poncho looking up at the comforting stars, my drifting mind floated down, all the way back into my body. It had remained outside all along, remote and detached, while watching my initiation into the hell of combat. I was drifting down from an adrenaline spiked high after my initial experience of sudden violence and death.

The grim reaper had apparently given me a pass today, I imagine he was preoccupied with some other poor suckers' predetermined doom. The atmosphere surrounding our camp was heavy. The air smelled of burnt foliage and cordite, smoke drifted by everywhere.

I was numb, tired, and drained of feeling, but somehow my spirit was still intact, and I was not just grateful but excited to be alive. I had survived the firefight, and that felt good. I had also performed my duties under fire, and I had responded to my combat training competently enough, it seemed.

You never knew whether you could or would do what was expected of you until that day arrived.

That day had arrived.

Captain Vowell, the Company Commander, was by my side.

"Doc, you did a damn fine job today," he said. "This was your first contact, wasn't it? Your baptism under fire?"

"Yessir, it was," I responded. My chapped lips trembled slightly, and I felt emotions that had been seeking release begin to well up inside of me.

"Well, son, I'm putting you in for the Army Commendation medal for gallantry and heroism under ground-fire, he said. You saved a few of the men's lives today with your response under hostile fire. Good job, young man."

"Thank you, sir. I was only doing my duty like everybody else."

"Also"- he continued, as though I had not spoken -"you are now the senior Company medic, so get your stuff together, you're in the Headquarters platoon now."

"But sir," I mumbled, "there are two other medics more senior to me…."

"Get your stuff, soldier." I gathered my stuff.

That evening, Private Plunkett was quietly spirited out amid the recovery melee on a re-supply helicopter. Probably by some quick-thinking officer. As if he could have slept out there among us anyway. He had, by his unprofessional misconduct, before we had even ascended that hill, effectively sealed the fate of Mike Vickery, a native of Tennessee, and John Rice, an Indianapolis preacher's son from the third platoon. Both of them were dead by 10:15 that morning.

These men were my first battlefield casualties in my first firefight. It was the first time that someone had died in my arms, resisting my desperate attempts to save them. Nothing could have been done to help either of these guys because their wounds were grievously fatal. Both John and Mike were hit at close range, directly. But the suddenness and finality of their losses would continue to weigh heavily on my mind for a long, long time.

Two of our platoon medics were also wounded in the ensuing battle. This effectively resulted in my becoming the senior company medic. I started the day off as the most junior of the five medics in the unit. By nightfall, I was in charge. Just like that. This was the Army, there's a war going on, and this was the way these things tend to happen in combat situations.

The sound of the fire mission's artillery shells passing over my head, one round every six or seven minutes hitting the top of the hill, was strangely soothing, making me drowsy. I slept fitfully as the barrage continued throughout the night.

At daybreak we went back up the hill to make our sweep - and mop-up operation of whatever or whoever was left up there in the bunker complex. Everyone, including the new senior company corpsman, fired their weapons in a standard "on line" infantry formation as we ascended the mountain yet again.

Chapter 2

This is What I Want to do, Uncle Len

I lay on the beach at the old Normandy Hotel in San Juan, Puerto Rico, with my mother and my stepfather, Len. It was November 1968, I was nineteen years old, and we were on holiday. It was a sun-drenched tropical setting, but that wasn't really the reason I was there.

I myself was from the small English-speaking island of Grenada, located in the southern Caribbean Sea close to Trinidad and Venezuela, population 110,000 at the time. I had recently completed my GCE (General Certificate of Education) Cambridge exams at my secondary school. Under our British system of education, this was equivalent to a US high school diploma.

Back home, I was a pretty good sports cyclist. I also rode a Honda motorbike, had a steady girlfriend, hiked, and explored mountains and lakes with friends. I sailed, swam and did my share of nineteen-year-old partying during holiday breaks. I was a normal lad in most ways.

I was told that my ancestors had come to the West Indies from two small villages. One of them was located in West Africa, and the other, some place near Aberdeen in

Scotland. Be that as it may, I only knew for sure where *I* was from–that indescribably beautiful island called Grenada.

My biological father had died when I was five. I was the youngest of three children. My mother had remarried, to an American, Uncle Len, as he would forever be called by our family. He was a veteran of World War II and later a stockbroker on Wall Street, but had retired early and sensibly, to the islands.

As a small boy, I was totally enamoured with anything military or anyone wearing a uniform. When British Royal Navy warships paid courtesy calls to Grenada, my friends Michael, Ian, Georgie, Champy, and I would go racing down the hill to the docks to see the sailors as they came ashore. We waited, excited and impatient for the official announcement of which days the warships would be opened to visitors.

We followed the sailors around St. George's tirelessly, like devoted puppies, until the ships weighed anchor at the end of their brief visits. Their uniforms made them seem larger than life, and filled our heads with fantasies of battles at sea and boarding parties.

My school had a cadet corps, which I joined when I was older. But maybe the stronger influence came from the two local movie houses that provided reel after reel of all the thrilling heroics a local boy with a passion for uniforms could desire. War movies, not surprisingly to me, were always the most popular fare.

I found out later in the service that the impressive John Wayne approach to solving military problems was better left and more suited to the silver screen. At the movies it was tremendously entertaining, like the man himself, and everybody always got to go home for their dinner, safe and sound in both body and mind, after an hour or two of thrills.

As I relaxed on the beach in Puerto Rico, I had been mulling over an idea that had been with me for a few days. The thought was not entirely new but was about what I really wanted to do with my life, and I was thinking maybe it was now time to actually do something about it.

I turned to face Uncle Len, who was lying peacefully on his beach chair, quietly snoozing; always a calm and collected person, that man. "Lenny, I want to join the US Army," I said, just like that. It was out, I had played my hand.

It was 1968, the height of the Vietnam conflict, a war that was escalating daily with ever increasing intensity. Earlier in the year, American armed forces fought the major Tet offensive at the Hue citadel against invading North Vietnamese forces. The outcome of this dogged encounter between two equally determined foes had been visually recorded, blow by blow, by the press.

Television broadcasts and newspaper articles for the first time took war live and direct from the field into people's living rooms and dining rooms. Although there was little if any of the romance that those John Wayne movies had depicted, I still wanted to join up.

Uncle Len took off his sunglasses, looked at me fixedly for a while then said, "Well, Roger, if you're sure that's what you want, I'll help you. You may be able to join up right here, if you want to." Puerto Rico was and still is a US territory.

I stared right back. "Yes, this is what I want to do Uncle Len." That was what I said to him. I was a "small-island boy." Maybe I was looking for adventure or my own way to experience the world. I didn't know what I would find—or what awaited me in the years ahead--but at the time I felt that this was the way for me to find out. I was only nineteen.

The day after agreeing to help me, Lenny and I took a cab to Fort Buchanan, the US Army Installation in Puerto

Rico. We inquired about the possibility of my enlisting right away. The response from the enlistment officer was quite favourable.

The fact that Uncle Len was a US citizen and a veteran himself helped with my eventual and expeditious acceptance. We were told, yes, I could be processed at the fort in San Juan, once I satisfied the necessary medical and aptitude requirements.

At eight a.m. sharp the next day, Mum and Uncle Len dropped me off at Fort Buchanan by taxi. It was raining heavily when we arrived at the citadel like structure located on an imposing promontory overlooking the old city of San Juan. Uncle Len handed me a five-dollar bill to "hold in my pocket" and shook my hand as men do. Mum hugged and kissed me between tears as women will.

I could feel the uncertainty in her embrace, but she was fatalistic about this whole army thing, because she had known, as only mothers can, that I had been waiting for this moment, like a racehorse at the starter's gate. She had never tried to discourage me. I was grateful to her for that. When I went off eventually, it was with my family's blessings, and their hopeful prayers as well.

I stood on the steps of the fort's entranceway feeling slightly abandoned as I watched my parents' taxi speed off. They were taking a flight back home to Grenada that same morning. I stared at their cab until it disappeared around a corner. I sighed, I was jittery. The icy breath of an emerging panic reached out to choke me. Roge, what have you done now? I thought to myself. But just as quickly I shrugged off the self-doubt.

I entered the fort and joined the first of a million long lines that I would have to get accustomed to joining. Queuing would become a regular pastime to be suffered with as much stoicism as a man could manage for the next three years of my life. The next twenty-four hours, however, were spent with only short breaks for food and the bathroom while completing a myriad of aptitude and IQ tests. Extensive and intrusive medical examinations were thrown in for good measure. This being the army, the probing continued on and on with no explanations of any kind given about anything--to anyone. "Go to that room there and drop your pants, someone will attend to you shortly," a detached sounding voice would order dismissively.

Day and night blurred into one homogeneous state, one tiring test followed closely by another and another ... In the physical examination, a stranger commanded you to bend over and "spread your proverbial cheeks." And this did not refer to the facial ones. I was so damn tired and confused by the end of it. All those banal tests and mind-numbing questions. Brain-teaser exams that required repositioning circles, eliminating angles and matching colours. After a while, it all blended into a foggy trail that led you listlessly and inexorably to join yet more endless lines.

In addition to this fumbling about in a maze, I experienced a most unusual problem at Fort Buchanan. I had to raise my hand each and every time the testing invigilator began to rattle off the written examination instructions to us in rapid fire Spanish, a practice he adhered to at the beginning of each round of tests.

Whenever he opened his mouth to speak, I pre-empted him by holding up my hand, beseeching, *"English, please!"* This humble request immediately brought the proceedings to a halt and initiated a firestorm of moans, chesty groans, loud "maricons," snarls and baleful glances, all shot with unvarnished hostility in my general direction from the other two hundred or so Spanish- speaking Puerto Rican candidates who were taking the same written Army entrance qualification tests as I.

Talk about isolation? I felt like a Lone Ranger without his Tonto. Be that as it may, the instructions were given in English.

I did quite well on the battery of written tests, unlike quite a number of my disillusioned colleagues who did not.

"I am afraid that your height and weight does not correlate, making you therefore disqualified." I was standing in front a pimply faced, gnomish looking official who was mumbling at me. Physically tired and mentally weary, it took me a while to process the stream of words he spilled my way. "I am what? What was that again, sir?"

I tried to fight off the veil of tiredness that had descended upon me, whilst thinking, my parents have left, I only had $5 in my pocket. What was I to do?

The world weary clerk, who looked as drained as I was, now impatiently explained to me that, for uniformity purposes (this being the Army), my measured height of 6 feet must correspond to a weight of at least 150 lbs. I weighed in, I was sternly advised, at an inadequate 146 lbs. What was I to do? The guy then looked up at me and pointed down the corridor towards a water cooler with as much indifference as he could muster. "Go and drink as much water as you can, and then come back here and weigh again." He then dismissively lowered his gaze to his waiting forms.

I looked around to see if anyone was snickering at this. But all I heard was "Move, man, hurry to fuck up, you're holding up the damn line here. Move your sorry ass along, *maricon*!" I slouched down to the water cooler, hope draining away on a rapidly ebbing tide. I drank and drank, and drank some more even after I was well past the point of bursting. I was drowning, drowning. Shit! *What in the world was I doing here?* This was pure madness.

I waddled back up the lonely hallway under the unforgiving eyes of my Spanish-speaking buddies. I approached the scale. I weighed, but I could not bring myself to look at the reading. Quasimodo scribbled something on my form. Finished writing, he looked up, handed me my papers then cast his eyes beyond me, wearily sighing. "Next!"

I looked down at my paper. I was in. I experienced there and then the same sense of relief that Atlas must have felt when he eventually shrugged. I had started to suspect that the whole thing was a plot hatched by the humourless Puerto Ricans to keep me out, just because I had caused half of them to fail the written exams.

We were driven to the San Juan Luis Muñoz Marin Airport and boarded a waiting C-130 Army cargo transport plane. Rumours (a staple of army life) had it that we were going to Fort Campbell Kentucky, to Fort Benning, Georgia, or to Fort Hamilton, New York.

The only thing we knew for sure was that we were leaving Puerto Rico for the US mainland at long last, and that we were in the army now.

Chapter 3

Fort Jackson Reception Centre

We landed in South Carolina in shirt sleeves. We were in the Southern U.S but it was November, and wintertime. But who had time to think of clothes? When I left Grenada, it was originally for a ten-day holiday in sunny Puerto Rico.

We were all freezing our cojonés off as we were trucked into the sprawling United States Army Reception Center at Fort Jackson. It was 0400 hours in the morning, and we all had our eyes glued and noses pressed to the windows. What we could make out was total symmetry. Wooden barracks freshly painted and precisely lined up. Pristine, perfectly crafted streets and pathways. Concrete walkways neatly aligned. There was exactitude and obsessive uniformity in everything we saw.

Every lawn was manicured, and each blade of grass seemed to be of similar height. The immaculately groomed sentry on guard duty at the gate looked unreal. His boots were polished to a glossy sheen, and his gloves were absolutely white. Everything was in place except us, and that incongruity was about to be ruthlessly corrected in very short order, too.

The process of dehumanization swung into full gear as we were shouted off our trucks by serious looking drill sergeants.

They were the bane of all recruits. If we ever succeeded in our training, we would have them to thank in a huge part for it. They would make their world our world by turning us into soldiers.

A drill sergeant was a career soldier of enlisted rank, somewhere between twenty-five and forty-five years old. Commonly known as a *"lifer"*, the army was his home, and he would be promoted up through the enlisted ranks to as high as maybe staff sergeant E-6 grade, or to sergeant first class E-7. He would spend at least two tours of duty in whatever war his country happened to be engaged in during his military career. He would complete twenty or thirty years in the service of his nation, before he was eventually through with his soldiering career.

His formal pre-army education would consist of little more than high school. He was strong willed, determined and lived strictly by the army's rules prescribed for a loyal soldier. He would likely, but not exceptionally be Black or Hispanic. He would have undergone Drill Instructor (DI) training at some opportune time between his overseas tours.

He was in fact the person who created and developed his nation's fighting men by first busting the ass of every recruit put into his "care"; by erasing the ways of civilian life from their very being and instilling the necessary attributes required to perfect the soldiers he could craft. He had to first break you down in order to build you back up, and it was that breaking down part that really hurt.

What these drill sergeants saw as we jumped off the trucks at the Reception Center predictably raised their blood pressure a few notches. Their nostrils flared at the sight of us. A bunch of long-haired, spineless, jelly-belly, soft-ass mama's boys. Civilian farts.

They surrounded us like hunters stalking game, or vultures circling carrion. We shivered from uncertainty and dreadful anticipation. They launched themselves at us with a punishing vigor. Did I fail to mention that they were men who enjoyed their work?

"Yes, you lily-white motherfucker." This from a very black DI to a very white, shivering boy from Tennessee. "Your ass is grass, and I'm the mower," a very burly Hispanic DI informed a hapless kid from Milwaukee. "What the fuck in heaven's name are you looking at, doofus. Did I give you permission to observe here?"

Another demonic looking DI walked slowly up and down our formation, shaking his head as he examined our ranks. He suddenly bellowed, "What a bunch of sick looking faggots. When we finish with you lowlifes, even your mamas won't recognize you."

We were treated to choruses of these welcoming remarks for about an hour, until we begin to get the disturbing picture of who was in charge and who else happened to be earmarked for some real rough shit for the next couple of months.

Having worked up a sweat, the exhausted DI's left us standing in formation as they scurried indoors to escape the cold of winter and to enjoy some coffee. Uninvited, we remained outside where it was winter too, musing about that same beverage that we once took for granted. We shuffled about and huddled closely together in the freezing weather. Besides the temperature, which seemed to be dropping by the second, we were hungry, disoriented and frightened. Some of the guys were already crying openly from the sheer frustration of the situation.

We never realized (until much later) that a very important aspect of our training had already begun out here on that cold and depressing morning. It was called dealing with pressure. Then someone groaned "Oh God, here they come again" as the DI's came back outside, unfairly refreshed and energized. "You mamas' boys hungry?" They taunted us as they marched us into a large building that was a mess hall with a seating capacity of about a thousand. As we hit the doorway, the warm, food scented air sent my weak and queasy stomach into an excited turmoil. But this is America. The very same guys who were blubbering and dying outside moments ago were soon relentlessly plowing through huge helpings of cereal, bacon and eggs, sausages, home fries, biscuits, milk, gallons of coffee, and even tea. I was just thankful for something hot to sip on. In our barracks, we were shown our bunks. Everyone immediately and wearily collapsed onto their designated beds.

My faltering eyelids had descended halfway downwards towards a deserving blink when there was an ominous crackle from loudspeakers strategically fitted into the ceiling of the barracks, directly above our heads.

An almighty blast of cursing exploded from out of these blaring boxes. The Drill Sergeants, threatening us with mayhem if we don't get our lazy arses up and at it. "Get to fuck up now, you sorry pieces of shit! How much rest do you little pansies need? You dip-shits think that you're on the French Riviera? Fall out! Fall out! Get your asses in formation outside of the barracks now, now, *now*!"

This was, by now, too much for some of the guys, and about six of the terrified ones bolt for the facilities' gates. I didn't know where they thought they were going. Running away from inside of here was now a Federal offense--we had taken the oath of allegiance earlier--and the FBI was routinely involved in rounding up potential deserters.

We spent the next four or five days getting our uniforms and gear ready for Basic Combat Training, taking more physicals and orientation classes, briefings, and lectures. With time, and survival, I developed a healthy respect for how the army's psychological program conditioned us. I came to see clearly what they were doing to us.

It made a lot of sense. They had intentionally made Reception Center such a hell, that all we could think of was getting out of there to report to our Basic Training units. Keen to get going where the real soldier training began. Of course, this would turn out to be another eight weeks of hell too, but at least it would be a different kind of hell.

Chapter 4

Basic Combat Training

A truck convoy took us up a hill to our basic training unit. In my case, it was to Company E, First Battalion, First Brigade—a unit with barracks located at the top of a steep hill ominously called Drag Ass Hill.

Fort Jackson was a huge military training complex of 52,600 acres, some 82 square miles. It was three-quarters the size of the island-nation I had come from, and contained more technology than my little island home could ever dream of. It was a virtual city onto itself. It was built on a hill overlooking a rolling expanse of pineland in the Congaree sand hills six miles east of Columbia South Carolina, and was named after General Andrew Jackson, a native of the Palmetto State, and the seventh President of the United States.

The fort had 53 firing ranges, 21 target detection ranges, and 18 train fire ranges. There were also churches, athletic fields, swimming pools, service clubs, golf courses, civilian taxi and bus services, banks, credit unions, a commissary, a hospital, hobby and craft shops, gymnasiums, fire and police services. It was a beautifully situated, well-operated and efficiently maintained facility. It was where boys were turned into finely honed fighting machines.

As our truck ground to a halt, I was about to enter a world of fitness, discipline, and knowledge acquiring that was unmatched in its sphere of training anywhere in the world.

I was about to learn the true meaning of the words strength, endurance, team spirit, and self-confidence as I learned to sweep, mop, wash dishes, and make a bunk so tightly that a coin would bounce off it when dropped from above. I learned to shoot (mandatory qualification with the M-16 rifle), run, dodge and jump over obstacles, and digest all manner of field craft, map reading, and hand-to-hand combat.

I would run five miles with a loaded pack on my back while carrying my weapon at port arms, yelling hoarsely, "The spirit of the bayonet is to kill," as they taught us how to best impale an enemy combatant. I mastered the art of polishing boots until their reflection threatened to blind an observer. All this while also learning to march and pitch a tent at night by the light of a flashlight, to fully disassemble and reassemble an M-16 automatic rifle in seven seconds (blindfolded that is), and to use a field radio in all conditions, day and night. All this in eight weeks.

Our driver had not yet fully engaged the handbrake on our truck when a giant, red-headed dervish from Hades stuck his massive head into the back of the vehicle and, without introducing himself, started screaming incoherently at us, spittle flying.

"Out, out, out, you sorry pieces of shit, get to fuck out here! Move it, move it, move it! What are you lazy, panty waist wallflowers waiting for--an invitation? Get to fuck down here now!" Despite all that had happened before at the Reception Centre, I was stunned by this premeditated onslaught "Move your asses, troopers.... Line up, line up, let's see some kind of order here now!"

The fifteen of us in my vehicle tried to get off the truck as fast as we could to please our tormentors. Unfortunately, all at once. In our panic, our heavy duffle bags fell all over the place, tripping us. The terrible shouting from outside escalated. "Move, move, move! Form up here, scumbags! Get your asses in line formation, now," a sergeant yelled. In line what? we wondered. What to do with our duffle bags. Let them drop at our feet or try to hold on to them? Who knows anymore?

There were about twelve Drill Instructors circling our truck, no doubt attracted by the scent of fresh meat. One of my friends, Rick Dalzell, had fallen while trying to scamper off the truck, and blood ran from a cut on his top lip as he tried to lick it away. Everybody was running every which way. The DI's took their classic in-your-face posture with us. They were dressed in their oh-so-neat uniforms and their impossibly shiny boots.

They wore their Yogi Bear wide-brim hats with the straps tightly bound around their chins. You couldn't see their eyes. Somehow, my quivering group of recruits had managed to line up in front of our company's barracks. "You little civilian shitheads think this is a joke, eh?" yells one of them.

We were introduced to our Company Commander, Captain Rowley, a buzz cut, clean-shaven, unsmiling man who graced us with an ultra-brief "welcome to E/1/1" and then left our ranks as suddenly as he had appeared from somewhere.

We then met First Lieutenant Weir, a pompous, Ivy League college man, and Second Lieutenant Hodges, probably a reservist as he looked more relaxed. Both of these officers were in their early twenties and revealed their patent inexperience as they walked around sniffing the air and parodying what they'd seen the marauding DI's do. For them, it didn't work quite as well.

Our Platoon Sergeant was Sgt Rivera. Short, and dark in both thoughts and complexion, he was a Mexican-American, bantam-sized package of wired intensity. He had an aggressively loud voice that enjoyed its own staccato resonance. The kind that would have made his own wife and children address him as Sergeant even at home.

Later in the scheme of things I would find Herr Rivera to be a fair minded man. But this was all very much further down the road from where I stood now experiencing a chill that was not weather related. There were twelve other DI's assigned to our training company. They ranked from corporal to staff sergeant E-6. In our minds they ranged in temperament from maniacal to sadistic.

"OK, you civilian shitheads, there are a few rules that you need to familiarize yourselves with around here," barked Sgt Rivera. "First and foremost, there are only two modes of transportation on this post. Whenever you leave a building, you will either run or you will crawl on your belly to your destination. There will be no walking whatsoever for the next eight weeks of your life.

"Next, whenever a cadre member tells you to *drop,* you do so instantly. Which is to say that you fall expeditiously to the ground and prepare yourself in the prone position, hands fully extended, feet straight back and your body supported by your toes and your fingertips--only! You assume this position, that is also known as the push-up posture, and then ask the question: How many, drill sergeant?"

Doing push-ups became a way of life for us. Just about every human contact with a DI automatically began and ended with the charming word "Drop." The number of push-ups we were ordered to do ranged from ten to two hundred. You counted loudly as you went along--"97, Drill Sgt, 98, Drill Sgt"--as every muscle in your body screamed in profound agony.

Occasionally, you were left wilting on the deck until your arms began to tremble, twitch, and buckle, then your brain rationalized, – screw this! as your arms gave out completely under your own weight. It sometimes got worse when you were left down prone and trembling on the frozen ground, and had to explain to a passing DI from another unit what the fuck you were doing *lying down* there when everyone else on the compound was busy doing pushups.

A scrawny little corporal on the cadre, who had a limp and an attitude to match, told about three of us recruits that if we ever thought we saw his car passing on the highway (about a mile away), we should drop and give him fifty of our best push-ups. Out of the blue one day, someone said, "Is that Corporal Jones' car going by out there?" We weren't sure. One of us replied, "Let's not take any chance, man." We all dropped and knocked them off before carrying on.

This was the beginning of the process of forging the necessary discipline and mindset that enabled a soldier to unquestioningly follow his leaders into harm's way at the issuing of an order.

The immediate area of our company training facilities comprised our living quarters. These were two-storey wooden barracks of World War II vintage. Old, but very clean and always freshly painted--cream and green. Each of the two barracks' floors contained two rows of twelve double bunk beds. A large, wooden footlocker was afforded each man for his possessions. The squad leader, a sergeant or a corporal, normally had his own small, private room located on the ground floor, where he could best control the disconsolate herd.

The "Orderly Room," the Company Headquarters, was just around the corner, a smaller building that housed the offices for the brass. The Company Commander's and the First Sergeant's offices were located here. The Charge of Quarters (CQ) function was operated from this location. This was a twenty-four hour job that controlled all aspects of life in our training unit, with a non-commissioned officer (NCO) on duty, and a CQ runner, one of us expendables, stationed there to run messages over the length and breadth of the extensive compound all day and all night long.

The mess hall was around another corner. It was a smaller, neater establishment of about twenty-five four-man tables. We ate in rotation with other companies but were always able to get in and out expeditiously for our three squares a day. Because Fort Jackson was specifically a training base, everything else was away from our quarters. What we couldn't run to, we were grudgingly driven out to in trucks.

We were awakened at 0300 hours each day for a five-mile warm-up run. Extensive calisthenics followed for about an hour. As you ran, you passed other units doing the same thing, running. Everyone sang morale-elevating, military-type ditties along the way. The singing actually helped to take your mind off the cold. It was still dark and frigid at that time of the morning, even if lights were on everywhere, and the place was huffing with activity. Over twenty-five thousand people lived here, spread across a housing plant of about two thousand buildings.

As I mentioned, our barracks were situated at the top of a hill called Drag Ass Hill. Every time we left and returned, it was steeply down and strenuously up. Our rifle training range was located nearby –(some five miles away). So we ran out in the morning, spent the day on the range learning the most basic and necessary trade of the infantryman, then ran back the five miles in the evening to our barracks.

Needless to say, not every civilian was born to run 10 miles a day in full uniform and boots while carrying a rifle. Some of our guys were plainly too damn fat to even properly walk one mile on a flat surface at this stage. Every evening, a few of us fitter guys had to drop back and literally carry some of the out-of-shape guys, drag them up the hill, hence its colourful name. The fact that I had been a competitive racing cyclist up until the time I had left home to joined the US Army, and had trained hard every day on my bike, paid me enormous dividends. I owed fellow training cyclists back home - Pokehead, Champ, Caca Genie, Copperthroat, the Evans brothers, Ian, Roger Steele - and Grand Anse, a debt I'd never be able to repay for all the strenuous, repetitive laps we rode around a track at high speed for long periods, all that "iron" that they made me eat every evening down at the Morne Rouge circuit.

Not only could I run, too, but for rather long distances. This was noticed early by the DI's, and I was appointed the company's "guide-on bearer": I carried our company colours (a pennant) at the front of the column whenever we marched, or more likely, ran, somewhere.

The D.I's had seen it all before. They stepped aside from hounding the poor, fat, struggling bastards they had been running alongside and haranguing at the base of the hill to allow us fitter guys to help them.

This was all part of the "buddy system". We were already unknowingly developing something here that in soldiering journals was called unit cohesiveness.

"Get your lard ass up that hill, fat boy" would morph swiftly into "OK, Byer and Dalzell, take over this gross piece of shit, but if he falls down again, his ass will definitely sleep out here tonight." We dragged our buddy up the hill with us.

He was one of us, and we'd been through Reception and all that shit together. We would not leave him behind.

Some of them, though, just could not make it and simply disappeared leaving an empty bunk to be discovered the following morning. They went AWOL (absent without official leave) from the barracks during the night.

These frustrated strugglers were usually rounded up and recycled to the next training class behind us, to do it all over.

We usually never saw those guys again. We learned our individual army serial number by heart RA (for Regular Army) with eight digits then that was made more difficult by adding our social security numbers, so that our number became seventeen digits to memorize.

One morning, we were marched down to the armoury, where we were issued our M-16 rifles. Finally, my own M-16. This beautiful, lightweight automatic weapon made by the Colt Company fired a 20-round magazine (5.56mm) on full automatic. It weighed only 7 lbs and was a great modern little ass kicker of a weapon. It was the standard issue, US armed forces military weapon for the infantryman. I signed for my Black Beauty. It had a unique smell similar to burnt almonds. I could not contain my feeling of raw exhilaration. This is what I came here for.

We cleaned our weapons at least four times a day. During the next seven or so weeks, we learned to disassemble and reassemble this weapon blindfolded in seconds and practiced shooting at green and brown camouflaged pop-up targets in the open forests, from intentionally staggered distances of 70 to 300 meters. No old time bulls eye ranges were used anymore. Only ranges equipped to provide modern automatic rifle, multiple target training.

Those green-and-brown, camouflage-coloured electronic targets popped up at any distance, and you had to quickly adjust your range vision to see them, and then fire accurately to score hits. Firing either single round or with automatic bursts as the specific drill called for. Every recruit had to qualify with his weapon in order to successfully graduate as a soldier from infantry basic training. It was a fundamental necessity. For those who went overseas to fight a war, this rifle would become an extension of their arms.

The drill was a simple one. The more successive target hits you scored in the variety of weaponry training exercises on the ranges, with the specified amount of rounds allowed for each drill, the higher your final level of qualification at the end of the exercises.

The targets had an annoying delayed reaction response built into them. When you fired at a pop up a distant 300 meters away and nothing happened, you always began to fret just at the very moment the lazy target began its reluctant descent.

The highest qualification was Expert rating 90 to 100 hits, followed by Sharpshooter 80 to 90 hits and Marksman 70 to 80 hits on the range. One had to qualify at the very least as a Marksman in order to graduate from the course. I worked really hard on the range and as a result of my efforts made Expert with the M-16 at the end of our live-fire exercises.

The Physical Combat Proficiency Test, or PCPT, was made up of five individual events that accentuated stamina and agility. The one-mile run, the 40-yard low crawl (on belly), the run-dodge-and-jump, the horizontal ladder, and the man carry, where you carry someone of similar weight to yourself on your back as you completed a 100-yard dash. These were in fact the most important tests for graduation, as points were awarded for speed and completion rates towards overall performance.

My friend Rick Dalzell and I, with some other like-minded pain lovers, went out in our free time on the winter evenings and pushed ourselves hard for two hours on the horizontal ladder and the run-dodge-and-jump course. Some of the other guys thought we were crazy and gung-ho, but this extra effort would pay off for a few of us later.

When you lived in close proximity to 100 men who started their day running at 0300 hours and ended it by running at 1800 hours, there would be a pressing need for some shower activity on a daily basis. One day we tried to bathe Joe Price after lights out. Joe was a farmer from Minnesota. A very nice guy, he did his job in a quiet way and never bothered anyone, but he did not like water. Farmer Joe refused to bathe and was not open to any form of subtle persuasion. Nor was he partial to any of the ploys that were concocted weekly to encourage him to drift towards the shower stalls.

I was responsible with five other guys for bundling Joe out of his bunk and shoving this hulk towards the showers. Joe weighed about 230 lbs. Not of fat, like the hapless Drag Ass Hill groaners, but of plough-generated muscle, as we found out to our detriment.

Joe fought back, of course, wriggling and lashing out. "Put me to fuck down. What the fuck you guys think you're doing? Stop!" he protested.

We had, by that time, somehow pushed and prodded the uncooperative farmer halfway into the nearest shower stall. We couldn't undress the spitting behemoth, so we tried, out of sheer desperation, to bathe him with his clothes on.

Having had enough of our feeble attempts at cleansing him, Joe erupted with a roar and literally threw the six of us off him, casually, up and over his head, and painfully down onto our disorganized asses. He plowed out of the showers, grumbling, shaking his great wet massive head on his way back to his overturned bed. Failed mission.

We went out daily to the close combat range for our bayonet training. What this entailed was the vigorous thrusting out of our rifle at a prop of a human silhouette, making ambitious forward and upward motions with the bayonet. This was a long, sharp detachable knife-shaped instrument that was attached to the business end of our rifle.

Every time we made a ballet-like thrust forward, we had to yell at the top of our lungs, "The spirit of the bayonet is to kill!" Our friendly neighborhood DI's, never satisfied, would march up and down our sweating ranks yelling encouraging cajolery like "I can't hear you girls. Louder!" "What did you sweethearts say? *Louder!*" We then repeated the dogmatic chant over and over as we grimaced and thrust away at the perpetually bored and uncaring cutouts in the December morning chill. It all seemed so pointless, until I got it.

Admittedly, it did take me a while to get it. This was because we humans could often hear things stated repeatedly without the message ever fully registering. But when this one finally did, I clearly understood the morbid rationale behind our early morning dance lessons. The bayonet drill was not about thrusting. It was intended to drive home the message that if we ever used our bayonet against an enemy in combat, we were required to stick it firmly into his chest and twist our wrist around sharply until he was dead from our action.

It was brutal and it was dirty, but it was also reality. We weren't the Boy Scouts of America learning to tie knots here. Our training was about combat - war and death, not building campfires. That meant learning how to kill people efficiently on the battlefield, and all of our training would have been useless if we refused to understand this fact very early in the program.

* * * * *

"Anybody here want to drive a truck?"

"A what?"

"A big vehicle with four wheels, birdbrains," yelled the impatient duty NCO as he ambled into our barracks one early morning. Every day, some of us recruits were taken from our training schedule to perform irregular jobs, like KP (kitchen police) duty. Besides being responsible for keeping our barracks and general area clean with a thrice daily "police call," where everyone lined up and went through the area picking up every errant match, toothpick, or piece of paper- wrapping of any kind not belonging or firmly attached to somebody, we had other extra duties that were sometimes fun.

"Me, Drill Sergeant! Me, Drill Sergeant! I want to drive." A number of us raised our hands as if we were in primary school. We were a bunch of little boys sometimes playing at being men. Ten of us were chosen. We hopped into the back of the large two-and-a-half-ton truck waiting outside, and off we went.

Fort Jackson was a massive facility, so for the purpose of this exercise we were driven up a three mile long road with a low rise. The truck was stopped along the way; someone from the back hopped out, went to the front, and drove the truck from first gear through the other gears, downshifted back, hopped out and got into the back. Then somebody else did the same thing. "Next!" the transportation corporal yelled.

That was the test for the army's truck driver's license. It was a very short one. Not surprisingly, everyone passed it in one sitting.

A few mornings later, I was sent to the motor pool to collect a truck to bring back to the company area to drive for the mess hall detail that day. It was wintertime, very cold, and dark at 0330 hours in the blasted AM. What was I doing here, Lord? I often asked myself.

When I got down to the massive motor pool facility, I had to find my truck from about 500 similar vehicles across 20 parking lots. I found it at last after half an hour of near panic. But then I had to scrape a ton of frost off of the windshield.

Oh Grenada! Oh Caribbean! Sunshine and beaches, why had I forsaken you for this self-abasement? I was freezing, as my numb fingers fumbled to start the vehicle. Fifteen minutes later, I found a button to press. The truck wouldn't start because the engine was frozen like me and every damn thing around the motor pool. Eventually the lethargic engine turned over. My problem then was to figure out how to get back up to the barracks with the truck. I had slept all the way down to the motor pool, you see.

Every so often, I was reminded by my fellow recruits that I was from someplace else. I was remorselessly teased when I declared, in my own Caribbean fashion, that my skin was "scratching me" not "itching me." Or there would be peals of hysterical laughter if I mistakenly asked for a "rubber" instead of a pencil "eraser." This periodic taunting caused me to reserve my own private place for my thoughts. It ensured, too, that I never completely lost my distinctive Caribbean personality, despite the host of extreme and demanding physical and psychological transformations we were forced to undergo on a daily basis. This forged a sense of determination in my mind that would help me to cope later on.

Some nights later I am assigned to CQ (Charge of Quarters) duty in the headquarters office of the company. I was actually the less glamorous *CQ runner*. The CQ that night was a gruff overweight *'lifer'* by the name of Sergeant Coltrane, like the jazz man.

It was December and it was North America so it was cold. The orderly room had a beautiful log fire but I would not be around long enough to form an opinion on its effectiveness against the winter chill as I was whipped in and out of the office on senseless and tiresome errands all over the compound. It was actually 0230 hours; I had started my day some twenty two hours ago so I was kind of tired and miserable.

The one thing that could have brought me some solace from my bout of self-pity would have been a cup of coffee.

Coltrane the Lucifer clone had sat on his substantial ass watching a basketball game on a little black and white TV whilst sipping coffee for the whole night. The only sign that he was conscious and maintaining some measure of contact with the land of the living came when he snorted a derisive "arggh" of disappointment at his team missing a basket. That man refused to give me a cup of his delicious smelling coffee, and the tantalizing smell of the brew had almost driven me crazy.

In that far off civilian world that I had once belonged to, I could have just walked up to the percolating pot and pour. Now, this action would probably have earned me a summary court martial and instant recycling to the next class of recruits that were behind my class. "Runner, here is a quarter - go get me a coke from the machine by the mess hall." So I stepped out in the nighttime chill to fetch him his bloody coke.

My CQ runner duty ended at 0600 hrs and I never did get my coffee. But I would work hard at my training, I would not remain a recruit forever, and I would show people like Coltrane, one of these days, that I too deserved a cup of coffee, at least occasionally.

Arguably the most dangerous part of our training up to that time was learning how to throw a hand grenade. We learned how to throw "live" ones at the hand grenade range.

We had to run out to the range, of course, and we sang at the top of our voices on the way. Regrettably, we were not always in perfect harmony, but it helped us to cope by distracting us from the early morning December chill and the full import of the exercise.

Our favourite song at Basic Training was Creedence Clearwater Revival's *"Proud Mary"*. There was something about singing while you ran. A cadence developed, you slid into a groove, and the world seemed all right for a while. This must have been one of the reasons why our slave ancestors sang throughout their tumultuous lives.

We got to the forest range without too many runners "falling out" of ranks and proceeded into an immediate outdoor-class environment. A sleep-inducing lecture on the principles of the grenade followed for about an hour. Not many heard it in its entirety.

After the basics had been highlighted, we were begrudgingly instructed in the more practical aspects of the hand grenade by a glowering, ill-humoured DI called Sergeant Bertwistle. A swarthy, robust, lifer who hailed from someplace called Butte, Montana. This man clearly did not enjoy teaching the "live" part of this course to numb-nut, butterfingered recruits.

As a matter of fact, he had become increasingly discontented lately and was rapidly approaching a permanent state of anxiety because of the hazardous nature of his job assignment: a risky area of work that exposed him on a daily basis, along with his colleagues on the training cadre, to the unorthodox practices of nervous trainees like us: sleep-deprived recruits who had, on past occasions, without much provocation or warning, dropped activated hand grenades from trembling and frostbitten fingers right at the participating drill instructor's feet.

Whenever this happened, it had a tendency to upset the DIs' composure, and always stretched their nerves to no imaginable end. This agitation usually produced an outpouring of wrath that was aimed unerringly at all attending recruits. So for this reason, if no other, none of the grenade-training cadre ever greeted recruits too warmly when they arrived for the segment of the course that encompassed live hand-grenade training drills.

We moved from the class area to the open range, where we diligently practiced the procedure of pulling the pin from a mock grenade.

Once you pulled the pin, you had to hold the grenade's handle down until ready to throw it, as the grenade's explosive was activated by the handle's release. Once you let go of the handle, the grenade would explode in about 8 to 10 seconds. Of course, the throwing of the grenade away from you was supposed to correspond with the handle being released from your grip.

We had to throw our grenades over an extended 10 foot high wall into a swampy area located behind a heavily reinforced sandbag barricade. A combination of prevailing factors could cause this training exercise to turn deadly.

This was my predicament.

First of all, the little hand grenade was considerably heavier than it looked in the movies. Then, my semi-numb hands were sweating copiously from the mind-arresting fear and a nagging premonition that I would somehow drop the grenade once I pulled the pin, and kill myself outright. But even more alarming was the harrowing concern that in the process of blowing myself to bits I would also manage, inadvertently, to kill a reluctant and inherently belligerent supervising DI by the name of Bertwistle as well. So the prevailing atmosphere was quite tense.

Sergeant Bertwistle, for his part, was just as nervous as I was that I would do all of the things that I was nervous about doing. Convinced that his longevity was threatened by my kind, he was as uptight as my Puerto Rican buddies were when they were forced by the intervention of some guy from the English speaking Caribbean, to write their Army entrance exams in alien English instead of Spanish. Because my hands were frozen rigid from the December chill, I was wearing woollen gloves - certainly not part of the customary daily attire in the tropics - and this affected my grip on the smooth, oval-shaped grenade.

Sergeant Bertwistle, behaving more and more like a man suffering from the side effects of spending many sleep-deprived nights thinking of some *other* line of work, remained mired in a very black mood. "If any of you butter-fingered recruit fuckers believe that you're going to kill me out here on the job today," he shouted, "well, just try it". "Pull any of your grenade-dropping stunts with me this time around, and see if I don't flatten your hapless asses and grind your pitiful faces deep into this mud. If you dipshits fuck this thing up out here, I'm warning you all: you will wish that you had enrolled in Julia Child's cookery school instead of the US Army."

I reluctantly stepped forward to throw. I heard the premonitory *Blamns! Blamns!* and felt the ground shudder beneath my feet from the vibrations of other live grenades exploding in neighbouring ranges. My pulse raced. The air thickened with a palpable tension. My turn was up. I walked to my mark, held the grenade to my chest, pulled the pin, cocked my hand, and threw hard. Just as I released, my world darkened as the 225-lb flak-jacket-adorned drill sergeant from hell tackled me into the mud, falling on top of me in the process.

My hand grenade arced through the crisp morning air, cleared the sandbag wall with an inch or so of daylight to spare, and exploded on the far side of the barrier where it was supposed to land.

I staggered to my feet gasping for air. What the hell? I thought to say but didn't, but I was sure he could read it on my face. Sergeant Bertwistle looked at me coldly and sneered. "Trainees," he muttered as he lumbered off. "I didn't like the way your eyes looked, recruit," he offered as a parting shot.

"You asshole lifer… I hope that you turn grey with frustration and die homeless out on the job-hunting trail," I mumbled, adding the appropriate knife-stabbing gestures as soon as I determined that his back was turned and he was safely out of hearing range.

On the flip side, there was a sergeant on our cadre team we all really admired. Sergeant Broderick was about twenty-five years old, a six-footer, about 195 lbs, trim and agile. He looked like an Army recruitment-poster model; his uniform always fit him like a glove. He walked with a lope and could be as reticent as a silent-movie hero.

The guy actually had the presence and stature of a Sidney Poitier. But what made us 19-year-old "wannabes" follow this sergeant around, was the fact that he had just completed his second tour of duty in Vietnam. Broderick a highly decorated combat veteran, had that look about him: a confident yet restrained air of fatalism that the other DIs did not possess. Although half of them had put in at least one tour "over there," he had experienced the real thing twice.

We all wanted to be like Sergeant Broderick when we grew up and graduated from our boot camp alma mater.

* * * * *

I had been put on the roster for KP (kitchen police) duties at last. You got this detail at least twice during basic training, and it was usually an unforgettable chapter in every soldier's life. Instead of waking up at the normal, luxurious hour of 0300, you now got up at 0200 in the morning to report to the head cook at the mess hall. We had been sent to a larger battalion mess hall than the smaller one we presently ate in. It catered to about 1000 men, providing three meals a day. Breakfast started at 0600, lunch at 1200 noon, and dinner was at 1800. In between meals you prepared for the next one.

The cavernous building operated like the insides of a constipated fat man's guts. There was the clanging of dishes and shouting of instructions from the kitchen. Food-making and drink-dispensing machines throbbed away beneath the consistent murmur of about 1000 hungry and impatient diners congregating in the same building throughout the entire day, three times a day. The mess hall was a feast of managed confusion.

There were 250 tables, each with four chairs. These four-man tables had to be set up with cutlery and so on for breakfast then taken down completely for cleaning and reset, and taken down again for lunch and dinner the same way. It was laborious. The entire mess hall had to be swept, mopped, and buffed to a shine, too, three separate times in between feeding the hordes.

The kitchen work was no less tremendous, having to prepare all those meals, and have the wares washed, dried and stacked for use again in triplicate. It eventually all blurred into a sort of madness. The work was dirty, backbreaking and mind-numbing.

Aside from meals and cigarette breaks for smokers, the mess detail stumbled from one exhausting set-up / take down operation to the next.

You entered this world of toil at 0230 and slogged straight on until 1900 hours. You never saw the light of day unless your job was "outside man" – garbage detail, which was actually one of the more coveted KP assignments, since you got ample supplies of fresh air as you drove to and from the garbage dump the entire day, getting rid of trash. The dining-room detail was the real killer, as you forgot after a while whether you were taking down or putting up tables and chairs, removing dirty dishes or laying clean ones. Was it lunch or dinner? Soon, I couldn't keep track.

This was KP, a blur of constant motion, of 1000 hungry people coming and going over and over again in a merry-go-round of noise and bustle. Hungry and impatient men. The people working in the kitchens were bullied by the cooks; not in an unfriendly manner but in order to keep up the back-breaking schedule. Everyone involved was under constant pressure.

The menu for lunch, for instance, would have roast beef and fried chicken, mashed potatoes, scalloped potatoes, and rice on it, including all types of vegetables, salads, and soups, too. There would be about three different types of desserts. The milk dispensers, both chocolate and plain milk, had to be constantly replenished.

The people running the mess hall also had to be on constant lookout for military health inspectors, who could pop in at any time of the day to run their white-gloved hands over something or the other only to shake their heads in disapproval.

Servers like me lined up to dispense the food as the diners came through the chow line indicating their choices. Sometimes not enough of this or that was scooped onto a slotted tray, and you were vigorously told something derogatory about your great-grandmother's undergarments or whatever. "Move along, move along now, and be smart about it!" you warned the ungrateful asses.

At 1900 hours, meals done for the day, we would limp back to our barracks in a sodden and bone-weary state, to collapse, spent and fully clothed, onto our bunks. It was a measure of how physically draining KP could be, that after a stint at it you got the entire next day off, free of any imaginable task under the sun, to sleep undisturbed and to hopefully recuperate.

* * * * *

We have been gassed! We have been gassed! I couldn't breathe. My throat felt like it was being torn to shreds. Tears streamed down my face. I was gasping for air, shaking and dry heaving violently. I had to escape the pain as I fled the wooden hut located somewhere deep inside of a South Carolina forest.

Were they really going to kill us out here? I was always hoping for a lifespan rather longer than that of Solomon Grundy. But I was having my doubts as we underwent our CBR (chemical, biological, and radiological) warfare training.

After some two hours of what-to-look-for and how-to-prevent instructions, we were shown how to put on and operate our gas masks, the most important but seldom used piece of equipment from our infantryman's bottomless kitbag.

The problem with this old rubber-and-mildew-smelling face mask for me was that when I put it on snugly over my face my brain immediately signaled asphyxiation. This led to the reactive ripping off of the mask seemingly always at the very moment our DIs began to enthusiastically gas us.

To be gassed was another of those unforgettable experiences that stayed with you long after basic training was over.

We were packed into a little hut for the demonstration. Our DI of the day, known to all as "Jolly Green Giant" because of his six-foot, two-inch frame, warned us forthrightly, "DO NOT TAKE OFF YOUR MASKS." But, remember, we were only until very recently, civilians. What did we know about tear gas? The demonstration canister went off with a pop followed by an ominous hiss.

Our tiny demonstration hut was hot, cramped, and filled with sweating and confused recruits. None of us had quite digested the procedural points in their entirety, as our ability to respond lucidly to simple instructions was seriously diminished by our lack of a decent night's sleep since entering basic training. We were supposed to remain in the hut as it filled with gas for just 10 seconds after the canister was popped. It sounded pretty easy. What were 10 seconds? A lifetime under these conditions.

We reacted predictably. Gas masks were ripped off blue faces, and we fled, gagging and spluttering. Of course, in doing so, we were then liberally gassed without the masks protection. But then of course, this is what we were brought here for in the first place, to experience the feeling of being gassed.

We were nearing the end of our basic training. We recruits had changed profoundly in the last eight weeks of our lives, and would surely change more. We no longer noticed that we ran everywhere we went. Push-ups were easily knocked off without breaking a sweat. As a matter of fact, when the DIs now told us to *"drop,"* we smiled in descent.

We disassembled and reassembled our rifles rapidly, with ease, without even thinking about what we were doing. We always seemed to finish whatever tasks we undertook with plenty of time to spare now. Some of the DIs even smiled at us, sometimes. Because they liked what they had crafted here.

But most of them still snarled at us. We had spent a lot of time learning hand-to-hand combat, which, of course, we would never use because it was totally out of sync with modern-day warfare, and not enough time with our M-16s on the qualifying range, considering where most of us were bound for.

Yet we resembled nothing of the bunch of ragtag civilian drifters who had arrived at the Reception Center two months before. Now, we were all fit and honed, finished products ready for some form of release. The domineering "drag ass" mount had reduced itself to a mere anthill in our overconfident minds. For most of us, a burgeoning arrogance existed concerning "the hill that was." "Didn't notice it there before. Did you?" we joked.

But it was good to feel good about ourselves, and we had sweated hard to reach this plateau. Some of us had figured out that our passport out of this place would be intrinsically linked to our physical fitness. So we drove ourselves real hard to achieve and then maintain a level of body readiness that would carry us through to the end.

We had already completed our night infiltration course, which was as close to actual combat situations as could be simulated. We crawled under and through barbed wire, over and around water-filled ditches, while explosive demolition charges went off over and around us. It wasn't live fire, but the next "closest" thing to it, we were told. Machine guns were fired with blank red tracer rounds, for effect, just over our heads as we crept on our bellies for about two hundred yards in complete darkness over the sprawling tactical combat course.

You had to keep your rifle dry and clean, right through the simulation. The rounds whizzing above our heads sounded the same as we imagined the real ones did, and this disturbed us. But this was not a cheerleading exercise. This was meant to be tough and exacting reality-based training.

A good sense of having accomplished something at the end of a night's drill was our ultimate satisfaction. We had also *sort of* completed our nighttime map-reading course. This called for us to be dropped off deep in the "boonies" forest on a conveniently moonless night; separated into random groups of three or four trainees; given a map, a compass and a flashlight, and cheerfully told, "See you recruits back at the barracks!"—located some twenty-odd miles away.

This was a very stimulating outing, our *terrain comprehension* exercise. We stumbled around in a state of confusion, hopelessly lost in the intimidating woods for the better part of the night, while trying to find some clue that would lead us back to base before daybreak.

* * * * *

We had our Physical Combat Proficiency Test (P.C.P.T.) at last: the one mile run, the forty-yard crawl, the run-dodge and jump, the 100 yard dash, the man carry, and the horizontal-ladder drill. This was what some of us had practiced extra hard for in our spare time when we were off duty on late evenings, throughout our eight-week training stint here.

There was an old tradition in our training battalion that stipulated that anyone who obtained maximum points in these five grueling disciplines of speed, stamina and agility--and this achievement had in fact been accomplished before, but not often--would not only earn his private's stripe to graduate proudly with, for we were still recruits and had not as yet attained rank at this early stage of our military life. But almost as alluring as this, was the unheard of promise that the Battalion First Sergeant would serve the high achievers breakfast in bed.

We did the run, dodge and jump--I maxed it in 18 seconds flat. Horizontal bars--200 rungs completed, well below the time allowed--maxed it. Low crawl--maxed easily. One-mile run with full battle gear, under allocated time--maxed it. I also recorded full points for the 100-yard dash, carrying a man of similar weight on my back. At the end of the testing, I had completed the P.C.P.T. with the highest attainable score: 100 points. One of two full-point scores attained during our entire 100-man company's qualifying drill.

The other recruit who made the honour roll for our company, and fittingly so, was my friend from the reception center, Rick Dalzell. And we both got our deserved stripe and breakfasts in bed as promised, but with a typically military Machiavellian twist to it all.

The day after the P.C.P.T., the company was lined up outside the barracks. Rick and I were reminded that the First Sergeant was serving us breakfast in bed. So we were told to just relax inside the barracks, not to bother to fall out for formation with the rest of the company. Some trepidation started to creep up on us by then. We sensed that something was about to backfire on us in some way, but what?

First sergeants in the US Army were legends. They were the most admired and highly respected men in uniform.

Tattooed Memories

They worked their way steadfastly up through the ranks and generally had at least 20 years in proven service when they made "First." They were referred to by everyone who possessed at least one functioning brain cell, in reverent tones, as *"Top" or "First,"* even by the unit's commissioned officers, who also treaded softly in their overwhelming presence.

Our "Top," First Sergeant Norman Nichols, was a big man of Irish stock, at least six feet tall and weighing 240 compacted pounds. He wore the standard military buzz haircut style, of course, and had glacial blue eyes that piercingly observed every living thing in *his* world, the entire 52,600 acres that comprised Fort Jackson, from a deceptively cherubic face. He carried his weight well and had a light step, as some big men do. He usually had little to say, so people familiar with him prudently did not engage him in unnecessary verbal discourse.

A bunch of people clambered too purposefully up the barracks' steps, and Rick and I *"braced"* (that is, we stood at an exaggerated position of attention with our chins pressed hard into our chest bones) next to our bunks.

We were sweating bullets by then. We looked at each other with fatalistic expressions of resigned acceptance as we waited for whatever unpleasant surprise was in store for us. Sergeant Nichols arrived on the scene first, followed by platoon Sergeant Rivera and about three other DIs from our company. All of them wearing knowing smiles while expressing an awkwardly alien air of fraternity. They cast about bonhomie tainted looks and tried to suppress their scarcely concealed mirth at some hilariously impending doom.

Behind the brass, two recruits on mess-hall duty trailed them, carrying two sumptuously laden breakfast trays bearing an assortment of delights like hot coffee, bacon and eggs, French toast and a fruit tray. Sergeant Coltrane, who was part of the delegation, looked directly at me and our eyes locked momentarily. He conceded a slight smile - I had earned that cup of coffee, and his ass knew it.

Sergeant Nichol says "Recruits Byer and Dalzell, you have done your company E/1/1 proud with your performances on the P.C.P.T., and I want to be the first to congratulate you and to also inform you that you have both been immediately promoted to Private E-1 rank. Congratulations. Your performances were outstanding, and in keeping with battalion tradition I want to invite you to have this special First Sergeant's breakfast in bed, at my pleasure.

"The only problem is that you had three seconds to eat this tray of food, and to get your sorry lazy asses downstairs and into the ranks of the morning formation for roll call. Now move it, move it, move it! What the hell are you waiting for? Out, out, out! *Now!*"

The chase was on as we darted for the staircase as if running for our lives. We were vigorously pursued by what seemed to be an unruly horde of screaming and laughing men in uniform. We hit the stairs running, trays spilling food all over the place. Half a step behind us, leaping down the stairs at full tilt, was a manic pack of baying DIs, jubilantly whipping up a raucous chant of "hooargh argh hooargh".

We flew down the stairs like bats out of their hell. Apparently, this was a major highlight of a DI's life, whenever it occurred, and they enjoyed it to the maximum, as they thought of it as being such a cute stunt. We knew we'd be the feature topic of "lifer mirth" down at the N.C.O. (Non-Commissioned Officers) club the coming Saturday night.

We careened, breathless, out of the building, stumbling into our waiting company formation. The First Sergeant followed in a more sedate fashion, a beatific smile on his amused face. Everyone was cracking up in ranks at our sudden misfortune. But you could not help but notice the lingering looks of admiration and respect that were cast our way, by recruits and cadre alike. Nothing or no one would spoil our day. We were not the butts of a joke here, just the rationale for it.

We didn't beat the system, but we surely matched it head to head, and came out at the top. Nobody could take that away from us.

We had worked hard and practiced after regular hours when others were resting. We went for it. We deserved our triumph and enjoyed our well-earned celebrity while it lasted.

My first promotion to private E-1 rank remained the most precious of the four promotions that I attained during my three years in the US armed forces. Even the two promotions I received in Vietnam under battlefield conditions were not as special to me as this first one was. I had started climbing inexorably up the rungs of the military ladder, heading with determination for that well-deserved cup of coffee. Look at me now, Sergeant Coltrane! I had begun my run.

Graduation day arrived, for most of us, we had made it. We had our pass in review parade in dress khakis before the reviewing stand, symbolizing our complete transition from civilian to soldier. It was a proud moment, marching to the beat of the drum on the wide open grassy parade grounds, and I felt like a complete soldier for the very first time.

After the parade, we the new soldiers mingled a bit with the few parents able to make it down for the ceremony, and we chatted with our former nemeses, the DIs. They kind of recognized us as people at last, now that they could no longer order us to "drop" anytime they felt like it. We also saw them as the consummate professionals they really were, men who could not afford to kid-glove us throughout the past eight weeks of training. We were almost friends now, but not quite.

Before we left for Advanced Individual Training (A.I.T.), we had three important things to do. First, we had to turn in our M-16 rifles and pass a rigorous inspection that would determine whether or not we walked off the base. To be safe, we used our toothbrushes vigorously on our rifles from butt to muzzle until they were gleaming. Even scrubbed, cleaned and spit shined for hours, it normally took about three tries before the weapon was acceptable to the duty officer to be handed in. Only then would we be allowed to leave the post.

The other two things we had to do were to be introduced to the Enlisted Men's Club on post. This facility was always there but previously off limits to us. Here, we could now drink endless overflowing jugs of frothing cold beer and get quite drunk. The last thing we did was descend en masse onto the city of Columbia, South Carolina, where we drank more jugs of beer and got drunker yet while sampling all the available clubs in town, that is, the ones that had girls, females or women in them, which most of them naturally did.

This partying was made possible by the fact we all had two months' pay to go through: the princely sum of about $130 in 1969 dollars. Especially not bad when your overhead expenses and cost of living were practically zero.

Columbia, like most towns in the US that existed in the shadow of a large service installation like Fort Jackson, seized on the profitable industry to be realized from being a GI town by catering to young servicemen's predictable and base needs. (The term GI really referred to anything that was Government Issue but was universally recognized as a nickname for American soldiers.)

There were banks, pawn shops, movie theatres, restaurants, and bowling alleys. The attractiveness of these facilities paled in comparison to what the many bars and discos had to offer: dancing girls or strippers who might satisfy the basic needs of young, sex-starved servicemen.

Nothing in the world seized, undividedly, the attention of a serviceman of about nineteen years of age, who had been training for eight weeks non-stop, more so, than the sight of a scantily clad female gyrating on an elevated stage. The finance office on base might as well have endorsed all of our paychecks over to the proprietors of those establishments.

* * * * *

Those of us who did well in our Basic Training Courses were actually given a choice of what we wanted to do for our Advanced Individual Training. Although soldiers were generally sent to the field wherever the manpower was needed most critically at the time of their graduation.

I chose the combat medic field, 91A10-MOS. (MOS stood for Military Occupational Specialty).

It never crossed my mind at the time, after basic, how dangerous a field this might be. It sounded like just another challenge to be tackled. It also seemed like something I would like to do.

I probably would have been sent for medic training anyway. I found out later, that combat medics were always in great demand, and would continue to be urgently required throughout the Vietnam conflict.

This was due to the high mortality rates suffered by corpsmen attached to infantry line companies. The units that were exposed to hazardous combat conditions in Vietnam on a daily basis.

Chapter 5

Advanced Individual Training

Arriving at Fort Sam Houston in Texas to begin training for my chosen specialty (or job) in the Army was nothing like what I experienced on arriving at Fort Jackson to learn my basic soldiering. I was a soldier now, a mighty private (E-1) proudly sporting my one stripe on my sleeves and not willing to be trifled with by anyone less than a mightier two striper.

We were greeted on base without shouts or taunts. Order and discipline already reigned. I was to report to barracks, and get signed up and introduced to a cadre of a different kind. This was a school, the US Army Medical Training Center, albeit still a military program. We had a schedule of instructions and course criteria to follow as if in college.

The training was no less regimented or intense here, but without the dogmatism or threats. Courses ranged from dispensary and hospital-ward disciplines to the application of injections and medicines. We learned how to make beds without removing the patients in them first.

The twelve-week course was a packed one. There were classes in clinical studies physical hygiene, basic first aid, and the use of battlefield craft expedients, screening and diagnosing patients for doctors, and quite a comprehensive knowledge of pharmaceuticals. I learned bandaging, splinting, stretcher bearing, and, of course, field-work applications with emphasis on helicopter evacuation and treatment.

The combat medic trainee had to absorb a wide range of information, and take this with him, ready to use, whether assigned to an aid station which is a small hospital or deep into the middle of a triple-canopied jungle. He had to be adept at setting up an intravenous drip in the field, applying a tourniquet and cauterizing a broken-bone stump. At the same time, he had to understand when and how to apply an injection by the intramuscular, intravenous, intradermal or subcutaneous methods.

The medics, especially the ones who found themselves in remote jungle situations, were really both their units' doctors and nurses. Their responsibilities were enormous, because the men in their outfits depended on them entirely. Added to this pressure, they were cognizant of their limited medical knowledge, and of their units' expectations that they would always be able to counter almost any damage inflicted by modern-day, high-velocity weapons.

The men of their units fully appreciated their presence and referred to them as their "Doc."

Every medic was Doc from the day he arrived on the battlefield until the day he left. When he resumed his duties back in the US, he was again referred to by rank. The very cry of "Medic" out in the field, itself a plaintive wail of urgency and hope, never went unanswered, as far as I know.

I really liked Fort Sam. It was very Texas, with big, wide open expanses and fresh air. It had an invigorating atmosphere, combined with the gratifying relief of not having to operate in the pressure-cooker of a training camp like Fort Jackson. This made learning easy and appealing here.

We settled eagerly into the demanding routine of acquiring the variety of skills we'd need to become capable combat medics. One interesting stage of our training program was when, in typical no-frills, no-nonsense military fashion; we were paired for practical applications. One trainee was to be the patient, the other acted as the medic for the first hour of learning.

This lead to the expected high jinks. Guys would remove a syringe from a vein after taking blood, leaving the tourniquet still applied. The resulting pressure would cause a fountain of blood to geyser up alarmingly to the ceiling, stopping the class to allow for the required mopping up before trying the procedure again. Instructors rolled their eyes and shook their heads with patient understanding. They'd seen it all before when dealing with a bunch of young men just out of high school.

Most weekends we were allowed off base, and the nearby city of San Antonio was a very exciting outing for all of us. I remember visiting the Alamo, which was located right in the center of town.

I was standing in an open plaza with my friend Pete Ryan when Pete said, "Roge, do you see the mission–the Alamo?"

I said, "No, but the tourist-bureau people said that it was right around here somewhere."

Like a lot of people, I had seen John Wayne and Richard Widmark defend the landmark fortress against hordes of charging Mexican soldiers. I saw this at the movies on my island home in Grenada, years ago. So I knew the place was supposed to be impressive, size-wise. Then someone came up and said, "You boys like it?" "Like what?" we answered in chorus. The person said, "What's left of the Alamo."

To our grave disappointment, he pointed to an unimpressive, crumbly looking parapet. "That's it."

"That?" I mumbled. I recalled John Wayne again, doing his thing against the attacking Mexican cavalry. General Santa Anna, their commander, would not have fought so aggressively for this little mortar anthill. The damn thing had to be bigger than this....

I also saw the premier of the shockingly classic horror movie *The Night of the Living Dead* in grizzly black and white, in San Antonio that same day. But, having been let down by our brief foray into cultural and historical enlightenment, we reverted to type and swiftly regressed to our habitual pastimes.

We spent the rest of our weekend liberty drinking beer and watching winsome, sloe eyed strippers at the tacky neighborhood clubs. We languished obligingly in all the naughty, disreputable dives around town that existed just for us.

* * * * *

It's February, and I was on guard duty, and it was damn cold in Texas. I wondered sometimes whether I would ever get used to this weather that other humans seemed to live comfortably in and blithely referred to as winter. Sentry duty was two hours on and four hours off in a 24-hour period.

We had a large wood stove with an impressive furnace in the guard hut. Wonderful to come in to, but it was hard to leave and step outside again to repeat those lonely, monotonous, windswept foot patrol duties.

We spent most of our time on guard duty hiding from the biting wind behind buildings or any available windbreak at hand. Tearing eyes peeped out of muffled scarves as we watched for the unforgiving officer of the guard and his sentry-inspecting jeep patrol.

It was all right; ducking for warmth wasn't treasonable. We weren't guarding Fort Knox, Kentucky, home of the US Government's gold bullion reserves. It was just empty parking lots. It was only training, so you could relax a little. As if intentionally, other sentries from the guard detail were dropped off in seemingly distant and remote areas. Positioned well away from each other, so that we never passed near a fellow sufferer.

My only companions during these lonely vigils were bands like Jim Morrison and the Doors. My low powered transistor radio pulsated bravely from somewhere deep inside the folds of my winter clothing, as I strained to hear the comforting words of "touch me". My only link to human warmth and companionship.

I recall also being on "Police call" detail and, therefore understandably, in a bored and recalcitrant mood, picking up pieces of paper and cigarette butts off the Post's manicured lawns.

It was July the 21st 1969, and a man called Neil Armstrong was about to step onto the lunar surface. We were hastily directed into the dayroom from our police call duties. This was a big moment of national pride in the US of A, and the wider world for that matter. Everyone squeezed into the room to squat in front of the large colour TV that was now only able to produce grainy jumpy black- and-white images.

A man stepped carefully onto the bottom rung of the lunar lander module's ladder and onto the dusty lunar landscape. We heard the now famous words "One small step for...."

Earlier, we had listened to this same man's scratchy and indistinct voice assuring N.A.S.A. mission control, "Houston--tranquility base....the eagle has landed."

I admired all of this and believed that it had actually happened. Attaboy Neil! I thought to myself excitedly. I had found a kindred spirit here. Although planets apart, Armstrong like me, was on a lonely mission far away from the comforts of home. Both of us would have to use our wits to survive our individual challenges. I was elated by this.

Suddenly and for the first time in quite a while I did not feel as lonely as I did before, because I had just realized that there was someone else out there who was stationed a lot further away from his home than I was from mine.

And because things seemed to be working out for him, I was comforted that I would be fine also.

But as I stepped back out into the summer heat to resume the important work assignment we had interrupted to witness this event of a lifetime, I smilingly mused about a news report I had heard recently concerning the impending moon landing. Apparently, in the Australian outback, when Aborigine elders had been informed of this historic event by bearers of the news from the cities, these wise old men politely listened to the important tidings, then, with a gleam in their eyes and in barely audible voices, they whispered back to the heralds, "Prove it."

* * * * *

I was at leadership training school here on the same base. I was selected as potential Officer Material. A one-week course, it was meant to sharpen the skills of people earmarked as potential leaders. It was a rigid, higher level of everything learned in basic training but without the debasement and hectoring unleashed on recruits.

Tattooed Memories

A memorable and amusing activity of this period was our method of reintroducing bored and yearning taste buds to that much appreciated and sorely missed American civilian pastime—the consumption of junk food.

Somebody came up with the clever idea of stepping out onto the nearby highway and hailing a taxi driver, who would be then roped into our clever plot. The driver would come to our upstairs barracks bathroom window at night, at a pre-arranged time. We would then lower a fire bucket to him on a rope (implementing recently acquired military leadership skills) with some money in it. He would drive to the nearby MacDonald's restaurant, purchase the off-limit grub for us, and return with it to the crime scene. We would then eagerly pull up our spoils through the bathroom window, always leaving a healthy tip in the fire bucket for the accommodating cab driver.

The drivers never absconded with our money. This was too much of a reliable, well-tipped business arrangement for them to make that mistake.

The only problem was that we had to immediately wolf down our repast. The wonderfully maddening smell of the burgers would much too soon permeate the barracks Sergeant's sleeping quarters downstairs, awakening and arousing his own taste buds.

He would come flying up the stairs like a homing pigeon, yelling, "What the hell's going on up here? I smell something! What've you got? Give it up!" He would have been a bit hungry and longing himself for some satisfying, diet-defying, non-GI grub, as we were all shackled to the same military menu here, both cadre and trainees alike.

Anyway, at this stage of the game, anyone with the smallest modicum of functioning grey matter knew it was 1969 AD, and if you happened to be wearing a US Army soldier's uniform, there was a really good chance you would be heading sooner or later for a trip in a westerly direction across the South China Sea.

Sometimes, Sergeant Brent (our junk-food sniffing barracks sergeant, who was quartered downstairs) would allow some of us to watch reports of the Vietnam War on television in his quarters. The war in Vietnam was the first to be regularly domestically televised in the US.

Americans saw their fathers, sons, brothers, and husbands "over there" courtesy of daily evening news broadcasts beamed into American homes by all of the major television networks. We looked distractedly at images of troopers jumping out of helicopters and struggling through swamplands, and saw the smoke rising up from air strikes and artillery fire missions.

But for some remarkable reason we never associated what we saw playing out on the little screen as the true script of what we would soon be part of. Even though we were the next group of actors waiting to enter from stage right, to play out our designated roles in subsequent installments of the ongoing live serial show that was the war in Vietnam.

Shortly, we would be the ones whose images would be beamed back into American homes. But we could not connect with that eventuality at this time as we watched the scenes been played out. They were to us only pictures of somebody else fighting someone else's distant and far removed war, somewhere far away, "over there."

Chapter 6

Maternal Instinct and the Leather Talisman

It was my second leave home to Grenada. I'd been in the United States Army for a year. I'd served at Forts Jackson, South Carolina, and Sam Houston in Texas. My orders were to ship out in thirty days' time to the Republic of Vietnam for a one-year tour of combat duty.

I was on my mandatory, pre-overseas, one-month leave before taking up my duties in a hostile environment. Nobody knew this except the Department of the Army and me. Or so I thought. Ever heard of maternal instinct?

Fifteen minutes after arriving home, I greeted my parents and settled down to have a drink and catch up. My stepfather, Uncle Len, came up to me and said, "Roger, what's wrong with your mother? What did you tell her?" I replied, "I don't know, and nothing."

"Are you going to Vietnam? Did you tell her this?" Again, I answered "Yes, but no."

My mother, a strong lady all her life, had sensed that something was different this time around on my latest visit home, without a word being said about the war. As a result of this, she had retreated to her room and was in fact lying on her bed in prostration. *She knew .... She just knew..* She had felt the emotion I was probably trying too hard to spare her.

At that time, being 20 years old and having no clue (as most humans didn't) of what a shooting war was all about, I was not unduly scared. Apprehensive and excited, yes, but frightened, no. I should not have been given off any alarming vibes to anyone, but my mother must have sensed an understatement or felt an undercurrent, some kind of disquietude, coming from me.

Later I would learn to live with fear, as an ever present, choking and menacing shadow that had to be shunted to one side, if not, it would cripple one's ability to function in the field, making you a prime candidate for the very doom that it so accurately presaged for you.

My parents had a good friend called Oswald Buxo. We called him "Uncle Ozzie," of course, this being the Caribbean. He was a wise older man, something of a seer. The type of guy who read the dregs of tea leaves at the bottom of cups at parties. He was soft spoken and deeply respected in our community. He read extensively and was a good conversationalist on a wide variety of subjects.

One evening, sitting on the verandah of our home at Belmont, overlooking the yacht marina and the inner harbor of St. George's, Grenada's capital city, and having a drink with my parents and a group of friends that included Uncle Ozzie, he had said to me, "Roger I have something here for you." He handed me a triangular piece of leather with prominent stitches on it where it had been sewn together. It had a hole cut through the leather to accommodate a chain. He said, "Wear this talisman around your neck all the while that you are over there, in Vietnam."

I thanked him for the token and said that I would wear it. Then I asked him, "What is it?"

"This is my going away gift to you, Roger. Your name is written on a piece of paper that has been placed inside of the leather pouch surrounded by other things, things that will protect you over there."

Uncle Ozzie then turned calmly to my mother, put his arms around her shoulders, squeezed them and, with convincing frankness, said to her, "Don't worry, Barbara, he'll come back home, I guarantee you this." There was not a dry eye on our verandah after that statement.

He said no more, in the way that self-assured people do. I respected his silence and thanked him again for my gift.

I wore that talisman on the same chain that I used to secure my dog tags for the entire year I spent in both Vietnam and Cambodia. I didn't wear it after that, but I kept it in a safe place with all my other cherished mementoes. I never opened the leather pouch to see what was inside it. I have never cared to know its contents.

I had many close calls both in Vietnam and Cambodia. But I returned home whole and relatively unscathed after serving my one year tour of duty in those war zones. I came back alive just as Uncle Ozzie had promised my mother I would.

There were quite a few instances when people died close to or around me in combat situations, sometimes in my very arms because of my job as a medic. The talisman was always there with me. I wore it every day, as Uncle Ozzie said I should. Its protective powers? Who's to say? I trusted Uncle Ozzie, as I had always known him to be a man of his word.

He had said I would return from the war *before* I went overseas, and because it was also my intention to do just that, I took that belief with me into harm's way and nurtured it for all the time that I spent over there.

Chapter 7

I Smell Asia

The chartered Seaboard World Boeing B-707 touched down gracefully on the wide tarmac of the airfield at the Cam Ranh Bay Naval base, located on the glittering eastern coastline of the Republic of South Vietnam. Our flight had taken more than a half day to get us here from Mc-Chord Air Force Base in California. About fifteen hours actually.

It was 0200 hours, November 29, 1969, when I arrived in Vietnam. Yet another very young soldier who had come to this country from a land far away to fight in a politician's war.

The interior of the aircraft was cool and the cabin lighting muted. This was no crowded World War II troop transport but a modern-day commercial jetliner, with comfortable seating and appetizing airline catering.

The flight attendants were all wonderful throughout the long trip across the Pacific. The service was impeccable. Fattened calves to the slaughter, I couldn't help but reflect.

As our aircraft taxied to the ramp, 200 US servicemen, aged 20 years on average, stirred sleepily and tried to gather their jet-lagged wits.

Well, I thought as I looked around the cabin, we are here. Some of us volunteered for this, didn't we? Others, the noticeably more solemn ones, didn't; they had been drafted. It didn't matter anymore; we were all here in this thing together now.

I couldn't see or hear anything from the outside as yet. Didn't think they were firing at us. The closest stewardess looked normal and unperturbed. She would know if anything was wrong. Right?

We finally stopped. The engines whined down as the pilots cut the fuel supply to the giant turbofans. The cabin doors were opened, and our lives changed forever there and then.

There was a pervasive sense of anxiety about getting off the aircraft and getting on with whatever we came over here to do.

"Get up, boy!" The guy sitting behind me joked to break the tension.

I unbuckled my seat belt and trudged along the length of the aircraft towards the beckoning passenger doorway. I wandered what was out there waiting for us?

I got to the door and stuck my head out and I was struck by a blast of hot, acrid air, reeking of rotten vegetation, burnt charcoal and some unknown sweet ambrosia. My senses felt assaulted and my brain cells suffused with this alien cocktail.

My mind reeled with the mixture of odour, heat, and confusion. I smell Asia, I thought to myself. So hello to you too, Vietnam.

I now had only 364 and a half days left on my tour of duty in the Republic of Vietnam. But who was counting?

Stepping off the jetliner at Cam Ranh Bay, I was weary but excited. I was really on the Asian continent at last. And it was warm. I was accustomed to warmth on my island home in the Caribbean, but warmth of a different kind. This was a thick pea-soup type environment, a stifling cloying presence.

There was no sea breeze present here like we had at home to circulate the air, only a prevailing stillness broken by a constant medley of chirping bush crickets.

As we descended the aircraft steps, we stared hypnotically at the ranks of soldiers waiting to board our flight to return to the US of A.

They represented everything that we aspired to be. Veterans who had survived a year of warfare in Vietnam. There was an expectant expression on their faces. Also, an unmistakable you-poor-suckers look that we could not misinterpret as they glanced our way.

Most of them had this deadpan look on their faces as if something important had been wrenched out of their souls whilst over here. Their bodies projected suffering, our suffering to come down the road. They were older and wiser young men now who had perhaps been forced to take a peek into some kind of hell. I wished Godspeed to them all.

A year from now, if I made it out, someone else would be staring at me the same way.

We ambled over to the line of olive-coloured army buses waiting to spirit us off to our accommodation. The heady scent of the land was cloying.

As we drove away onto the base's large roadways, there wasn't much to see at this early hour of the morning. Still, we swivelled our heads around to stare with fascination at every passing local Vietnamese that we saw.

We were intrigued by actually being in the country and finally seeing the people at last.

Whether the people we saw were local base workers or allied national policemen working at the military installation's main gate, it didn't matter: they were still our first Vietnamese experience.

There would be more time in the future for encounters with slimly built people wearing what looked like pajama clothing, large conical hats and a generally inscrutable expression.

The never-ending lights mesmerized us as we concerned ourselves with predictably wild thoughts of what really was out there on the base, but, far more importantly, what was out there *past* the base's wire fences on the other "side" that represented an open, enigmatic landscape where there was a war being waged as we arrived in- country.

Chapter 8

Byer, Get Your Shit Together – You're Going Out

"Byer, get your shit together. You're going out."

"Tuffy", our company's venerable Hawaiian-born First Sergeant was shouting very loudly. We were about to open a door that would lead me down a path towards unfolding events I could never imagine.

Once I stepped through this doorway I would forever have a tattoo burned into my consciousness concerning what lay ahead of me. In fact, the events that I would face would leave me for the rest of my life with a series of tattooed memories, born strictly out of my experiences in Vietnam.

I had been at our base's Medical Aid Station at Quan Loi, which was Third Brigade headquarters for my assigned unit, the First Battalion Fifth Air Cavalry Division of the mighty First Air Cavalry Division Airmobile, for three days.

Here, my slow-moving brain, still befuddled by new surroundings and sensations, had only recently begun to grasp and sort out the reality that Quan Loi, comfortable though sometimes rocket besieged, was not to be my home away from home or, at worst, my final destination. I had come here from the large Cam Ranh Bay facility, only recently arrived from the U.S. of A. At Cam Ranh, I also suffered the naïve notion that I was going to be based there. But I was destined for something else, much further away.

Cam Ranh would have been nice, though. The huge, well-equipped American naval base, located on a dazzling white sand beach on Vietnam's east coast, provided a natural deep-water berth for the navy. Multi-purpose airfield facilities coupled with the harbour's gargantuan cargo handling capacity made Cam Ranh one of the most important dual-purpose military bases ever to be operated by US armed forces in South Vietnam.

Cam Ranh was always teeming with new equipment and busy looking noncoms (non- commissioned officers) briskly marching new in-country arrivals all over the place, as if to dispel any misconceptions that something very important wasn't always happening right there all of the time. Accommodation for servicemen was provided in stateside-style barracks, with electricity, running water and ice, that godsend to the sweltering tropics.

We had air conditioning, bunks with clean sheets, permanent leak-proof roofs over our heads, hot meals, and movies at night. I could have done my year there without suffering from too much homesickness. Especially since the servicemen stationed at CB got the same overseas combat hazard pay, the extra sum of $65 per month, as the poor bastards just a little ways up the road that were fighting the real war.

Medics with my military occupational specialty or "job" in standard English, could be assigned to various areas in Vietnam. We could work at regular base hospitals, offshore hospital ships, aid stations, dispensaries, clinics, or clearing stations located at the rear. All of this was generally out of harm's way and at a distance from major hostilities. If all else failed, as happened quite frequently in the military, we could be sent into the jungle to fight the war out there.

I would later surmise that, yes, my prospects over there were fairly clear at the time. But then I didn't know what to look for or where to look to make sense of them.

I had arrived at Cam Ranh Bay on a comfortable civilian jetliner. From there, I was flown out to Quan Loi on a C-7A De Havilland Caribou, a smaller but marvelous workhorse of an aircraft built in Canada by the De Havilland company.

En route to Quan Loi, the countryside had started to look progressively rougher. There was a lot less utilization of planes. Aside from the 0V-10 Bronco, some C-130's and Caribous, this was all helicopter country.

Helicopters arrogantly command the airspace: the giant CH-54 Sikorsky sky crane, a heavy cargo lifter that was aptly renamed "The Jolly Green Giant"; the stealthy and deadly AH-1G Cobra attack gunship nicknamed "Blue Max" which was the senior partner of a shrewdly conceptualized helicopter duo of death exercise for the enemy.

This was how it worked.

The heavily armed Cobra would circle above ground at about 3 000 feet, hiding in any available clouds. A smaller chopper, an LOH, in obvious radio contact with big brother upstairs, buzzed around invitingly and temptingly at treetop level. This inadvertently drew ground fire from a group of Vietcong forces onto this innocent looking helicopter. Fired upon, the LOH would peel away to safety and the Cobra would plunge, like a screeching harridan towards the ground, unleashing a devastating hellfire of rockets and mini-guns on the enemy snipers.

The lay of the land transformed itself before my eyes as I looked down from my vantage point inside the cabin of the Caribou I was riding in. The terrain seemed much denser and somehow more threatening from up here. I could not shake the unsettling feeling that I was being slowly drawn ever deeper into a green mass or an entity of doom.

Huge swaths of jungle appeared below, with very large trees. It was an evergreen ocean that spread as far as the eye could see. We passed over an expansive rubber plantation, quite possibly French-owned and operated. Many rivers cropped up, and there was a noticeable scarcity of recognizable buildings of any type or shape anywhere. Large, liana-suffocated trees reached up to the sky as though trying to escape the tendrils of creeping ground mist that encircled their massive trunks possessively.

This was definitely chopper country; there weren't many fixed-wing craft around at all, mainly rotary wing. The Huey UH-1, the workhorse helicopter and sky trooper carrier of the First Air Cavalry division, was the most predominant, and I would find out soon enough the indispensable role of this aircraft. The Huey would play a major part in every facet of our operations. It was our main mode of transportation in and out of the "sticks," as we called the jungle; it was our re–supply ship, medical evacuation and gunship air support facilitator, or sometimes simply a most welcome ride for worn-out legs and aching backsides.

The helicopters were always there for us. I was glad I joined the cavalry long after they had given up those damn cumbersome mules as a division's premier mode of transportation.

I had, by this stage, changed into my full jungle fatigues from the khakis that I had arrived in. I carried all of my gear now on my person. My M-16 rifle, which I had qualified with in what seemed like ages ago at Fort Jackson, never left my side. Basic training was now a blurred and somewhat distant past, although it was only a year to the month since I had joined up.

Everything around me now was green, interspersed with the ever present red mud that I first would learn to hate and then later fail to notice. By then, I would be totally preoccupied with a host of daily, daunting and life-threatening challenges, any one of which may have caused me to miss that end-of-day ritual of marking off another day spent on *my short-timer's calendar*, which would indicate my success at another day completed, while still breathing and surviving in Vietnam.

Chapter 9

Let me Tell you About Quan-Loi

My C-7A Caribou aircraft dropped onto a hard-packed, dirt-and-asphalt strip that had been cut out of a somewhat level area in the surrounding rubber trees. This strip had been hacked and scraped out of the jungle by redoubtable combat engineers, bulldozer driving skilled madmen in uniform who had the reputation for building amazing things out of nothingness even when under enemy fire.

Our division garrison at Quan-Loi was located close to the large Michelin rubber plantation, whose dominant trees would later witness numerous violent skirmishes between our forces and the stubbornly committed Vietcong units that frequented the immediate area.

Just before this tooth-rattling arrival, I had glimpsed a sea of Quonset and wood-frame huts slipping by below me. All precisely and militarily lined up with the necessary outer sand bag protection ring around them. Now, every fixed object was encircled by a sandbag or 6000 sandbags in Vietnam. The problem with this type of architectural design was the mandatory need to fill them all before using them. I must have filled a million or so, give or take a couple hundred thousand, of these sandbags during my one year stint in that place, and that would have been routine.

I stepped off the aircraft and lugged my increasingly heavier gear towards the arrivals area, a row of small huts draped in the usual GI type haphazard and irrationally loud confetti. Most of us were, after all, 19 years old.

Some guy was trotting briskly towards me. He stared directly at me. He seemed to have zeroed in on me and cut me off from the rest of the pack for some reason. He sported one of those Fu Manchu-type of moustaches that disappeared accommodatingly into a supporting beard that obliterated any sight of his chin. His green uniform was stained completely brown with red mud. His appearance definitely signaled that he'd been around country, out here in the "big sticks," for quite some time now.

He was about five-feet-six in height, one hundred and twenty pounds if weighed when fully clothed and soaking wet. His eyes were wild and burning, his gait was frenetic, but most disconcerting to me was the fact that this apparition from Haight-Ashbury (the hippy haven in San Francisco) was grinning directly at me. He was enjoying some private joke inside of his shell-shocked and, most likely marijuana-addled skull, that included me.

"Shit, what now?" I murmured (this talking to myself was becoming a habit of mine). "Here I go again."

"Hey, are you the FNG [new guy] replacement for Charlie Company?" the guy shouted directly at me. "You're a medic, right?" I nodded in the affirmative.

"Good, let me help you with your gear." Help me? I mused, h mmn…

Something was definitely off- kilter here, but I couldn't figure out what, yet.

"Great stuff," he said. "I'm John Stevens - everybody calls me John. Welcome to Quan-Loi, soldier. I am a medic too, and I believe that you're my replacement."

During the ensuing year of my involvement in the war, I would be better armed to put all of this into proper perspective—our encounter and brief exchange—but I had to be John Stevens first, out in the jungle, to fully understand the gravity of his words. Stevens hugged and kissed me before I could protest, then grabbed my stuff enthusiastically, leading the way to the heavily bunkered underground medical aid station.

There I met Lieutenant Levy, a rotund, Coke bottom glasses wearing Jewish gentleman from New York who sported a Pancho Villa moustache. He was the medical officer in charge. I found out later that Levy was an officer indeed but he was in charge of nothing. He was a complete and non-apologetic coward who spent all of his waking hours cringing in fear, hiding from our enemies' wrath in the base's underground bunker.

"Tuffy", our First Sergeant, and who was also the Medical Sergeant, was there. He was in fact really the man in charge and certainly no coward, and Miguel Perez, a street-smart and charming Puerto Rican medic from a very different part of New York to where Levy hailed from. It was a matter of affluence. Same city, but one was from Uptown the other from Downtown.

Perez was never in charge of anything in his life, never would be, and really couldn't give a flying fart about it either. He was "short," meaning, almost over with his tour and halfway home, with only a few days left to board the "Freedom bird" (the civilian airliner that flew soldiers home at the end of their tour of duty in Vietnam). He was a lucky man and would not mess up his "short" schedule by volunteering for anything or taking on unnecessary responsibilities that may have put him in harm's way.

Everyone was friendly, welcoming me and showing me the ropes. I immediately felt again that I wouldn't have minded serving my tour of duty here.

Yet there was something going on in every "in country" veteran soldier's eyes, a repressed message, when they met an FNG like me. And their faces just couldn't succeed in showing a too-welcoming smile. There was only so much they could tell you, and too much they couldn't really tell you, all because you may or may not live. What were they going to explain to you? Which tree to hide behind? Or that everything was going to be OK? They could never know any of this even for themselves. We all knew that "tomorrow never knows." The Beatles told us that in song, didn't they?

The Medical Aid Station was a deep expansive hole dug into the ground, a bunker supported by wooden beams with stairs hacked out of the dirt and covered with crate tops. It comprised a well-equipped medical treatment center containing an electrical powered generator used primarily for chilling beers and occasionally for emergency lighting requirements.

Ample stores of medical supplies and about six cots had been provided for patient treatment. The roof and sides were heavily reinforced by laboriously filled sandbags. There were other smaller underground bunkers that were used for sleeping quarters, and for hiding from enemy mortar fire. Hot meals were served up three times a day, provided by the base's mess hall.

This was all part of the larger base, which had its own artillery section, re-supply services, helicopter operations and cargo re-fitters, not to mention an ammunition supply dump (Charlie's bull's eye), military police (MP) facility, graves registration, and a host of other units whose sole mission was to keep the lowly "grunt" infantryman well fed and heavily armed to continue to fight the real war "out there," on behalf of everyone else who was sort of safely ensconced back "in here."

They got regular mail from home, and enjoyed ice cream and movies, too. OK, they had incoming rockets and mortars fired at them two or three nights a week to contend with, but there was a war going on here.

John, who was known as John, had become my perpetual shadow by the time I settled in. The guy was afraid that I might contract food poisoning or something and die before I had officially replaced him. He seemed to be willing me to live for a while longer, at least. Take his job first and die later if I must, but please just not during our transition watch. If anything happened to me, the poor sucker had to go back out to the jungle to replace himself. I was in fact his only salvation, his way out of there. The means for the continuation of his life. Because I was *his* replacement.

I spent a day or two at the base, eating, sleeping, bonding, learning jungle theatre speak, and storing my other non-combat gear in a huge shipping container. I hoped someone else would not have to pick up my belongings for me. I was stripping down, morphing into the grunt combat soldier's basic war machine. Ready to fight or go wherever I was sent. This was what I had trained so hard for. Little did I suspect how truly staggering the events to come would be. Little did I know how blissfully secure I was in my ignorance.

I was destined to spend the next 11 months of my life as an infantry unit's medical corpsman, on continuous air and foot patrol operations between my brigade headquarters at Quan Loi, in the relentless jungles, and on numerous landing zones (LZ's) and fire support bases (FSB's), traversing doggedly the entire First Air Cavalry's III corps area of operations in Vietnam.

    I would taste combat in places with amazing names like Phuoc Vinh, Loc Ninh, An Loc, Tay Ninh, Song Be, Serges jungle highway, Ho Chi Minh trail, parrots beak and fish hook areas. Our terrain expanded to include the un-bargained for Cambodia, when our (US) forces invaded that neighbouring country. These lands were strange and beguiling to me. I would make a few short assignment stints back into Quan-Loi for medical re-supply purposes, but those trips were never for an extended period. I would not get to see much of my home base again because of where I was sent on assignment.

    John, the erstwhile hippy from San Francisco, became a much more relaxed and *relieved* veteran combat medic a few days after my arrival at Quan-Loi. Still, taking no chances with my physical well-being, he escorted me out and insistently *onto* the waiting "Dust off" Huey UH-1B chopper that was going to take me out to join my unit in the field. Besides the crew and me, there were crates of ammunition, food supplies, water, precious mail from home, and yet more ammunition that went "out" on my flight.

    John's smile was tinged with a little wistfulness. He gave me the popular clenched-fist salute, the one we all had copied from the Black Panthers movement and adopted as our own. He hopped from one leg to the other in anticipation and yelled above the whipping rotors. "Go give them motherfuckers hell, Doc."

    As the chopper lifted off, I watched John's figure dwindle to a distant silhouette. I settled down on the floor, my back resting uncomfortably against a case of white phosphorus fragmentation grenades. My legs dangled adventurously out of the helicopter's open hatchway. This was it; I was on my way at last to engage in the war.

The two pilots flying my helicopter looked like 17-year-old boys. But the pair of eyes that glanced over me just once, registering everything about me instantly, told me they were seasoned war veterans. They were probably in their early twenties anyway, if that much.

I tried to remain calm, to concentrate and somehow keep focused on my increasingly twisted emotions. I was tense but also meditative as I headed out determinedly towards something unknown waiting somewhere out there for me. I was ready for this, wasn't I? I had to be, and I would definitely see it through to the end, whatever that might be. I grew determined and resolved not to be overwhelmed by my present circumstances.

I gripped my M-16 rifle tightly, my knuckles white. My little island home in the Caribbean, Grand Anse Beach in particular, was a long way off now, so distant and removed from me that it might as well have been situated on some other planet. I hoped it would be all there waiting for me to return to one day when all of this was over with.

In Vietnam, you never approached, you arrived. The reason for this was that it was always necessary to get in and out as expeditiously as possible. All landing zones were targeted for hostile fire by the enemy; in and out were the only workable alternative to being shot down in flames.

The LZ was where all our operations started and ended for the 1st Air Cavalry, since we did everything by helicopter. Whether it was a medical evacuation, sky-trooper insertion, re-supply operation, or trooper replacement. The threat of being shot down always remained the same, and the possibility of this danger was always present.

The chopper pilots normally hovered at six feet above the ground then said, "OK, boys, you have arrived home…." In other words, jump the fuck out. Like right now! If necessary, the chopper crew chief or door gunner assisted the decision-making processes with a strategically and timely placed boot to the small of your back. Applied pressure and the laws of gravity usually took care of the rest, and you were out of there.

Exiting a helicopter hovering six feet above the ground when you were carrying a rucksack fully loaded with all your food supplies and clothes, M-16 rifle in one hand, your medical aid kit in the other; two twelve-clip bandoliers of ammo and four full water bottles strapped around your torso; wearing a heavy steel pot helmet, dealing with a swaying platform and the backwash of other choppers flying nearby; along with the possibility that you are already taking hostile fire, and scared shitless as was routine on those occasions—well, it always struck me that there had to be a better way.

But tell that to the pilots who had to sit there hovering and being shot at while we (in their minds) seemingly slow danced off their sitting duck stationary helicopter at our own leisure. It was obviously a question of perspective.

Inserting 100 men into or extracting them out of an area took time, and helicopters were noisy beasts. Their disturbance encouraged energetic little black pajama-clad fanatics to come scurrying over from the tree-line hideouts to try to kill us off during these manoeuvres whenever it was opportune.

They loved to do this. To take the opportunity to have us at a disadvantage. They had studied their enemy--us--and they knew our ways. They knew that when a chopper went down, others would always come to rescue possible survivors, thereby providing them with multiple targets. We never left anybody behind, dead or wounded. We came in together and went out together, every time.

They took advantage of this situation, but we repaid the courtesy, too, anytime we could do so with all the energy that we could muster, because this was a war.

You could imagine them. "Minh, you get to shoot down the next one. Here, take the RPG-40 launcher. Remember to aim for the pilots; the helicopters won't fly too well without them. Heh heh heh!" Great sport for some, I guessed.

We casually referred to the enemy and his people by disrespectful names like Gooks, Slants, Slope heads, and Dinks.

This may sound callous to a civilian reader today. But this harsh categorization of our opponents was intentional: it was a lot easier to do battle against someone you had depersonalized with an alias, rather than consider them someone's father, brother or son.

This was the norm for both sides of the conflict. Their references to us were similarly unflattering. Back then, having pressing longevity concerns to contend with, I wasted nary a thought on the name calling thing.

Chapter 10

Pop Smoke

"Pop smoke!" was the common cry of US forces servicemen waiting to receive a helicopter approaching a landing zone anywhere in Vietnam.

Someone in the expectant unit on terra firma detonated a colored smoke grenade on or near the spot where they wanted the chopper to land. The approaching pilot, once on station (in radio contact and in close proximity), identified the color of the smoke he saw through radio transmissions with the ground unit. Thereby confirming he was coming into a friendly drop-off or pickup zone, and not in fact into an ambush site.

The latter had been known to happen. Hence the necessity for the smoke routine.

Because of the dense terrain of triple canopy jungle, steep mountainous rocky escarpments, and, of course, unforgiving swamps and glutinous marshland with which our area of operations abounded, most of the time an LZ had to be physically cut out of the jungle by hand, meaning, with machetes and knives. Sometimes, a chopper could not land at the required location. An insertion or extraction had to be accomplished by repelling, or, in the case of wounded, going out winched up to the hovering helicopter in a basket-like contraption.

My arrival in the field was imminent. I was about to become an infantry combat medic.

The combat medic's job in Vietnam was referred to with whispered reverence, even with some head-shaking awe, in certain military circles. It had the glorious distinction of being one of the most recognizably and indisputably dangerous lines of work in a war, especially in that brutal and indiscriminate man-made conflict known as jungle warfare.

We were grunt medics (the grunt being the lowly foot soldier of history's pages), who always ended up mopping up politicians' messes and doing all the dirty work but who didn't always get the credit when due.

Medical corpsmen inexorably joined the casualty lists by the very nature of their jobs, which was to immediately get to the point of fighting to provide that vital, initial life-saving first aid to soldiers: the quick treatment of a sucking chest wound, or the proper application of a tourniquet to a shattered limb, combined with a quick response medevac helicopter extraction to a highly equipped, expertly staffed base hospital in the rear areas. This was the difference between life and death for many wounded infantrymen.

In a contact situation, meaning any skirmish with enemy forces, a medic had to get to the fallen fast, then know what to do and do it quickly and correctly, every time, if he was to accomplish his job of saving lives. In other words, when the shit hit the fan, the combat medic had to run towards the middle of the firefight in order to carry out his mission, while others in his unit might take well-recommended cover. Some combat units flatly refused to venture out without their full allotment of medics.

Medics were also targeted by the Vietcong as vital people to get rid of early in a battle, along with the unit's commander and the forward artillery observer. "Veterans of the long stare" would tell you that whenever this deliberate personnel culling was accomplished, immediate chaos would ensue among the unit's ranks. Morale, in such a confusing scenario was rapidly eroded, resulting in a castrated and floundering unit left exposed to the enemy's mercy or, more likely, lack thereof.

Note that, of the aforementioned trio slated for "chop chop" in Charlie's war manual, the medic was the next in line after the Commander. And right up there for just plain, everyday run-of the-mill death at the hands of the enemy forces. This was just another morale-boosting, confidence-building, fireside warming tidbit I had learned from Lieutenant Levy while he huddled safely in his bunker at Quan-Loi prior to my being sent out to the field.

I guessed that he must have seen all of this on armed services television before coming overseas.

Mortality rates were astronomically high among our ranks.

Our helicopters flew at treetop level habitually to frustrate enemy ground-to-air fire. By the time the would-be ambusher heard the sound of the quickly moving craft, it was usually well past his position and out of his sights.

In truth, I couldn't claim to have seen anything "much" during my first trip out to the field as my helicopter hurtled just above the green jungle expanse.

The company of about 100 men that I was joining, waiting below, would be tactically out of sight anyway, with only a small squad of eight to ten men assigned to meet us. Their job was to rapidly unload whatever or whoever was coming in and then to move away from the "hot" pick-up zone as expeditiously as possible. The rest of the company would be already widely dispersed, manning perimeters, approaches and flanks that were set up around the LZ. Always quickly, in and out. Choppers didn't hang around the drop-off zone, ever.

My circling Huey finally started making an approach to somewhere. I craned my neck around to try to see where, but I couldn't see a damn thing except verdant lush foliage, and more unbroken jungle. The same scenery I had been seeing for the past half hour. Where the hell were we going? Was this a slow crash or something? Had we been quietly shot down? Stupid thoughts from a sensory-starved and disoriented brain. I soon made out a slender thread of green smoke drifting about indifferently, somewhere far below us.

The helicopter's nose pitched upwards for its pre-landing approach. Tree branches tore the shit out of my foolishly dangling legs. Pull them in while you still have them, boy. The door gunner slapped me firmly on the back. "*Get ready!*" he ordered. What the fuck was he talking about, get ready? We were still way up in the air. I couldn't see anyone or anything properly, not even the ground.

The door gunner then said, "*Stand up now and prepare yourself!*" I looked around the cabin for support but there was nobody else in here but me. We were lower now. I glimpsed some ghostly blurred faces peering up at us from the tree line. The perimeter happened to be swathed in eerie wisps of ground fog. We were about six or eight feet off the ground then, I supposed. Who could tell? The homicidal door gunner finally said to me: "*OK, man, this is it! Good luck! Jump out now!*"

At this juncture, any rational civilian would have said, "NO," and cited some reasonably convincing human rights convention as a persuasive argument for his reluctance to deplane from such a threatening height. But this was the military, and this was what all of our training was about. A soldier jumped when ordered to. So I jumped.

The air was hot and humid, dusty and unfamiliar. I was being dropped off somewhere in the middle of nowhere. Who was down there, friend or foe? I hadn't really seen anyone or anything clearly yet; only taken the word of Mr. Death Wish, my belligerent door gunner, who never had to jump off anywhere on any given occasion, ever. So it was all very well and good for him to tell other people to jump. I was the only sucker getting off at this confidence-building stop at a time when I was feeling as confident as a snake cornered down in a mongoose hole. Lord, what a thing!

I couldn't say whether I was in fact eventually nudged out of the hovering aircraft or leapt willingly, but I came down heavily. When I got up from my unmilitary-like spread eagled embarrassment, I worked my way up to all fours, stumbling and groping around frustratingly in a dust storm of images and unfamiliarity. Propeller blades jackhammered above me—had to remember to keep my head down. My helmet, living up to its more homely name of steel pot, was breaking my neck - had to hold on to my medical bag. My rifle was glued to my other hand as usual. I felt nothing but dust, heat, disorientation, and noise. My head was spinning wildly.

Disembodied voices yelled out indecipherable instructions to somebody from somewhere very far away. People materialized from the tree line, kind of looking like Americans: Green fatigues now bleached brown, bead-wearing hippy types in floppy hats. It could *only* be Americans dressed and looking that way. I was safe!

Someone came up to me, collected me, and spirited me away to firmer and saner ground. More than likely out of everybody's way. He said to me, "You the FNG medic replacement assigned to First platoon!"

It was a statement not a question. "Yes," I mumbled, breathless, "I am."

The company was by now stirring in a no nonsense fashion, beginning to move out expeditiously. The receding chopper's blades were already somewhat muted from the impressive distance it had wasted no time in putting between us. In and out. Always carefully in, and very rapidly out. The silence that replaced the throbbing rotor blades was deafening the first time that one came to grips with the suffocating isolation of being in the middle of nowhere, cut off from every vestige of civilization we once so easily – took for granted.

All supplies brought in with me had been recovered and distributed among the four platoons already. We had to move out of there right away. You didn't hang around a used LZ for too long before hearing that soon-to-be-familiar - *thump, thump, thump* of incoming mortar rounds.

I was hastily introduced to my new platoon sergeant; a confident-looking guy named Tom somebody or the other. Shit, he looked younger than I. He said to me, nonchalantly, both hands on my shoulders, "Come with me, doc, you walk along right here between these two guys. Don't hyperventilate on me now; you'll be all right; talk to you later." And with that said he was gone, swiftly melted away into the forest's yawning gloom. I did not see him to talk to again for another four days.

I really hated the fact that my arrival to join my first combat unit in the field was performed with such indelicacy, but much later I was told of the many generals, some of whom had even graced the cover of *Time* magazine, who had also fallen on their asses after exiting helicopters on their arrival in the field, and in circumstances very similar to mine.

I still couldn't help but wonder how many of them had also had an unsympathetic door gunner to put up with on their trip out. I also pondered whether any of the guys out here would allow me to even put a band-aid on their pinky fingers now. Shit!

* * * * *

Charlie Company, 1st Battalion, 5th Air Cavalry Division Airmobile, or C/1/5, was an infantry line company of approximately 100 to 110 men. Changes occurred in unit strength because of death, number of wounded or sick. This unit was now my parent company, my home away from home.

Four platoons of about 25 men each made up the company. The platoons were further broken down into approximately three eight man squads. The company commander was normally a captain, and the platoon leaders were 1st or 2nd lieutenants. Each platoon had a sergeant of staff E-6 or E-5 rank. The squads were led by a corporal or SP-4 (specialist fourth class) rank trooper.

Each platoon was assigned a medic or corpsman, plus a senior medic (normally the longest serving in the unit) who was assigned to the Headquarters platoon with the company commander and fire direction observer, or F/O (an artillery service lieutenant). The company sergeant stationed at the HQ platoon was of E-7 sergeant first class or E-8 first sergeant rank. These men were known as "Lifers": they spent their entire existence in the military. They wouldn't go home until they retired 25 or 30 years down the road: Not before most of them completed at least two or three tours of duty in a war sometimes.

They were indisputably recognized as being both omniscient and omnipresent; hence they were simply left to run their outfits without challenge by anyone.

They were in fact the heart and soul of any operation. Nothing got done without them. Orders were passed on to them by officers, but *they* made the men carry them out. An army could not function without these men. Sensible officers stayed out of their way and, by doing so, remained in their good graces while getting their own jobs done more efficiently.

Each platoon had an RTO, a radio telephone operator, with radio of course. HQ platoon had one extra, and the F/O had his own operator specifically for calling in fire missions that were necessary at times when we were pinned down in the bush and needed help. Artillery support batteries fired from a nearby firebase, usually directly onto the heads of the very people responsible for our being pinned down in the first place.

Sometimes we had a Chaplain (Padre) out here with us for a while. Also tracker dog teams that came and went. These lovely, highly trained German Shepherds never went home from the canine unit because of disease carrying viruses they contracted or may have contracted while serving over here. We tried not to get too close to them emotionally.

Five companies made up our Battalion--Alpha, Bravo, Charlie, Delta, and Echo. We operated in the III-Corps region Northwest of Saigon, in the infamous "Parrot's beak" area, very close to the Cambodian border. Our mission was primarily *"search and destroy."*

Our main assignment was to prevent infiltrating North Vietnamese Regulars and their material from journeying down to the south from communist North Vietnam, along the Ho Chi Minh trail and the Serges jungle highway. Both were popular infiltration routes for artillery, vehicles, food and medical supplies, and, of course, the manpower. All vitally important to wage the ground warfare which was fought entirely in the southern part of the country where we were deployed.

The US military was in South Vietnam to support the supposedly democratic South against North Vietnam's communist aggression. The North, in turn, claimed they wanted to unite both territories under one flag—that flag being the one bearing communist colours, naturally.

Our base for operations was a fire support base (FSB), or landing zone (LZ). You would hear of LZ's called "Vivian", "Baldy" or "David" that were carved out of dense forest or the sides of mountains. Locations were picked entirely for strategic purposes, never for their aesthetics.

The typical LZ was hacked out of the jungle and crafted into a circular-shaped fortification, with a bare strip of open land extending around it for three hundred and sixty degrees; well out to the ever present tree line. Protective concertina barbed wire strands were laid right around this perimeter, and the wire was heavily booby trapped with claymore mines, trip flares and an assortment of noise makers.

Defensive machine gun emplacements were set up right around the entire outer perimeter ring of the fortification. Within the compound were sandbag- fortified bunkers, work and living spaces, some wooden buildings built above ground with sandbag protection for the various uses required by all the supporting services.

First there was the tactical operations center (TOC): headquarters of the battalion commander, a lieutenant colonel, and his support staff. Then there were a medical aid station, a mess hall, and the vital helicopter landing pad for operations.

There was at least a battery or two of 105mm or 155mm artillery gun emplacements, with their computerized fire direction centers for fire support for troops out in the field. We had pits for mortar crews and areas for all-purpose supplies, including large water vessels. All of this was required to keep the five-line companies supplied with food and all the necessary war-waging equipment during their entire field operations scheduled rotations out in the dense jungle.

The helicopter pad serviced all the choppers, from the giant CH-54 Crane heavy transport to the CH-47 Chinook 30-seat cargo/transporter and, of course, the UH-I Huey, our workhorse sky-trooper transporter. It was sometimes also an operations base for the fiery AH-1G Cobra "Blue Max" gunship and its little mate in the hunter-killer team of destruction, the single-seat OH6A-LOH.

One line-company was assigned the responsibility for base defense, which was as the name suggested, while the other four were deployed on patrol/mission sweeps—sent out to work in the field, so to speak, to find, capture and or to kill the enemy.

We rotated missions, so that every company got a week in after three or four weeks out in the bush. The LZ provided hot meals, mail from home, cold beer, running water to shave and shower, a change or two of clean clothes, and music. All that was sadly lacking out there in the field. Without this periodic relief, creeping insanity would have held sway among the men, eventually.

Ten or 11 months of a grunt's 12-month Vietnam tour would be spent out here in the jungle.

Except that everyone was eligible for a two-week "rest and recuperation" (R & R) leave, which could be taken in Hawaii, Hong Kong, Bangkok, Japan, or in Australia. No one was ever known to come back "rested" or "recuperated" from R & R. Usually, the men returned seriously and definitely worse off for wear, very tired, and depleted in body and soul from these sojourns into paradise.

Most of them engaged in understandable self-indulgences on these trips, taking advantage of the wide range of physical services on offer that young men required from time to time and could not be regularly found in the jungle. These destinations catered to a burgeoning sex trade.

Young soldiers on leave from an ongoing war with considerable quantities of internationally recognized US currency begging to be spent, were always welcomed by the proprietors of the many bars, bordellos, restaurants and hotels at these randy locales.

Besides these recreational breaks, the LZ became a much appreciated home away from home. The words that "we are going in," spoken while out "humping" in the hot, wet, muddy, mosquito-infested jungle, were always immediately welcome to all who heard them because of what they represented: a refreshing pause, away from the sweltering and threatening boondocks.

Surprisingly, we had some meals out in the field that were quite palatable. We called them LRRPS. They were in fact the dehydrated food that the long range reconnaissance patrol units traveled with. We were sometimes lucky to get these meals in addition to our C rations, the definitely not so palatable tin food that unfortunately made up the bulk of our food supplies.

The C rations were anything that came in a tin, from luncheon meat to spaghetti and meatballs to pears. Once opened, you could either warm them in the tin itself or pour the contents into your canteen cup and then warm the contents on a prepared fire.

The difference with the LRRPS was that when you opened the package, helpfully labeled either chicken and rice or beef stew, all you saw inside was some dried out and dehydrated pap that looked suspiciously like a baby's fecal matter. But when you poured some hot water over this mess a meal literally formed before your eyes. More to the point, these meals were absolutely tasty, quite unlike the C rations, which were certainly not.

The C rations were also quite heavy to carry. The challenge was always to be balanced; by not taking too much from the supply helicopter to hump around on your back in the suffocating jungle, but taking just enough to last until the next re-supply flight to avoid starvation.

Hot meals provided on the LZ's were unforgettable affairs. Just the smell of real, cooked food, washed down with cold drinks and sometimes available ice cream, could only be properly appreciated if one had to do without these pleasures for a period of time.

Another thing about our meals was that everyone ate together. There were no longer barriers of rank or pecking order for food. We all lined up and waited our turn together. It was virtually impossible to suffer from hunger in the US military. Impossible. Those people liked to eat, and eat they did, whenever and wherever it was possible to do so.

Yet, despite this never-ending supply of food, we all yearned to be rid of the place. The popular 'Animals' song of the day "We gotta get out of this place" was sung by all soldiers, primarily when half drunk. It was our favourite tune of all time, a one-and-only anthem that meant the same thing to everyone. This was what we all lived to do, to make it back to where we came from and where we belonged as soon as our tour was up.

Another famous saying of the day reminded us we "owed it to ourselves" to do this, though sadly not all would.

Mail from home, whether from a girlfriend, the wife or a neighborhood pastor, especially letters with pictures, was a welcome thrill. A letter reminded us of that distant but promising real life out there waiting for us to resume someday. It was the necessary link that kept many a disillusioned soldier focused on seeing out the end of his hell tour.

But it could also be a heartbreaker on occasion. The resupply helicopter brought in mail. Mail call was always filled either with hopeful promise, or it could tailspin rapidly out of control into grave and traumatic disappointment for a soldier a long way from home. On a no-letter day, your mental isolation was immediate. You couldn't help but feel cut off from humanity or anything real. Peter Harris, an inimical jackass from Detroit, would look across at me and say loudly enough for the whole of southern Vietnam to hear, "Nothing for you again today, Roge?" whilst gleefully brandishing a thick pile of pretty colored sweet-scented envelopes.

You couldn't help then but wonder at the sneer on his face. And your mind would race. Did he know something you didn't? Was it "Jody", that perennial replacement boyfriend back home who allegedly took care of business with your wife or girlfriend while you were away? And if so, did he know something about it? Self-doubt and fresh worries start to seep into the crevasses of your mind. When did she last write you? Was there a subtle undercurrent in the tone of that last letter from her? Were there hidden clues that you missed before? Where was that damn letter anyway?

The gulf between this experience and that of hearing "Byer, got something here for you" was tremendous. No matter what the news might be, you took your letter and walked away to a private spot to read it if you had time before the company moved out. Or you waited until you had time and prayed for enough reading light left in the day. First, you examined the handwriting, recognizing the style as hers, and you drank it in. Then you smelled the envelope for any lingering traces of her familiar perfume. Then you carefully opened the letter, and ingested its contents.

This was an intentionally drawn-out ritual, prolonged in order to savour and maximize what a letter from a sweetheart or wife represented to its recipient. It was an immeasurably great boon and boost to a soldier's lonely state of mind.

Because of this, I unrepentantly damned those self-centered partners who selfishly wrote gut-curdling "Dear John" letters, telling a soldier embroiled in jungle warfare like ours, that they had found someone else or were simply breaking up with him.

To me, regardless of the circumstances, it was cruel and dispassionate: Out here? Where you could not compete or even respond with a clear head? To be told sorry, go take a hike? Too cruel.

Chapter 11

A Typical Force Insertion

A typical force insertion would take place when battalion intelligence got wind of enemy "movement." They then sent us out from the Fire Support Base to counter this. If we were already in the field, we just "humped" as we would more normally say towards the expected trouble spot from wherever we were, in order to engage the enemy promptly.

"We have movement" was without a doubt the most gut-wrenching, bone-chilling, closer-to-thy-maker warning ever uttered from a soldier's lips in our normally silent but tense jungle environment. The words were usually expressed by the point man, the unfortunate guy walking in front of the entire unit and therefore the most likely person to hear anything or succumb to any hostilities first.

Traditionally, it was the newest guy in the unit who was awarded the grim distinction of being allowed to walk point: Always until someone newer than him joined the company. (This could take weeks sometimes.) Needless to say, this position did not encourage longevity. Everybody got their chance at it, though. Continued survival in this position depended on a giant- size portion of personal good luck.

At the sound of "movement," all normal brain functions ceased. Any coherent conversation was immediately disrupted. Every previously ongoing action was immediately abandoned. Faces tingled, then became numb, and nervous stomachs churned acid.

This could happen anywhere, anytime. It could occur in the middle of the night, during a rest break, while on ambush, or on radio watch. Or, most exasperatingly, while pissing in the bush or taking a crap.

Because of the thick jungle environment in which we operated, we seldom saw the enemy. You could only hear him. That fateful sound, be it the snapping of a twig underfoot, the rustle of clothing or the clinking of exposed metal, was the signal of an imminent confrontation. An entire unit of 100 men prepared instantly when alerted. We got our weapons ready, hunkered down and waited for all hell to break loose. It usually did. You never had to wait too long either.

The entire company was loaded onto Huey UH-1 and CH-47 Chinook helicopters at the LZ. Six to 10 men aboard the smaller bird, about thirty on the larger one. Five to 10 helicopters at a time lifted us to our drop zone. As we approached the area, the helicopter door gunners would "prep" the tree line by strafing with machine-gun fire to try to dissuade any waiting enemy from greeting us in kind.

When we were dropped off, we raced into the tree line from the unprotected landing site and set up a covering perimeter for the other troops arriving behind us. This whole operation could be pulled off in minutes, if no enemy resistance was met on arrival.

The company moved out swiftly for us to carry out our task. As we moved deeply into the silent jungle, we were soon swallowed up by the dark, brooding, and seemingly patiently waiting trees. We began our mission keenly; our shoulders burdened by heavy equipment, our minds by lingering trepidation.

We moved towards a predetermined point on the map, humping three to five kilometres or what we called "klicks", a day. The distance covered was actually determined by the prevailing terrain and, of course, enemy activity in the immediate operational area.

What we encountered was dense triple-canopy jungle, riddled with leech- infested and mosquito-swarmed swamps that we had to ford, chest deep, while keeping the one thing that must always be kept dry, our rifle, extended achingly high above our heads.

The undergrowth produced clinging and vicious ankle-twisting vines : Interspersed with various species of poisonous snakes and many varieties of insects, all contributed equally to the agony of our marches.

Bloodsucking swamp leeches would attach themselves to a man's body, painlessly gorging itself on his blood. Thankfully, the tip of a lit cigarette was sufficient to dispatch those voracious vampires.

The infantryman carried everything necessary for his survival in the jungle with him on his back: Until helicopter re-supply could be arranged at an opportune date. The machine gunner carried his heavier weapon and all his extra ammunition belts. His assistant disdainfully carried much more of the same.

Every soldier had a rucksack (backpack), with a towel placed under the straps to prevent blistering on your shoulders, containing your change of uniforms: shirts, pants, socks. No underwear because of chaffing and crotch rot that wearing underwear caused in a jungle environment. We carried all our food and water, about three bottles per man.

The radio operators carried their standard radio sets, the PRC-25's. Of course, these sets would be forever labeled

"Prick 25's." The radio operators either walked next to the company commander, their platoon leaders or the artillery forward observer, ever ready to add to or receive the never ceasing stream of radio transmissions.

Everyone was equipped with an air mattress, a retrenching tool, and a poncho and liner (the latter was a rubber sheeting used to make a half tent cover for sleeping under in foul weather conditions). The crew-served heavy weapons sections, M-60 and .50 caliber machine gunners, and mortar crews had heavy tripods and rounds to "hump", along with their personal gear. As the medical corpsman, I had a fully outfitted aid bag, with bandages, morphine syringes et al, to carry, in addition to my personal kit, rifle and ammunition bandoliers.

All metal surfaces had to be wrapped in cloth or securely taped to prevent clinking or jangling noises. The sound of metal on metal that carried for miles and resonated audibly in the quietude of the jungle could alert the ever listening enemy to our location.

One had to communicate in muted whispers all the time out there. The entire atmosphere was that of a silent, surrealistic survival dance routine. As we humped along, a squad of men were periodically dispatched out from the main body for general scouting, or ambush duties along incursion trails that looked like well-trafficked routes used by the enemy.

Claymore mines and early warning trip flares were tactically positioned at a key junction along a visibly used trail by the ambush party. The claymores dispatched steel ball bearings in a 100-foot swath of instant death when a hand-held detonator was squeezed, so as to send an electrical charge through an attached wire to the explosive end. Two squeezes, of quite audible "clack-clacks", were all it took to unleash this hellfire.

The men then took up their vigil of the enemy along the staked-out area.

At the chosen ambush site, machine guns were emplaced to produce the most brutal effective onslaught. Merciless, interlocking bursts of raw firepower were carefully aimed at anybody who walked down the targeted trail.

This was nothing less than a killing field. The squad of men settled down, determined, to annihilate anyone who would appear on the scene and become "step ons", our way of referring to the enemy dead.

I never saw an NVA regular or Vietcong combatant walk away from one of these deadly mantraps, once they had been effectively sprung.

This was how it happened on a cool, quiet, sedate jungle morning.

The birds would stop singing, the crickets stopped chirping, and silence weighed eternal. Four men stepped around the corner of the trail and were cut to pieces by the ensuing enfilade. Just like that. Once they stumbled into the kill zone, they were dead meat.

Maybe mercifully so, it all happened fast. They could not save themselves, but they did not suffer longer than necessary. Our weaponry was high-powered and modern. The result of this action was no Hollywood production. The men had been clinically mowed down. Their remains were pulpy and grotesque, with dismembered body parts and splattered brain matter everywhere. War, was a dirty hell. Ours was a killing situation. So what was the point of trying to clothe it in justification bullshit? We did what we had to do. Others, in future wars, would do the same again in similar circumstances.

Our daily patrolling started at dawn. Aside for short water breaks, a pause for a bite of food, or to receive a scheduled helicopter resupply flight or medevac dustoff, we humped until about two hours before dusk.

We then stopped and pretended to set up our overnight bivouac. This was a vital safeguard. It was the old you-think-we're-here-but-we're-actually-not ploy. We made some boldly exaggerated settling-in noises for effect, except that we were not staying. We moved away at least a kilometer from this location to our truly chosen overnight stop area. Invariably, the first location received mortar fire sometime during the night, once there were enemy patrols in the immediate area. This enabled us to sleep a bit more comfortably where we actually were, a relatively safe "klick" away from attack for one night, at least.

We would finally dig in just before nightfall, which literally fell in the jungle with an abrupt finality. This sent us scrambling to complete our nocturnal preparations. Trenches had to be dug in the ground to take cover in case of an attack on our positions during the night.

Security perimeters had to be established, and mines and trip flares selectively emplaced. A command post was set up, and our coordinates (position on the map) radioed into battalion headquarters in case we needed a fire mission or a helicopter medevac extraction during the night.

Radio watch, keeping in touch with our headquarters, was shared by everyone. One of my first nights on radio duty, I sat squirming on the hard wet ground, moping to myself about the injustice of being constantly stalked by a host of determined little fuckers wearing black pajamas. Suddenly, across the sobering airwaves came this deeply contented, bass, stentorian voice breaking into my sleep-deprived consciousness with a silky rendition of "Fence Post 7" (our company's call sign), General Motors 65 (battalion HQ's call sign), your SITREP? Headquarters was calling to get our situation report. Were we still alive out there, or were we pinned down in a firefight with superior enemy forces? The short reply of "Negative SITREP" would reaffirm our status quo. We were constantly in touch with headquarters, every minute of the day and night, while out in the jungle. This was routine.

I keyed the microphone to scream "Yes, you warmly secured, steak-eating, cold beer-guzzling, two-movie-a-night-viewing son of a bitch, we're still out here." But all that came out on the tail of a wide yawn was "General Motors 65, Fence Post 7, negative SITREP."

Nights in the jungle. They were dark, wet and cold, but perhaps most disturbing of all, eerily quiet. The jungle treetops were so high that they blocked out not only available light but sometimes obliterated the entire sky as well. There were no stars out there to reach out to or attempt to hold onto—disturbing indeed for someone like me, hailing from an island always covered by a star-filled Caribbean night sky.

When we lay down on the ground at night on our chosen lonely spot, our thoughts came ricocheting back at us loudly. Hearing ourselves think was the only conversation available at times. So we got used to it. We talked to ourselves, and then rolled over and got some rest until it was our turn for radio watch.

During the monsoon season, which spitefully and inconveniently lasted half the year, the rain fell in relentless torrential sheets. We woke up in the rain, ate, pissed, crapped, ate again, and went back to sleep in the same rain. Sometimes, we had to fight in it, too. Then it continued the next day, and so on, and on, and on, same drill.

In the mornings we rolled up our air mattresses, shook the water and dew out of our poncho/pup tents, sacrificed a little precious drinking water to wash the kisser and brush the teeth. We listened for the birds, crickets, and frogs to begin to chirp or croak their morning song. This was always subconsciously noted by everyone. The sudden absence of their symphony most accurately forewarned of the approach of the enemy. A little C-4 explosive (I know, not army approved) to light a fire between two stones. Add a package of cocoa, sugar, and cream powder to the canteen cup with water neatly balanced over the illegal flame; open a tin of luncheon meat, add some biscuits, and we were about good to go.

But I was down to my last pair of dry socks. I had to throw out all the other ones from my rucksack: what the leeches didn't invade, dry rot infected. I wondered if Chief would lend me a pair.

Chief, Francis Billy, was a full-blooded Navajo Indian. A short, quiet, brown-skinned man with a big heart, and a winning but tentative smile that he issued sporadically, he was trying his best to survive in a war zone that bore no resemblance whatsoever to his Native American ancestral tribal grounds.

I loved Chief. He had taken me under his veteran wings when I first arrived out in the field as a struggling FNG, when I was green and most at risk of drowning in an ocean of pathos. He allowed me to place my bed roll next to his the first couple of nights out. This was, to me, akin to being breastfed as a baby. I wanted to cry out in relief and heartfelt appreciation in those gloomy first days and especially challenging nights out in the bush.

I would always be grateful to Chief for taking a little time to care.

People understandably stayed away from FNGs, an endangered species because of their tendency to do foolish things their first time out. With naturally alarmingly high death rates, a soldier didn't improve his chances of survival by hanging around them. So FNGs were kind of avoided out in the bush. It didn't matter that everyone started out their jungle assignment as an FNG, scared and inexperienced.

You just prayed to God you didn't *end* up as an FNG. It was like how you really learned to drive a car only about three months after you actually got your driver's license. This was accomplished through sheer cumulative experience. Out here, you had to try to survive while you became acclimatized to everything overnight. There was no grace period. So it was hard, but that was how it was in the jungle, hard. In times of great stress, we reached back to memories of better days.

Having lived on a Caribbean island for most of my existence, the sea had become an intrinsic part of my life. My home at Silversands was literally located on the famous Grand Anse Beach.

I always saw the water when I looked out of my classroom window at the Grenada Boys Secondary School, down at the wind-rippled lagoon that formed part of the sheltered inner harbour of the capital city of St. George's. Grenada's largest sporting facility, at Queens Park, where I competed as a cyclist, was also by the sea.

The St. John's River passed within feet of the main stadium on her one-way journey to the beckoning, blue waters of the Caribbean Sea. If I wasn't next to the sea at any given time, if so desirous, I could be on its shoreline within five minutes.

Now, every day and night, I was suffocating out here in this thick green jungle, a sea of trees, an ocean of a very different kind. I felt smothered by this stifling and impenetrable triple-canopied gargantuan that never, ever seemed to leave me. I yearned for real seawater. It was in my blood, and I missed it dearly.

The sea to an islander is like what a park depicted to an urban dweller. The park was a place to sit, read a book, have lunch, feed pigeons or walk babies in strollers. The seaside a place to swim, stroll on a beach, or have a picnic with family or friends.

For the city dweller and the islander our familiar places of routine were always comfortingly there. Although you did not consciously pay attention to them, you knew, and reassuringly so, that they were still there for you whenever you needed them. I yearned for my island now.

Chapter 12

Incoming

One of the most recognizable and unanimously heeded declarations in the Vietnam War was the excitedly expressed and sometimes panicked shout of "*Incoming.*"

Because we existed in a war zone, explosions occurred all the time. Sometimes, it was that warning yell of "fire in the hole." This heads-up warning was given by combat engineers as they proceeded to blow up something for construction or land-clearing purposes. Or it signalled the necessary detonation of old, captured or damaged enemy munitions.

The warning of "incoming," though, was a confirmation that we were indeed under attack.

Our artillery pieces on the LZ's and FSB's were normally 105-mm or 155-mm howitzer batteries that provided fire support missions for our units out in the field around the clock. Therefore, loud bangs and explosions were synonymous with the way of life on these bases. Especially so if we were fortified with long-range, self-propelled artillery howitzers, like the 8-inch 'cherry picker' or the 175- mm gun. These large artillery pieces manoeuvred on tracks like tanks and made deafening noises when discharging their huge missile payloads.

It was firstly vital to know whether the explosion was outgoing or incoming. This crucial, early warning had to be given by the first person who recognized the trajectory of the rounds in question.

Knowing the direction that the rounds were heading was nothing short of life prolonging. This warning was then announced by simply screaming at the top of one's voice, to all points of the compass, "Incoming!"

This was guaranteed to get everyone's attention. All action stopped, and a predictable human stampede ensued with only one thought in mind: How to get to the nearest underground sandbagged bunker position. The wailing of warning sirens (where available) was further confirmation of an attack.

The cry of "incoming" also changed the entire base's posture as preparations had to be made for the real possibility of a ground attack (an all-out assault on a fixed base by infantry ground forces).

A decision had to be made as to whether the barrage of mortars or rockets being received was an opening gambit for a more sustained attack, or just probing fire by the enemy. The wait was never a long one for stark clarification of these matters to be confirmed.

Chapter 13

A Bunker in Binh Long Province

Try to imagine this. It's 0130 hours on a muggy, starless morning. We are all trying to listen to 'The Beatles' fantastic new album, *Abbey Road*. Albeit, without much success, because there's an ominous disturbance. It's Vietnam, and they're hell-bent on having a war out here.

We were in a sandbag-reinforced underground bunker on our brigade base camp at Quan Loi. The base was on condition one – red alert. Sirens were howling and sphincters were contracting, as would be expected under the circumstances. The music was being played on Miguel Perez's phlegmatic, battery-driven cassette tape deck. We had to listen really close in order to decipher anything clearly.

Underground bunkers were used principally for combatants' protection on nights like tonight, when the local chapter of the Vietcong vigorously and convincingly reminded us of their unswerving commitment to the war effort by raining down a merciless barrage of 122-mm rockets and 82-mm mortars on our friendly neighbourhood Division Garrison, without either invitation or forewarning.

The indoor lighting provided for our musical interlude was by somewhat waning candlelight. Additional outdoor lighting and complementary sound effects were the result of constant illumination from our own perimeter observation flares, and the incessant shell blasts and impacting incoming rounds of enemy ordnance.

The $64,000.00 question, as always, begged: Was the incoming firestorm a precursor to the graver and more foreboding threat of a fully fledged ground attack intended to breach, then ultimately overrun the entire base's fortifications?

What should we do? Collect our weapons and ammo as ordered, don our steel helmets and flak jackets and report to our pre-assigned defensive positions on the base perimeter? Or should we just continue to hunker down and blissfully listen to John Lennon sing "Come Together"?

Maybe the Vietcong would just get tired of it all tonight and go away.

"Hey Miguel, bro, anymore cold beers in that cooler, man?" Uhmnnn...ahhh....... *"Here come old flattop, he come grooving up slowly....". A* rocket exploded nearby, just outside the bunker complex, and the little cassette player droned on in the underground bunker.

Chapter 14

Xmas Day 1969

When I got up on Christmas day, the morning seemed similar to all other jungle mornings. I was stiff as usual from sleeping on the damn hard ground. The air mattress and poncho bed were of no help to my perpetually sore backside. I was in a grouchy mood. It was cold and it was damp as the morning mist slowly raised up in cloying wisps off the surfaces of mold and rot-infested lichen and flora.

"Get up and be gone with you," I mumbled. I would never get used to sleeping on this damned ground.

The massive treetops were entwined in their early morning torpor. There would be no warming welcome sunlight slipping through, if they had anything to do with it.

The depressing gloom had to persist, they would see to that. The jungle was so dank and grey, so frigid and unprepossessing. The sameness of the day was disheartening, and it was supposed to be Christmas.

A platoon leader reminded someone to pass the word around, lest anyone negligently forgets, that Battalion Headquarters had informed us earlier by radio that today was a cease-fire day.

There would be no shooting today, because we were supposed to be having a truce with the enemy. How ludicrous! No shooting, eh? We were operating north of An Loc at a map grid reference somewhere without a name.

We'd been humping around for a week and had only seen some wild pigs foraging beneath the trees. We were not engaged with anyone, so how were we to disengage? There was no one with whom to cease fire with. I was getting madder by the minute.

More worrisome was the question of who, actually, was going to inform the North Vietnamese regulars, who had left their barracks in Hanoi a month ago in groups of five to ten, all of them romping down the Ho Chi Minh trail on their way to kill some Americans as so ordered, about our cease fire?

They most likely were not in touch with their command and control centre. Were we to kindly ask them to please take their fingers off of their triggers, too? Maybe in tandem, on a count of three?

The absurdity of it all and the inevitable drudgery of the day made it impossible for us to wish each other even the most token merry anything. Standard radio blackout procedures killed any idea of carols. Who was going to sing them anyway?

We looked at each other with sad, knowing smiles. We would not give in to the ridiculous notion that it was Christmas Day today; we refused to accept the idea, when it was clearly a day like all the others out here.

There would be no Xmas in 1969 for us, it won't happen. We will have our Xmas some other time, and we are willing to wait for this opportunity.

Two things that we knew for sure. That it would not happen in 1969, and that whenever we did get the chance to do it right, that it would be a really great one.

Chapter 15

Field Extraction

"Just put your finger on that hole and squeeze down hard."

"Jesus, doc, fucking blood is pumping out," my friend lamented.

"That's why I want you to press down firmly here for me," I said, encouraging my buddy. "The blood's from an artery. I'm preparing a pressure bandage then I'll tie a tourniquet on the wound. Just stay with me on this. I have to splint the leg, too. A compound fracture, but I'd finish much faster if I got some help around here. You just give me a hand with this."

I turned back to my friend. "It will be fine."

"Oh, my God, Jesus, doc, am I dying? Tell me the truth." This was from our 2nd platoon point man, Jeb; I was trying to treat him with a little reluctant help from one of the guys.

"Not yet, Jeb, you'll be OK. We'll have you out of here real soon, I promise." I bullshit further -"A dustoff is inbound already," I said with a grim smile. Not true. There was no Medevac yet, but I had to embellish to keep his spirits up; this was vital. We'd been calling for a medevac for a while, but no luck so far.

Tattooed Memories

"Doc, I can't—"

"Mark! What's wrong with you, man? Just keep your fucking finger on that damn hole, like I showed you. Stop acting like a damn pussy. You helping me out with this or not?"

"OK, Doc, OK." Mark reluctantly replies. "But hurry the fuck up, man; I'm not a fucking medic. All this blood and shit….I can't take too much more of this."

Our point man had been shot in the upper thigh by a VC sniper as we patrolled through some rubber trees near Quan Loi about a half an hour before. No sign of the VC yet, but we were looking. I needed to medevac Jeb out soon; I was getting worried about his blood loss.

I neutralized the wound, then kept him warm and comfortable. Got him to relax by exaggerating how close his pick up medevac chopper was to our position. I had to keep him quiet to prevent the onset of shock, a serious battlefield condition which happened often when someone was hit by high powered weapons.

Eventually "Hey, doc, the dust off is on station now," somebody yelled. Thank God. It was a UH-1 medevac Huey, now overhead, but it had to hover because there was no open area for the pilot to land among the rubber trees. In situations like this we extracted our wounded in a basket litter on a winch extended down from the helicopter.

As the litter was winched down from the helicopter on a "jungle penetrator" device, I flashed back to my training class at Fort Sam. The practical class that taught us to do what I was doing now. Except, out here I was performing the exercise, not with a training dummy, but with a wounded man whose life rested squarely in my hands.

But it all seemed so long ago, my training.

The Huey swayed and steadied itself. It had to stay immobile as we winched up the litter.

God forbid if we started taking hostile ground fire in the middle of all this.

I banished the thought and got to work, slowly and gently winching Jeb up, up, up. The operation seemed to take forever, and the noise of the hovering chopper was stupendously loud.

General Giap, the NVA's top general and military strategist, could lean out of his back door in Hanoi, and he would be able to hear us quite easily, I thought.

Jeb was finally winched up and into the medevac chopper.

The on-board medic was already setting up an IV(intravenous) drip, and no doubt critically assessing my field craft handiwork. Whatever.

I got my man safely out of the field. I was sure he'd be OK, and I felt good. That was what I came here to do. I liked my job out here sometimes on days like this, when things were going well for us, which happened on occasion.

Chapter 16

The Company Commander and the Medic

The company commander of my unit, Charlie Company 1st Battalion 5th Cavalry (C/1/5), was a man called Captain William Vowell. He hailed from the southern state of Mississippi, but grew up and was schooled in Alabama U.S.A.

"Six," was his designated unit codename. He was 6 feet, 2 inches tall and weighed about 230 pounds. He spoke with a raw southern accent that could instantly curdle good milk. An impressive figure, he was in fact a fine soldier, the epitome of the celebrated fighting man in the true American tradition.

We would follow him anywhere, and we actually did. We loved this man just as strongly as he fiercely protected our interests, fighting tooth and nail for our every need. He defended us, led us forthrightly, and was a father to the 100 people under his command, which was not an easy accomplishment in sometimes extremely trying circumstances.

He, the old man, must have been all of 25 years of age at the time I came to know him.

Captain Vowell carried the larger and heavier wooden stocked M-14 rifle that fired a 7.62mm round and was touted for its stopping power. This rifle had been since replaced as the standard armed forces weapon of issue by the M-16, the smaller, more modern and lightweight 5.56mm round-firing weapon that most other people carried. Yet Six insisted that he preferred his older dependable M-14.

Who was going to take the older, non-regulation rifle away from him anyway?

He was forced to leave our unit out in the field several times to go back into a Fire Support Base for fortnightly battalion company commander briefings. On three occasions during these meetings, we made enemy contact while he was away from us.

He went berserk one time in the rear area when this happened, and he literally refused to take "No" for an answer when his superiors argued that his company would be OK out there under the command of the executive officer, so he should remain on the base and continue the meeting. He commandeered a helicopter to fly him back out to us immediately. Meeting with superiors be damned, that could wait, he had openly stated.

We raised our heads in the middle of a raging firefight to look up gratefully at our "Six," arriving back to the field, standing on the chopper skids blatantly disregarding his exposure to enemy ground fire and brandishing his big M-14 in his giant fists, looking exactly like the avenging God of War that he really was whenever his unit's nest was ruffled. You felt like singing out and shouting for joy at this sight, getting up and charging the hill. But you did not do so, because that action would invite instant death. This was not the movies.

His very presence among us meant everything. Once he was on board, we were all immediately ready to rumble: to go anywhere at anytime, once Six was the one in command of our unit.

Bravo Company, a company from our battalion, was once pinned down on a hill just outside the village of An Loc in a grim firefight. It was a typical situation in that they had taken heavy casualties and had to pull back down the hill that they had been patrolling to regroup.

They had to leave their dead on the hilltop in order to escape the withering and overwhelming firepower they had encountered from a well dug in NVA heavy-weapons platoon. After a day and a half of unsuccessfully trying to go back up to retrieve the bodies, taking more and more casualties with every futile attempt, Bravo's commander, Captain Jarvis, a somewhat taciturn and surly man whom I had seen around the FSB before, was now at extreme loggerheads with the agitated battalion commander, Lieutenant Colonel James Anderson, who wanted *his* hill cleared NOW.

Finally, after much disagreement on tactics, Captain Jarvis put his foot down. No more pyrrhic sacrifices for him. He was not going back up there, nor would he ask his men to do so again. Jarvis, never known to be a man to mince words, had just about had it with his superior officer. He informed LTC Anderson: "Sir, if you insist on having *your* hill cleared, irrespective of the prevailing circumstances, I suggest that you go on up there and do so for yourself, but not with *my* men."

This act of insubordination was a predictably and consciously enacted career-ending move on Jarvis' part. He was relieved of his field command on the spot, as was expected. His *insubordination* would have curtailed his prospects, in terms of advancement, as a career officer in the US Army Officer Corps.

To our consternation and temporary discomfort, but to no-one's surprise, battalion "borrowed" our company commander, Captain Vowell, to "take the hill" and get the bodies of the Bravo company soldiers off of it.

This harrowing feat we accomplished by 1600 hours that same day, without taking major casualties in our unit, thankfully. We had used a clinically directed combination of stealth and firepower orchestrated by our C.O. Capt. Vowell that had worn down the enemy forces eventually. This enabled my fellow medics and me to help our colleagues, the beleaguered Bravo company medics, to evacuate the fallen men and to prepare the retrieved bodies for a dignified transfer from the field to our graves registration unit in the rear. It was the beginning of a long journey back home to the US for those unfortunate boys.

This was the type of man of action our commanding officer was. He was a soldier's soldier, a man who took hills when ordered by a superior officer to do so.

But who was right? Was it the dour Captain Jarvis, who resolutely chose to sacrifice his own military career for the sake of protecting the personnel in his unit from a cause he no longer believed in?

He had decided that he would not waste anymore lives simply to enable some colonel, sitting somewhere safe in operations command, to conveniently move around a little red pin on a situation chart in a way that was pleasing to him.

Or was it our hero, Captain Vowell, always driven and dependably capable of winning the hill of the day? He may not have asked himself what we were winning the hill for on that day, or for whom or for what real, meaningful purpose. But we asked ourselves those same questions as we tended to our wounds that night. Was it worth it in the end? Any of it?

Tattooed Memories

* * * * *

Since the firefight in Tay Ninh last January, I had been elevated, at the unseasoned age of 20, to the post of company senior corpsman. I was now a vital member of the unit's headquarters decision-making team, operating within the company structure. The company commander and his RTO, for tactical purposes, slept a couple feet away from me every night now while we were on patrol. In other words, I was beginning to appreciate the complexity and futility of command decision making.

Overall responsibility for the four other medics and the rest of the 100-man unit in my area of "expertise" was all mine. This charge of accountability was an awesome one. We were not planning a Christmas party or a weekend beach picnic during school holidays; we were making life-and-death decisions.

Some nights, Six and I would agonize long into the morning hours over tough questions that confronted us. In the medical cases, I actually had the last word, which didn't necessarily make my decisions any easier.

Should we bring in a helicopter tonight to take out a wounded or sick man? By doing this, our entire 100-man position and the chopper crew would be openly compromised, exposing everyone on the ground to mortar attacks, and the rescue aircraft to hostile surface-to-air fire. The din made by a hovering helicopter, especially in the stillness of early morning, was nothing short of earth shattering, and the wrong kind of people quite often did take notice of this kind of disturbance.

If we did not bring in the chopper to take that wounded man out, would he survive until the next day?

"Can we wait until morning instead, doc. What do you think? And how bad is the sergeant's bullet wound?" "Is the loss of blood too great for the wounded trooper in second platoon to make it without a surgeon's immediate attention? What are his real chances of survival?" "What about the two men that were sick with diarrhea this morning, would they have to go in, too?" Our company commander would direct these questions at me, begging for answers, during our weekly crisis situations.

I had at my disposal a grand total of 12 weeks of packaged medical training from the Brooke Army hospital at Fort Sam Houston Texas to help me decide what I should do about some poor soldier's life-threatening wounds, a roasting fever brought on by a bout of chronic malaria, or some debilitating jungle infection picked up from the brackish swamp water that we lived in.

There was no one else to say what to do about it but me. I was the unit's doctor and nurse, even though I was technically neither. But I was a combat medic, the unit's senior medic, and I would simply have to do my best.

Decision making can be lonely and harrowing especially before one's twenty-first birthday. The majority of these judgment calls were life threatening and company endangering, but someone had to make them.

The only thing we could not afford to do out there in the jungle, was nothing. So between us, Six and I, we deliberated long and hard on those stress filled nights, then decided to the best of our abilities what to do about each and every situation we were faced with. But I have to admit, on some nights, the calls that we made were not necessarily the right ones.

Chapter 17

Mad Minute

We were awaiting the signal to start the night's Mad Minute. And some of the guys were also getting plastered in the interim.

Of course we were singing our pet song, the only song we seemed to know or cared to know, because of the profound relevance of the lyrics to our prevailing circumstances. It was called "We gotta get out of this place", written by a rock band called The Animals. We sang this same song over and over again, no matter where we were in Vietnam.

Our singing tonight was a balm. Everybody was choked up. An atmosphere of depression pervaded the company's ranks. We sang, we grieved, and we sang some more.

We had received news of deaths within the company's family. So those of us who were not completely inebriated were well on the way to arriving at that plateau. It was only a matter of time.

Earlier in the day an insidious gloom had descended on our FSB, Vivian, with the arrival of some really bad news for us in Charlie Company, concerning the tragic deaths of some of our sky troopers.

We were in for our rotation of base defense and should have been happy; what with the promise of one week's hot food, cold beer, showers, mail from home, and nightly "Mad Minute" drunken entertainment. All this after three frenetic weeks in the boonies, where we made sporadic enemy contact on about four occasions and took only minor casualties along the way.

About a month ago, what we thought was a break and good news for some of the guys from our artillery attachment in the field with us, now appeared to have been the sounding of their death knell.

It was the much sought after "transfer out" of our own forward artillery observer Lieutenant Bridgman, F/O as we called him, and his two radio operators, Francis Billy (Chief) and Sp4 Bob Layne, to the comfortable and supposedly safer assignment of an artillery battery unit: Even if the unit was based on some FSB in Tay Ninh province, an area that was very close to the Cambodian border.

Humping in the jungle was at the lowest end of the stick, the hardest and most unforgiving assignment in Vietnam. We had all thought they were lucky to get out when they did. They, ironically, got the break to go in because they were all "short" at the time of the transfer, with only a few months left in country.

LZ Illingworth, the FSB they were assigned to, was overrun by a battalion strength ground attack force of North Vietnamese army regulars only a week after they arrived there. Lieutenant Bridgman, Chief and Layne were all killed in the ensuing battle for the base. How tragic life could be sometimes. Chief was my protector, and at first my only friend when I came out to the field. He was the guy who was kindest to me when I was at my most vulnerable FNG stage. I could not believe this. I could not bring myself to visualize a death mask placed permanently over my friend's gently unassuming face.

I grieved deeply over Chief's death. It was something I was unprepared for. It was the greatest personal loss I suffered while in Vietnam. I would miss him dearly. Then F/O, my pal, the teddy bear Lieutenant who used to poach chocolate bars off me, and was sitting with me on that day in January past when I experienced my very first enemy contact on that horrible death trap of a hill in Tay Ninh province: How could I ever forget F/O, too?

The other guy, Bob Layne, was from Tennessee and no friend of mine. He had sometimes giving FNGs a hard time when they first came out to the field. I still did not wish him his sad fate, though. He had done his time out here in the bush and deserved to go home on his own two feet like everyone else did.

Chief and F/O, both gone together.... I could not stand the thought of it. Such really nice guys. How could this have happened to them: When we all thought that they had made it out, had gone back home already, and were safe and sound?

I had to have the company commander tell me himself. So he did. I was crippled inside by his grim confirmation, and sick with grief. Upset at the bewildering arbitrariness of the whole fucking thing. In Vietnam, there was no clear demarcation of front line or rear safe areas, as in other conflicts. You could get it anywhere over there, and that was what had happened to my two good friends.

We still had our Mad Minute that night on base defense. We could feel it deep in our bones that tonight's power show would be a special one. For me, it would be dedicated to F/O and Chief. The decision for the tribute to our friends was unspoken; everybody just knew what was called for. A Valhalla type of farewell ceremony, perhaps.

We were going to make our weapons fucking howl. The whole area would feel the brunt of our passions expressed in true warrior fashion. My head was by now heavily suffused with a dangerous cocktail of bloodlust and excessive alcoholic consumption. We had to relieve some of the pressure building up or we would have simply burst apart.

The Mad Minute was a simple idea that sometimes worked because of the sheer unorthodox manner of its implementation. I cannot state for sure whether it was first conceived by the US Armed forces or whether it was started by someone throwing stones over a mud barricade back in medieval times. But we did it regularly.

Remember, a fire support base, or a landing zone like Vivian, which we presently were defending, was also our battalion headquarters. All support services for our units out in the jungle were operated from right here.

The base was carved out of the ever present jungle, and although we had purposefully cleared 360 degrees of area all around it, flattened it, heavily mined and booby- trapped the environs, there was always an eventual tree line, where the jungle always rose up again, obstinately, no matter how many times we chopped it down.

Creepy crawlers of the two-footed kind tended to come visit us out of that mysterious dark forest, bearing death offerings, especially at night. We tried our best to cater to and to receive them in as embracing and welcoming a manner as we could, whenever possible. In a sense, that night was really no different from any other.

At a given signal, sometime between midnight and 0400 hours, the entire company assigned to base defense, about 120 men, and any cook, vehicle driver, helicopter pilot, or, for that matter, any other breathing and willing human being on the base, was invited to fire off every available weapon on the base directly into the omnipresent tree line.

This meant everyone fired everything they had right around the entire base in a 360-degree barrage for one unbroken minute of sheer weaponry-orchestrated bedlam.

Besides being tremendously noisy, it was great sport. Especially so for the non- combatant cooks and the like on the base, who got a rare chance to play John Wayne.

We would sometimes find some decomposing bodies in the wire and out in the tree line the next day. The faces of these dead enemy insurgents' all wore fixed expressions of surprise and grave consternation.

The company commander gave the signal this morning at 0137 hours, and instant Armageddon ensued. We began firing everything, at random. Some laughing and screaming in a frenzy while crying hysterically. By now everyone was even drunker than before.

We ran from one gun emplacement to another, trying to fire as many weapons as we possibly could, exchanging rifles for, say, bazookas. M-79 grenade launchers coughed repeatedly and lobbed shells out in an arc, a subsequent *blaamm* confirming impact, out in the hostile darkness.

I fired a big rocket launcher that night, or maybe it was an M-40? Or was it a .45 revolver? Maybe the big .50 caliber machine gun?

Was I even awake?

I was floating around somewhere, in that nether land between tipsy and falling down drunk, or was that getting up?

The sickly sweet smell of pot came wafting up from a bunker, where some hysterical maniacs were firing light anti-tank weapons (LAWs). Shit, I wondered for a brief moment, who was really down there?

A noisy rocket launcher fired a double blast into the trees. Its probing high explosive rounds impacted resoundingly and then bellowed around inside the dormant greenwood. The earth shuddered and erupted with the force of our deliberate assault.

Loud cackling, alcohol- and no doubt dope-tainted laughter, burst from the underground bunkers. A power-maddened driver of a mule—(a small, sled-like vehicle used for offloading supplies from large transport helicopters) tried gamely to hang on to a large .50 caliber machine gun. *Bup, bup, bup, bup.* The little guy was shrieking maniacally as he punished the bushes with large-caliber rounds. He swung the heavy fixed-tripod weapon to and fro, hanging on to it gleefully, whilst trying not to lose his grip on the precious bottle of wild turkey he was also clutching hold of.

Somebody was throwing hand grenades over the berm now. Probably that crazy old platoon sergeant Pop Frag. He was the only man mad enough to throw something when you could just simply squeeze a trigger. Fingers of red tracer fire lanced across the bare strip of no man's land, pounding the tree line.

Incandescent flares turned night into day for a while as they floated back to earth, as thousands of high- powered rounds of ammunition sliced through the air.

Fires were being lit in the bush. "Let them burn," someone spat. "Right on, burn muufucker," a blissfully stoned voice agreed from the darkness.

We were having fun, but we only had about 30 seconds left. "Take that, you slopes," a born-again cook yelled, his voice shrill and stoked with excitement. Rocket-propelled grenades and relentless machine gun fire continued to shred the night sky. What the hell were the villagers in the nearby town thinking? Who cared? They could all kiss my ass I thought.

The forest beyond the tree line was well lit, and burning fiercely, a conflagration from the firestorm of heavy explosive tracer rounds and illumination flares.

We shot off every and anything we could lay our hands on, and then some more.

This Mad Minute was for the three guys we lost. But for me, it was especially dedicated to F/O and my Chief. They were my friends, we had shared a lot together both good times and bad, and then they were gone, forever. This mad minute was our company's unspoken farewell salute to them.

I prayed somebody was out there, trying to sneak up on us. Preferably sometime within the last sixty seconds. That would have made our show all the more worthwhile to us.

I would find out for sure tomorrow at daybreak whether we had surprised any nighttime intruders when we inspected the barbed wire perimeter fences and went out to reset our claymore mines and trip flares for the subsequent night's Mad Minute. I would know soon enough.

Chapter 18

Night Ambush

Battalion headquarters had assigned our company the task of "sweeping" the heavily trafficked roadways approaching our brigade's base camp at Quan Loi, like Highway 13. We provided manpower and security capabilities for the daytime mine-sweeping details as they tried to keep those important highways free of landmines for the safe transit of our essential supply- and troop-bearing convoys that used them incessantly during the day.

For the past few days, we had been deployed around a small hamlet called Binh Long, which was located in the shadows of the giant Michelin rubber plantation.

Patrolling through rubber plantations was eerie. We had to move through rows upon rows of perfectly planted trees that stood straight and huge, for miles. These imposing and magnificent trees towered above us like time worn colossuses, which in fact they really were.

Imagine, after stepping around the fortieth row of sameness, being suddenly confronted with black pajama-clad insurgents? Talk about breaking symmetry. Hard to contemplate meeting the enemy in this setting? But we did, and quite often, too.

Before we left Quan Loi, we witnessed another elucidating wartime situation.

A helicopter equipment loader sitting on the steps of a hootch (building), taking a quiet smoke, noticed a Papa San, or older Vietnamese man, walking up and down in front of him. Something just did not seem right as he watched the old man walk. He appeared to be striding over the same area repeatedly and counting steps or looking for something.

Then it all snapped into place for the observant GI. Papa San was in fact measuring the distance between the base's ammunition dump and the western fence line, beyond which the densest rubber trees lay. This mild-mannered daily worker was either a Vietcong or an informant for their cause.

Here in broad daylight, he was casing the joint. His actions, if not interrupted, would have certainly resulted in the base's receiving a barrage of well-targeted 122-mm rocket or 82-mm mortar fire descending on it with a devastating vengeance later that night.

Papa San was part of the regular civilian workforce on the base that laboured as cleaners, or handyman types. They left the base for their homes in a nearby village at 1800 hours every day. Papa San, of course, would have called in sick the next day had he not been caught by the alert trooper as he deliberately paced out the grid for the enemy to accurately target our weapons bunkers and ammunition storage sites.

We watched, intrigued, as the frail-looking old man was arrested and taken away for interrogation. The face of the enemy was sometimes closeted in a most disingenuous guise. A frustrating problem in this war.

Papa San mumbled begrudgingly as he was led away, "American GI, *number10*." This meant everything and anything bad in Vietnam. "I no do something. Papa San good man. *Number 1,*" he pleaded. Number 1, of course, meant everything and anything good in Vietnam.

One of the MPs who escorted the old geezer paused only long enough to reply, "Di di mau, Papa San—let's get out of here--Not only are you a bad boy, but you're now also a fired one. "

I was going out on ambush with a squad from third platoon. Ten of us in all. We had to leave the hamlet just before dusk, as we would not have been able to come back into the compound after nightfall because of the unreliability of the road at night, and the general tactical disadvantage posed by having a small unit out, alone, away from the main body of the company, and wandering around in the dark. So once we positioned out, we'd stay put.

If anything happened to us during the night, a rescue party would not come out to assist us, either, because of the flagrant exposure this would cause them. So we would have to hunker down out there by our lonesome, until daybreak the following day. This was even if some shit hit the fan out there. Because we would have had to deal with any threat by ourselves, we made maximum preparedness for this a top priority. We would go out heavily equipped, ready for a fight, and able to manage as independently as possible as a small force.

Between the ten of us, we carried three M-60 machine guns and enough belts of ammo to feed them. About 12 claymore mines, a dozen trip flares, and two radio packs. We each had our individual M-16 rifles with us, and about six to ten (20) round clips (magazines) of ammunition each, and three M-79 grenade launchers. Just a small party but a heavily equipped one. We traveled light, no field packs. Only some water, energy bars and extra ammo.

The purpose of the ambush was to discourage the active Vietcong forces in the area from mining the roadway at night and to dissuade them from sneaking up on our company to launch a surprise attack on the main body's nighttime bivouac inside the hamlet.

Another reason was the fact that, from the first minute of our road-sweeping operational activity in the area, the VC knew we were there, and pretty much what we were doing, courtesy of their intricate network of local spies. Unlike the jungle, where we moved about three to five klicks a day in any given direction, making our position hard to detect at any time, camped in the village we were more static and hence patently exposed to insurgent attacks. Our unit's permanently sited position was vulnerable to nighttime attack, and only a well-placed blocking ambush could successfully defend against this eventuality.

It was about 1800 hours when we left the hamlet's compound, comprising mainly small, thatched roof, peasant huts with mud walls. Everyone checked each other's equipment. Our squad leader for the mission was sergeant Neville Burton. He was a lanky, easygoing 22-year-old veteran grunt, a farm goods truck driver from Arkansas in a previously far less demanding life. He got his call signals and emergency procedures down pat with both his platoon leader lieutenant Dan Barlow and our company commander Captain Vowell. Last minute advice and encouragement, too, no doubt.

The children followed us to the edge of the town, as the leaden sky darkened on its way to rendezvous with a purple sunset. Then, having shrugged off twilights feeble grasp, the waning day settled down.

The kids were our pals. We gave them chocolates, and they bought "tiger piss" beer for us from the bevy of small, local enterprises lining the roadsides. Little Nguyen was my favourite. I was convinced that this bony little racketeer *par excellence* would one day open a chain of department stores in

Vietnam with all of the candy bars and cigarettes he had fleeced off of me since we arrived, for the benefit, according to him, of his six starving siblings and his poor, handicapped and ailing Grandfather. Yeah, right.

Nguyen, skipping along merrily beside us as we left the village, yelled, "Hey, doc, where are you guys going to set up your ambush tonight?" Oh, brother. The whole damned village knew already what we were going out for. "Nguyen, you scrawny little bastard," I replied in mock exasperation. "You really think that I want your uncle, who masquerades as the village schoolteacher during daylight hours, but who is really a VC guerrilla after dark, to know where I am going tonight, so that he and his pals can come out there to kill me in my bedroll later on?"

I searched the faces of the adults, who wore conical hats, and were all bowing and waving cheerfully at us as we went by. I wondered whether I would meet a few of them at the ambush site later that night wearing much less benign expressions. I gave what I hoped was a smug-looking, see-you-later smile as I walked past the cheerful but observant village crowd, just in case....

We walked out of the hamlet in an easterly direction through the ever looming and seemingly threatening rubber trees. It was almost dusk, and the land was cooling fast. Cooking fires were being stoked, and the local villagers were settling in comfortably for a restful night. We, on the other hand, were anything but settled as we searched for an ideal spot to set a trap - A pre-emptive one that would give us the jump on killing the men that may come out to kill us tonight.

We eventually found a spot where a well-worn trail intersected the main road about a kilometer from the hamlet. The trail also conveyed potential users to higher ground that overlooked our main camp. Looked like a real good possibility for nighttime infiltration.

We went about setting up our site expediently. Darkness would fall suddenly, with a vengeance. Trip flares were run out encircling our area, and claymore mines carefully placed on likely approaches. The three-crew served machine guns were positioned, laid to provide interlocking fire on the targeted trail.

We broke into two-man teams that carefully covered the entire 360 degrees of our small perimeter. Anybody or anything that walked down that trail would set off a trip flare. Explosive claymore mine blasts, simultaneous machine gun, automatic rifle, and M-79 grenade launcher support fire would subsequently decimate the infiltrators. Our killing ground was set, but the waiting was another matter.

It was dark, and it was quiet. The night would be a long and tense one. Most jungle noises had settled down, not so our pounding hearts. Only the constantly chirping crickets and croaking frogs continued to harmonize as usual.

We tried to calm our nerves by talking to each other. The air was thick with a palpable tension. There was the coppery taste of fear on our tongues as our hearts thudded against our rib cages. You could hear and feel its feverish thumping. Swallowing was a normal procedure earlier today, but all of a sudden, there was this big lump in our throats. Stomach muscles tightened like a vise.

The jungle quiet was deafening. Fear of death and bloody mayhem in the dark smothered our thoughts. Our bodies emitted that acrid smell indicative of all-pervading fear.

My buddy Mark Fogerty and I were crouched low behind a log facing the culprit trail. The waiting and the premonitory atmosphere of grave expectancy was mind-numbing.

He whispered to me. "Doc, what manner of man leaves his warm bed at night to come out here to kill?"

I didn't know, but I replied anyway, just for the sake of talking. "What manner of man crosses an ocean to come over here to prevent killing by killing?"

Deadpan, Mark responded, "Shit, doc, you have something there. But mind you, it's probably more of that usual deep shit that you like to throw out on people's asses all the time. But OK, I can dig man, I'm hep. I'm into your philosophy bullshit, too, but not now, man, not tonight, please, it's too damn tense, you dig?"

I agreed. I had thought that talking would take some of the edge off, but it didn't really help. Only two things would: the man you didn't want to have spring your laid trap coming and getting the shit over with once and for all, or the first rays of morning light that you wanted to see real badly, likewise, signaling that the wait was over.

I knew that if we made contact tonight, that it would be sudden, loud, horrifying, and death-dealing for someone out here. The waiting itself was a slow killer. It grew colder, and the tension tightened as Mark and I waited on, in silence now.

I had also thought earlier, while feeling sorry for myself, that patrolling through mystical rubber trees was eerie. But waiting for death in those same rubber trees in an ambush setting on a cold, moonless, suffocating jungle night wasn't just worse, it was downright mind-blowing. Eerie would have been just fine right about then. Oh, for a simple daytime jaunt through the rubber trees. I promised I'd never complain of those excursions again: If I ever got the chance to take one again.

Our radios chirped mutedly in the early morning gloom as we reported in our hourly SITREP to the company. Although we were too close to the hamlet for a fire mission, if we needed one anyway, we still had to keep in touch.

I figured they still needed to know just where we were. They wouldn't want to have to expend too much energy looking too far and wide to retrieve our bodies in the morning.

A sudden popping followed by ear splitting explosions *"pop, pop, blaam blaam!"* rocked me out of my reverie. Our claymores had gone off. Gunfire erupted as automatic weapons, both M-60s and M16s fired off frenzied bursts of firepower all over the place. "Shit, we have gooks in the... oh, fuck, man, we have....."" More intermingling bursts of shooting deafened my eardrums. "OK, OK, cease firing, men.... Stop the fuck, people, it's over, it's over," someone screams.

"What?"

"Jesus Christ...."

"MEDIC....!"

"Hey, doc, we have somebody hit here."

"Oh fuck! This looks real bad."

"Meeeeh....diiiiccc...!"

We had *contact*. Two Vietcong had walked into our ambush. The first one tripped an illumination flare, that made a *pop pop* sound, and one of our guys on the ball set off two claymore mines instantly. Machine guns responded with a deafening firestorm of lead and everybody else had entered the fray with their M-16 rifles on full automatic fire.

The Vietcong, amazingly, still had the presence of mind to get off two B-40 rocket-propelled grenade rounds at us. They must have had the B-40's at the ready when they walked into our net. I had not even succeeded in getting my weapon's safety lever off before it was over. In about 45 seconds it was finished.

Heart pumping overtime, I crawled rapidly over to the wounded trooper, Mason Evers. A slightly built, gentle red-headed guy from Mississippi, Mason was dead--killed instantly. The poor guy took a direct blast from one of the B-40's. He was positioned less than ten feet away from where Mark and I were lying when he was hit.

I had actually felt the warm blast of air from the round as it passed ever so closely by us. My eyes were burning. I looked down at my fallen comrade.

One never really got used to the weighty sadness of losing a fellow platoon member. Because we were so closely knit and depended on each other for our very survival, a loss was always frustrating, and hurt badly, every time.

Half of Mason's side was torn away, and his stomach was gutted from the blast. His shirt and pieces of his M-79 grenade launcher were smashed and embedded inside the massive wound. He had bled out. I checked for vital signs to validate what my probing eyes had already confirmed for me. I could not find a pulse.

I remembered speaking with Mason just that morning about where he hoped to go to on his upcoming R and R. I also saw him stop to give a kid some candy as we left the hamlet that very evening. Poor Mason would never go anywhere or stop to give anything to anyone again: Because he had just given the very last thing that he had had to give, his life.

"Hey, Burt," somebody called out softly to the squad leader, "we have two "step ons" down here".

The two Vietcong who had walked straight down the trail and into the ambush were dead. Both short and slightly built, the infiltrators were dressed in black pajamas, and carried two B-40 launchers, two AK-47 rifles and an 82-mm mortar tube with base plate and accompanying rounds.

They had been completely ripped to pieces by the ambush's firestorm.

Having taken the full brunt of the deployed claymore mines, M-60 machine guns and M-16 automatic rifle fire, the two VC guerrillas had been torn to shreds. Their frail bodies were no match for the screaming bullets that had greeted them under the dark and eerie rubber trees on this fateful night. Their once whole bodies were now skewered all over the area in distorted and unmatched pieces of fetid and disrupted flesh and gore.

Shattered bones and soiled torn pajama cloth material were also scattered haphazardly everywhere. An overwhelming stench from their vented bowels and ruptured organs prevailed. The smell of exposed guts and torn flesh mixed in with the sickly sweet scent of viscous blood invaded our aroused nostrils, raising bile and revulsion swiftly up our throats. Some of the patrol guys were instantly sick from this overpowering sensory onslaught.

The Vietcong resembled violated rag dolls. All of the bushes and trees around them were distorted and scorched from the awesome blasts and powerful impact of our spent munitions. The surrounding shrubbery in the immediate area was still smoking from the firepower. We immediately called in our situation to our company command post (CP) back at the hamlet. We also reported in the one "line one" and two "step ons".

We were told what we expected to hear. We had to stay out right where we were until dawn, hunker down quietly with our eyes wide open. Our position was now fully blown, but it was unlikely that any small group of insurgents would continue to work our area that night now that everyone's element of surprise had been compromised.

We wrapped up Evers' corpse in some ponchos, as securely and with as much dignity as we could accomplish in the darkness. We laid his body only a short distance away from us, too tired to move him further away. Why bother anyway? We would all sleep together close by to his body. Sort of assuring him that we were still there with him, our buddy. We would carry his body back with us at first light, back to the company command post from where we had all left on our mission into the dark jungle earlier on.

As the adrenalin seeped out of our bodies, we felt the weight of death and of unavoidable responsibility settling heavily onto our young shoulders.

The atmosphere felt a lot chillier. We had to salvage some rest from what was left of the night, because most of our brain controls had already begun to shut down, or go on auto pilot, as numbness and a sense of futility threatened to overwhelm us.

All of a sudden, I felt like screaming, but I couldn't summon the required effort. So I dry heaved instead. The well was dry, and there seemed to be nothing left inside of me that was available for release. I was tapped out of emotion. I was only 20 years old. What the hell was I doing in this place, anyway?

I was so damn tired of being tired all the time, of these recurring hostilities, of fear, sadness, blood and harrowing death from the shadows.

I wondered, wearily, not for the first time, as I glanced down at my blood stained hands that were trembling slightly, whether I possessed the requisite fortitude to continue doing my job, and ultimately, to make it out of this hive of madness in one piece. But it was in fact that very fear of dying that would keep me alive.

Chapter 19

Sergeant Grumbler and the Wild Pigs

We had a platoon sergeant in our unit called "Grumbler". His given name was Darryl Crowthers. He was a Cajun from Baton Rouge Louisiana. He was also one miserable son of a bitch: a nitpicking, fault-finding granny of a platoon sergeant, who was always inclined, it seemed, on making life more difficult for his charges.

He was also "short", which meant he had almost completed his tour of duty. He only had six weeks left in-country, and he was hungry for any opportunity to get into the rear area to, ultimately, safeguard his passage back stateside.

He made the mistake once of arguing with me on the only subject I had full, unquestionable control of in the field: the daily consumption of our malaria pills. I had to follow his ass out to his personal commode behind a tree and wait patiently as he relieved himself. Grunting and groaning with his efforts, and bitching about damn young medic upstarts, and the damn grainy toilet paper that the damn army was issuing people these damn days. He paused from his bowel relieving activities to shout out expansively to me from behind his chosen tree.

"Doc, I'm not the hard ass damn people think that I am. Just a sore ass, and you here bugging me with those damn pills doesn't help."

Six, the company commander, would sometimes take him on. "Crowthers, the amount of time that you spend quarreling and threatening the men, just how are you going to get their cooperation to get them moving during a firefight?"

"How? Easy, Sir." Grumbler was always sure of himself. "With my size 12 boots planted up their damn asses, that's how. You watch, sir. They asses be moving swiftly, doan you worry none about dat dere situation, sir. Leave it to me.."

As the company settled down for the long tense jungle night, the only identifiable sounds were the ever present chirping of the crickets and the lazy croaking of a seemingly contented bull frog. The radio squawked mutedly as we let Battalion HQ know we were still around. Perimeter claymore mines and trip flares had been run out, our only protection and early warning against the possibility of nighttime attack on our bivouacked position.

The sudden tripping of a flare as an insurgent stumbled into our camp, followed by claymore mines going off loudly, caused a man to swim up from a deep, exhausting sleep into a frenetic and troubling consciousness, clutching his weapon, turning expectantly to the sound, the direction, of imminent danger.

The ominous bark of an AK-47 chicom automatic weapon normally confirmed who our nighttime visitors were, and left no lingering doubts whatever as to their intentions.

Once that flare was tripped, we knew we were in deep shit. Our stomachs churned, and our hearts pumped like pistons. It was 0300 hours, quiet in our jungle encampment when our flares tripped, and the claymores exploded.

"Oh God, we have contact!" someone yelled. Everybody jumped up.

"Shit! Shit! Shit!"

"What's happening here? Are there gooks in the wire? What's going on? Are we taking fire?"

Adrenalin pumping, hearts thudding, I heard the patter of footsteps running. "Oh God. Jesus fucking Christ, Lord, Lord Almighty." Silence, then that patter again.

"Jesus Lord, get them off of my ass. Somebody help me out here! Please, ohhhh…. Shit! What the fuuuuh…. Oh God, they're killing me." There was the patter. And grunting noises. Then silence.

Two wild boars had inadvertently wandered into our camp of 100 sleeping men, tripping our security flares. Spooked, they both ran right over Sgt. Grumbler, who was peacefully asleep in his bedroll, and dreaming of his watery bayous, no doubt.

In their state of confusion, the boars, unbelievably, turned around and ran right back over Grumbler again as he was furiously attempting to untangle himself from his bedroll, only halfway recovered after the first surprise stampede.

One man out of a company of 100 was chosen for this humiliation, twice. Makes you wonder.

Grumbler got his wish to be transferred to the rear and out of the bush earlier than he had expected: Because his ability to lead a platoon of snickering sky troopers was permanently nullified after the boar-trampling incident.

*

Photographs

*

Private Byer at Fort Jackson, proudly sporting his first stripe

Roger Allan Byer

Visiting home in 1969 before deployment to Vietnam

Tattooed Memories

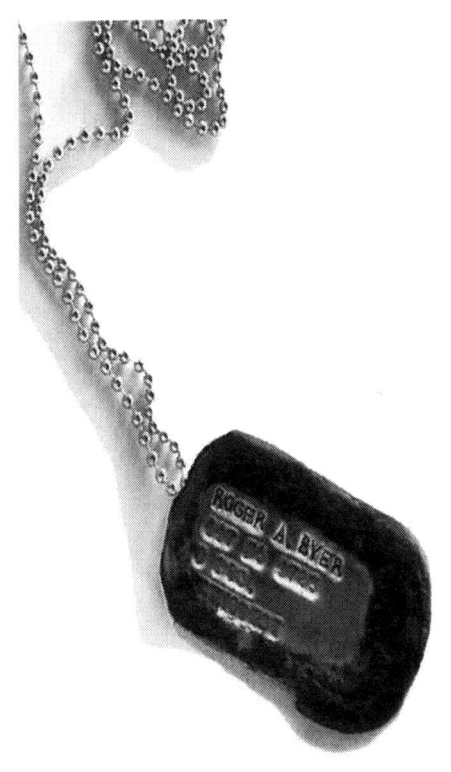

My official Vietnam flight information notice

My Dog tag

Roger Allan Byer

Jungle fatigues

In front of the Aid station at Quan Loi

Roger Allan Byer

Unwinding in the underground bunker at Quan Loi

Captured SKS rifles from the Cambodian campaign

Front-center – our underground bunker at Quan Loi

An M16 and a coke on "FSB David"

Resupply by Chinook helicopter on "LZ Prudence"

Rocket damaged Blue Max Cobra gunship

Incoming: Vietcong launched 122 mm rocket attack at Bien Hoa

One of our "Kit Carson" scouts

"Some guy" brandishing an M-60 machine gun

One of our "Kit Carson" scouts

"Some guy" brandishing an M-60 machine gun

'Doc' relaxing on a UH1-"Huey" Medevac helicopter

Holding an M-79 grenade launcher, whilst waiting to be airlifted out on patrol

Our Company Commander, Capt. William Vowell

Roger Allan Byer

"LZ Vivian"

A Cobra gunship over "FSB David"

A field extraction

An approaching Medevac helicopter

Papasan - Montagnard village elder

Tattooed Memories

Montagnard woman and child

Group of Montagnards, and Charlie Company soldiers

Tattooed Memories

Two Montagnard Villagers strolling

Roger Allan Byer

Cuts Down Reds
Hurl Back NVA Attack

By SPEC. 4 SETH LIPSKY
1&S Staff Correspondent

FIRE SUPPORT BASE DAVID, Cambodia — Heavily armed North Vietnamese Army troops, working under cover of darkness, drizzle and fog, struck an American outpost here early Sunday and battled American troops in a fierce two-hour exchange of rifle, grenade, mortar and rocket fire.

The uniformed NVA company slithered up through grassy approaches from the east and north, cut through a coil of wire and rushed toward an inner dirt dike, flinging grenades and firing B-40 rockets, according to officers and soldiers here. Many of the enemy were mowed down by American machine-gun fire, they said.

Despite heavy American fire, soldiers here said, some of the enemy actually reached the berm and, kneeling behind it, sprayed the camp with rifle fire amid what one soldier called "constant grenades thrown from both sides."

Two soldiers said one NVA soldier firing an AK47 rifle made it onto the fire base itself before he was cut down by M16 fire.

At daylight, American troops counted 28 enemy dead between the inner perimeter and the wire and on the slopes outside the wire. Some of the bodies were sprawled grotesquely at the base of the dirt berm itself.

No Americans were killed in the attack, according to officers here. In Saigon official American military spokesman put the number of American wounded at twelve.

Fire Support Base David, four miles into Cambodia and 115 miles north of Saigon, is the northernmost major outpost of the 1st Air Cav. Div. Cambodian operation. It sits on a wide grassy knoll amid rolling green hills.

(Continued on Back Page, Col. 2)

Cambodia, June 1970. Newspaper report on the June 13th ground attack on "FSB David."

My sleeping quarters on "FSB David" <u>before</u> the ground attack

My sleeping quarters on "FSB David" <u>after</u> the ground attack

SP5 Byer at Fort Devens 1971

Awards and Decorations

Type of Award	Awarded for
Good Conduct Medal.	Exemplary conduct in Armed services
National Defense Service Medal.	National Service in Armed forces
Purple Heart	Wounds received in action
Bronze Star Medal (with V device)	Heroism in ground combat
Bronze Star Medal (with first oak leaf cluster)	Meritorious achievement in ground operations against hostile forces
Two Army Commendation Medals (with V devices)	Heroism
Combat Medics Badge	Medical service in a combat zone
Air Medal	Meritorious achievement while participating in aerial flight
Vietnam Service Medal	Service in Republic of Vietnam
Vietnam Campaign Medal with 60 Device	Service in Republic of Vietnam
2 Overseas Bars / 2 Presidential Unit Citations	First Battalion Fifth Cavalry Unit Award
Expert badge M-16 Rifle	Rifle qualification rating

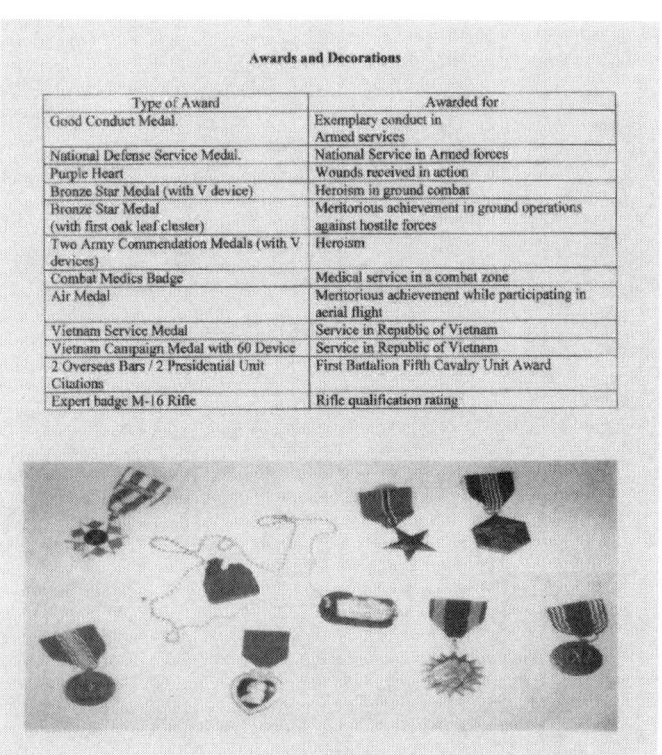

Some of my medals and awards

U.S. Detainee Compound notice (Grenada) 1983

Roger Allan Byer

The author's hometown, St. George's, Grenada

Grand Anse beach, Grenada

*

Chapter 20

Snake in the Hole

The tedium of daily life in the jungle, most intense between bouts of shooting and mayhem, was relieved when we were airlifted out of the boondocks to provide base defense for a new LZ being constructed on a lush jungle hillside, somewhere in central Loc Ninh province. This was something new and interesting for us, as we normally provided the defensive arm for an up-and-working, established LZ, not for one still under construction.

As we went smoking along at the usual treetop level in our UH-1 Huey helicopters, our legs dangled out, brushing branches at 120 knots, there was an old feeling of juvenile exhilaration in the air. We were out of the sticks, even if only for a while. We had made it again, for now. We weren't killed and left forgotten out there in the God-forsaken trees, to rot in lonely despair.

All of us grunt infantrymen believed that if we were to die in this war, we would be killed in the hot, humid, snake-infested jungle. We could never picture our demise occurring in a clean rear area or even on an LZ. So we had escaped the bush again, if only for the time being. Our exhilaration knew no bounds.

Our choppers circled over something. I was accustomed by that stage of my jungle life, and as a sky trooper in the First Air Cavalry Division, to arriving somewhere that you could not see. Par for the course. But what revealed itself below was an astounding sight even to us airmobile helicopter insertion veterans.

The spot chosen for the birthplace of LZ Prudence was the summit of a two thousand-foot mountain, heavily clothed in triple canopy forestry. Thick vines and robust liana abounded. They even had clouds on location up there.

As we circled overhead, construction workers were using heavy duty bulldozers and jumbo earth movers (all airlifted in, of course) to topple giant trees. The trees were then simply pushed over the side of the hill. Simultaneously, controlled explosive detonations were set off by the combat engineer unit in charge off the whole show.

This action converted large swaths of smaller, mud hills into dust storms that handily blanketed everything in a red whirlwind mess of blowing detritus. A muddy, almost flat piece of ground was already passing for a helicopter landing pad. Food supplies, artillery pieces, water, ammunition, and construction material, not to mention millions of sand bags, were already being airlifted in around the clock.

We approached with our eight-bird helicopter flight, adding more chaos to the existing confusion on the ground. Each chopper made two round trips back out to the pick-up point to complete our company's airlift in from the field.

Large CH-54, Jolly Green Giant, heavy-lift helicopters were hard at work, accurately but most expeditiously placing the 105-mm and 155-mm howitzer batteries exactly in the positions selected for them on the base. They would be up and ready for fire support missions that night: Most probably for Echo Company, who grudgingly replaced us on patrol by going back out to the field that morning after their one-week stint of base defense was completed on Prudence.

Once established on the ground, we dispersed quickly to set up perimeter and other necessary defensive measures before nightfall. The four platoons took assigned responsibilities for individual sectors of the fire base. Machine guns were emplaced, extra wire run out, the required trip flares and claymore mines swiftly positioned in the already established concertina wire fences that too loosely and haphazardly surrounded this dangerously incomplete and therefore vulnerable base.

We had to mould all of the confusion into proper and functional shape at once. Doing that included building a small aid station and adjacent sleeping areas, using lumber and galvanized inverts and the usual million or so available sandbags that, unfortunately, had to be filled by somebody with the available dirt.

So everybody was into construction. The place was buzzing like a hive of demented bees, and things were starting to take shape. Of course, it was the height of the monsoon season, so there was the good old red mud to contend with also. When it was briefly dry, it was the dust whipped up from the constant helicopter movements that we had to avoid.

I was always impressed at what the human brain would retain under the most trying situations. Even when not consciously paying attention to something, our mind's eye would have already processed that 'ignored' information and set it aside for later dispensation.

Take the large hole that was located about six feet from the entrance to our one day to be finished, definitely before the end of the war, hopefully, but still under construction, aid station. Every one of the 40 times a day I passed by that hole, I looked at it for a millisecond longer than the cursory glance it should have deserved. But I didn't know why I did so. It was, after all, just one of the natural holes on the LZ that adorned the landscape along with the many manmade holes that pockmarked the camp. Or was it?

But life on a fire support base construction site could be attention demanding. We needed to fortify as quickly and as efficiently as we could synch with the actual building of the more permanent facilities, like the aid station, so as to have secure defenses up and in place if attacked by the enemy while still in a primary building phase. For those reasons, that hole I kept encountering was gradually pushed to the back of my mind.

Jonas Pugh, a fellow company medic, and I had been working hard on the aid station's construction with the other medics. We'd been digging a lot and filling sandbags all day long. We slept at night on the bare ground on sandbag beds.

A mechanical excavator had dug out the main trench already for us, and we had manpower assistance for the serious building tasks. We just had to scoop out the dirt and round it off a bit. Then we put the floorboards down - upended crates, worked pretty well.

So there was a lot of digging, hammering, landing of helicopters, and driving of heavy earth-moving equipment about the place, combined with constantly falling trees. Enough noise and disturbance to wake the dead. Or maybe just the sleeping.

Sometime around mid-morning, about four days after we arrived at LZ Prudence, the base started to take shape. We were toiling inside the aid station trying to put in some serious constructive efforts when a loud and very excited voice just outside our soon-to-be-completed, maybe this very century, aid station's door exclaimed, "Shit, what the mother.... Jesus Christ son of a bitch. Hey, you guys, come quickly."

Living in a war zone, and being now seasoned combat veterans, everyone reached for his rifle on cue.

We all dashed outside in expectation of any kind of threatening situation imaginable. We came stumbling out of the aid station, eyes screwed up from the sun's glare, looking about apprehensively. We focused on the scene. Our mouths dropped open.

"Shit, look at that...."

"Man, what the...?"

"I've never seen anything so big...."

LZ Prudence, our temporary home, apparently was also the home of a 12-foot, reticulated python. That yawning hole that was located so, so close to our aid station entranceway was, in fact, the main egress to this snake's much maligned sleeping quarters.

The giant reptile must have been trying to sleep off a meal of wild pig or deer it had swallowed a week or so before our noisy arrival. Not only had we come uninvited, we had been digging the hell out of its natural habitat for days on end. Controlled explosions, falling trees, helicopter movements, and trampling, boot-clad feet. Angry? Of course it was angry, and it was finally coming out of its hole, its rest disturbed.

The snake's head looked ominous as it protruded up from the hole. Then, as if to say, "Let me see just who had been causing me such aggravated indigestion," it swiveled deliberately for 360 degrees to survey us all.

We all experienced the chilling feeling that the snake was looking directly at each one of us, individually, with squeezing and ingesting thoughts paramount on its mind. Its head was large, stripped grayish brown, with vivid rings....

Since I was one of the many people on earth undeniably and unabashedly afraid of snakes, I kept my distance.

I tried to find a high enough vantage point well off the ground whilst trying not to dwell on the fact that this was the very same ground I had been sleeping on every night since arriving at LZ Prudence. The problem was, all of the observation positions not situated at ground level seemed to have been already taken by like-minded cowards, who like me feared reptiles. At least three quarters of the LZ's population were already standing on or clinging to something, once it was well elevated off terra firma.

This being the American Army, I was waiting for someone to volunteer something. Someone in the crowd stepped forward. "Hey, I know what to do. Lemme through, guys." It was a red neck. A skinny little bespectacled guy from somewhere in Florida, maybe Gatorland? He came skipping up to the hole. There was plenty of room for him to pass through the onlookers. Nobody else was foolish enough to get too close to that large, irritated creature.

As he walked up to the hole, he'd already fashioned a noose of some length of rope and was swirling it deftly in his hands. This lunatic then calmly bent over the angry python, slipped the noose over its neck, drew it tight, and began to pull the snake up and out of the hole. Up, up, up, the madman pulled, and the snake came forth. More, and more, and more snake emerged and kept on coming out; forever, it seemed. Unassisted throughout, the little lunatic from Florida pulled and pulled out even more snake.

We finally saw the large bulge in its belly, the shape of whatever wild game it had swallowed. This caused the creature to be sluggish as it came to the surface. Eventually, out of the hole emerged 12 feet of a monstrosity. It was too big and slow to try to run away. But we wanted it off the base by nightfall, or no man would dare sleep here tonight.

That same afternoon, some low quarter (rear area) general with nothing better to do actually sent out a "conveniently available" supply helicopter equipped with a cage to remove the snake from the patently uninhabited part of the LZ where it lay tethered, to a Saigon or Bien Hoa rear area location. To be put on display, no doubt, to entertain impressionable visitors in some lazy ass officers club back there. The brass heads could have it. The further away from us they kept that war trophy, the better.

The hole was rapidly filled in, and the largest available boulder enthusiastically manhandled into place over it. We brave combat veterans were taking no chances. Suppose the creature had a mate? Who knew under whose booted feet she might be lurking whilst searching for her missing partner?

I slept that night on a pile of sandbags elevated only slightly higher than Jonas's stack. It was about eight feet high and six narrow inches across. I refused to look at or even acknowledge the spot where that nightmare hole was once located.

But the real problem was trying to figure out how I was ever going to be able to sleep on the bare ground again. We were due to go back out to the field in a few short days.

As soon as we completed the construction of our aid station, our one-week stint of base defense would be over on LZ Prudence. And I would not be able to carry my sandbag perch out to the field with me. Christ almighty, what was a guy to do sometimes? Maybe if we could find a way to further delay the construction of the aid station..?

Chapter 21

Mechanical Dinosaurs

Some weeks after our base defense stint on LZ Prudence, our company had been deployed to work with a mechanized armoured unit. I hoped it was not for long.

Those cumbersome, prehistoric-looking beasts were mainly modern, light-armoured tanks and armoured personnel carriers (APCs).

We were tracking through some forests near Phuoc-Vinh with them, so assigned by our division for a three-day period of something called "joint tactical operations."

The pride of US Army mechanized might, some M-48 and M-42 tanks also lumbered in the rear of the long column of vehicles.

As we trudged along, fully immersed in the swirling dust storms created by these incredibly noisy tin cans, we could not breathe or see where we were going. We could only inhale dust and thick fumes as we humped along in the sweltering heat behind these aggravating behemoths from some hell.

The difference between this type of patrol and our accustomed infantry type manoeuvres was profound. We operated with stealth and precision.

They seemed determined to wake every generation of Vietnamese dead with their clanging, the screeching of tank tracks, and the groaning of straining diesel engines gasping and wheezing black smoke—as if to indicate to the enemy that if you could not hear us, at least you could see us by our toxic emissions.

We, on the other hand, were accustomed to speaking in whispers and using hand signals to minimize noise levels whenever possible in our usually hushed and somber jungle combat environment. This shit, on the other hand, wouldn't work.

As a marriage of convenience between infantry and the mechanized, our pairing was doomed to be short-lived, heading inexorably towards a rocky lee shoreline.

The goggle-wearing men of the mechanized unit, sitting in cushioned seats, shaded from the sun, wondered just what we were fussing about.

Our infantrymen, who were choking to death on dust and fumes, whose vision was impaired and bodies were sun scorched, endlessly marching on weary legs, in turn wondered at the mechanized unit's blatant lack of comprehension concerning our unsatisfactory plight.

"You infantry boys are too damn soft," they shouted down dangerously at us.

"Oh yeah?" we responded. "Well get your pampered, mechanized, oil-sucking backsides down here in the grit and smoke and let our soft infantry asses sit up there on your luxury perches, just for the next five miles. Deal? No, not really? Thought not. So fuck off goggle eyes," we barked.

As we bivouacked on our first night together, we tried to stay as far away from the mechanized unit's confusion as we could. We were glad that we had been assigned full perimeter duties, and it was a very wide one that we formed.

We knew we would be mortared by the enemy sometime during the night; our experience assured us of this. It was inevitable, unless they were all stone deaf.

I hoped we could get away from this disorganized mess before too long, without any of our people really getting hurt, and return to our quiet and almost predictable jungle environs, where we at least exercised some semblance of control over our own unit's fate. That night we were mortared.

Chapter 22

Into the Trees

It was an unremarkable day as we assembled in a small jungle clearing near a village outside a large rubber plantation on the outskirts of Phuoc Vinh.

We waited to be picked up and airlifted back out to the boondocks to replace one of our infantry line company's on routine patrol rotation.

Now that we had completed a seemingly never-ending, patience-testing, one-week stint of joint unit patrolling with a mechanized outfit, our entire company was actually anxious to get back out to the bush.

Talking excitedly and nonstop, as was their habit, the local village's hawkers milled around busily selling trinkets and knick-knacks, and some hot French beer nicknamed "Tiger Piss", to the unit's bored and restless soldiers.

This beer was always guaranteed immediate consumption on sight, by the same critics who claimed that the brew had really earned its name.

A few young girls materialized in the clearing, giggling and fawning. So some of the older guys (in terms of their time in- country, not their age), suddenly no longer bored with life, a new found spring in their step, knowingly slipped off into the trees with them..

I really wanted to go off, too, into the secluded forests together with those guys and our new friends. But instead, I remained transfixed and mired in doubt, a mere observer of the developing situation.

I was stuck in a fog of indecision, because for some inexplicable reason all five of the company's officers, including the company commander himself, appeared to be staring directly at me while I contemplated the consequences of making my move into the tree line.

Christ! Would you believe that shit? The damn first sergeant, of all people, seemed in open collaboration with the officer clique and apparently unsympathetic to his own troopers' recreational needs. He too was also focusing in unerringly on my position.

I was certain as I stood there being observed that President Nixon, his defense secretary and the rest of his cabinet were pondering my present location vis-à-vis the tree line , at the White House's national security advisors' daily presidential breakfast briefing on the critical Vietnam war situation.

The radio in the command post squawked urgently. The company commander continued looking my way as he took the call, except that he was also nodding compliantly now.

I thought, it must be that nosey division commander General Casey, calling urgently from division headquarters to enquire directly of the CO as to whether Private First Class Byer had gone off into the trees to fraternize with the locals.

This had to be some kind of conspiracy unfolding here.

But how time flies when one is rooted in indecision. Suddenly it was over.

The braver guys who had just upped and went, were returning from the tree line, all wearing foolish grins of relief and satiation on their heavily beer-soaked mugs. *Negotiations had been successfully raised and brought to satisfactory fulfillment*, I concluded.

But I promised myself, never again. Oh no. There would be no preventing me from going into the trees the next time the opportunity arose.

That was, as long as someone or something could somehow distract those damn officers from constantly staring at me whilst I was trying to decide what to do.

Chapter 23

I'm Sorry, Thanh

Early in the morning, as the company stirred and trooper resistance levels were low, I performed one of my more ordinary but important corpsman duties not entailing dodging bullets or disaster. We, the company medics, distributed the daily anti-malarial pill to every member of our unit for immediate supervised consumption.

That meant from the company commander on down. Everyone had to swallow their pill every day literally right before our eyes. This was a direct and rigidly monitored order from Divisional Headquarters to all line units operating out in the field. A very sacred and important ritual. In the past, many a sky trooper had, on occasion, sort of accidentally forgotten to take his pill and had suffered the imposition of being sent in to the base hospital in the safe rear areas after contracting a bout of malaria out in the field.

Some suffering: Back there, a sick man was pampered by pretty nurses and enjoyed hot meals while watching stateside relayed TV programs. This imposition sure beat staying out in the death-dealing jungle and dutifully facing the wrath of the local Vietcong, or the NVA's bevy of snarling chicom

AK-47 automatic rifles and the blasts of B-40 rocket-propelled grenade launchers.

The medic was God in such circumstances. "Sherman--hey, hey--where you going?" I shouted. "Stand right there, man, and swallow the frigging things down. Yes, both of them, the big orange one, too!"

This second pill had to be taken on a weekly basis. "Oh Doc!" Sherman groaned.

"Oh Doc, my ass, man, hurry up and drink the damn things down, let's go now! There you are, that's a good man."

We had Kit Carson scouts out there with us in the field. Friendly South Vietnamese allies. They were indigenous, so they supposedly knew the lay of the land. They acted as our tracker scouts and went out with us on our extensive patrol operations.

Our scout in C/1/5 was a likeable, smiling little chap named Thanh. He lived with us out in the field for almost a year. Out there, we experienced and survived many hazards together, including firefights and skirmishes with the enemy. He was as close to me at times as Chief was. We shared some good laughs together. Believe it or not, funny was funny anytime or anywhere, even out in the jungle.

Then one day seemingly out of the blue, military intelligence, in their frustratingly dogmatic manner, informed our unit that Thanh, who had lived so closely with all of us for so long and who had been to our hell and back with us, was in truth and in fact a Vietcong spy! So much for early detection and intelligence oversight.

I saw Thanh close to the end of my tour (by then, I was "short" and thinking only of my coveted boarding pass) at a rear-area, outdoor movie show. He was under investigation but free to move about the base's environs. This, too, made one wonder. He called out cheerfully to a group of us passing by. "Hey, doc!" he said to me. I turned my head away from Thanh. I froze him on the spot by not responding. I regretted my action then and still do to this day.

Thanh was a man I had shared my life with out in the field. Sometimes, we chose adjacent spots to spread our ponchos and put down our air mattresses for the night. We'd heat up one block of C-4 to make a small fire for our evening meal, which consisted of my chicken and rice ration put together with his tin of C ration pears for dessert. He'd have a last package of cocoa powder, I'd have the cream and sugar, just barely enough to make two canteen cups of hot cocoa for us to share. How many days and nights like this?

Then, maybe because he was not one of us, we were told by our people, who had arrived here the same way we did, that he was our enemy. That we were to break off relations, just like that. After all the shared meals, human warmth, laughter and stress and real peril that we experienced together in the jungle.

Before the sudden "intelligence" revaluation, Thanh was our friend and unit companion. What if it was all true, and good old Thanh was in fact a VC? Did that mean we had not in fact shared all those profound times together as friends? If it was indeed all deception on his part, all along, did that now justify unforgiving ostracism? This was all very confusing to me back then. But in wartime situations, sea changes came fast at you, and you had to move with the tide in order to survive.

Nevertheless I would remain haunted by the sight of Thanh's familiar and ever present smile crumbling from his face for the last time. For me, the situation was not dissimilar to witnessing a death in the family: Because the death of a friendship, a relationship and everlasting trust had taken place. To be replaced by the acceptance of a hurtful and lonely lingering confusion.

If only we could rewind the clock of life in order to have another chance at it. What if military intelligence was wrong about him? He was our friend—I believed that and I should have stood by him. But I was a soldier and had to obey orders.

In a combat environment, we had to comply exactly as we were told to. This kept us alive in the main.

But I regretted my actions toward Thanh all the same, and I still do.

Whatever became of him after the fall of the South in 1975? Nothing bad, if he was in fact a Vietcong. For this reason, I sometimes hoped that he was. But no I did not. Who was I kidding?

Did he survive the grim re-education camps of the period if he was not a VC but was captured by our common enemy? I would never know.

But I pray that somehow my friend made it safely through the war; because I would always be sorry about the way I treated him, due to the fact that I was a soldier who obeyed his orders.

Chapter 24

Being Short

The only time I have known when everyone wanted to be short was in Vietnam.

It was the most admired, dreamt of, envied, respected, and sought after circumstance imaginable, and arriving at that state of virtual security was tirelessly pursued by every soldier over there, barring none. This pursuit transcended rank or race or anything else.

Everyone in- country had a short-timer's calendar or several. Every day of a serviceman's three hundred and sixty-five day stay over there was meticulously and tirelessly marked off. Either at the beginning or at the end of each and every day. Rituals varied with an innovative flair that sometimes bordered on the macabre.

Varieties of calendars or almanacs were created and worn on helmets, kept in private diaries, taped to the stock of a weapon, or secreted in ammunition tins, the only truly waterproof containers in the entire country. Everyone had two or three calendars. So sometimes you marked off the same day three times to make yourself feel extra good.

Officers had them, too, but they kept theirs hidden from us lesser mortals to try to prove, to God alone knows who, that they liked the jungle and wanted to stay there forever.

Madness. A short-timer would be excused almost any transgression. He had earned the right to be foolish, lazy, forgetful, greedy, aggressive, a little touchy, or just downright mean-spirited.

An FNG might say to a veteran soldier one day, "Look, man, I don't want to sound out of place here, but that guy over there, Sergeant Mayers, he's been standing completely still and staring at the same tree for the past ten minutes, and everyone else is passing by without pause or notice." To which the veteran soldier would reply: "Oh, Sergeant Mayers? That's Ok, he's short, so don't worry about it." End of conversation.

A short-timer would get to go in for any job that opened up in the rear that would get him out of the field a month or so before going home. So people with more time in-country would get the available jobs in the rear. Not that there were many, but it was the fairest system of all.

A short-timer, someone with about two months left in-country, would not have to walk point or would hardly ever be sent out on ambushes. It was a given that he be protected as much as was possible. Because he had come so far, he deserved whatever breaks would get him out of the field in one piece.

This was a sort of tribal rite aimed at protecting our own. We all looked forward to these same breaks once our calendars started to dwindle, too.

Soldiers greeted each other with the usual slap of hands, more so black troopers, but everyone had their version. "How much time you got left?" The reply would be brief. "Forty-two days and a wake up, man. And you?"

To those who were not so short, or not short at all, a tersely mumbled reply to the question sufficed. The longer timer would shuffle off in dismay and surly despondence, frustrated at the unfairness of his not being at least a little bit short too.

Chapter 25

Pop Frag

Pop Frag was a staff sergeant in our company. He was also a former weightlifter from Alabama who must have studiously and faithfully followed a Joe Weider exercise regime in civilian life.

His body was one of chiseled muscularity. He was about five feet, eight inches tall, weighed 230 pounds, had steely grey eyes, brown hair cut to regulation buzz, of course, and swaggered about, as all muscular men do.

He was baptized Jonathan Flagler. The "Pop" came from the fact that he was an ancient 36 years old by the time he joined our unit in the field. The "Frag" referred to explosive fragmentation hand grenades that were his weapon of choice.

At all times, he carried six to eight of these grenades strapped to his torso along with the necessary bandoliers of ammunition for his CAR-15 modified rifle strapped around his body. He was a walking arsenal.

Pop's first tour of duty in Vietnam was a regular and uninspiring one during which he served with an infantry line company from the Americal division. His second and third tours, the latter served with our unit, were driven by hatred and bitterness; they were personal odysseys for Pop.

He had a twin brother, Peter, who had served with the First Air Cavalry division. Peter was killed by enemy infiltrators at the A Shau Valley in 1968. It was one of the major battles of the Vietnam campaign.

Pop, being a lifer with some influence, got himself transferred to his brother's old unit, which happened to be our company, C/1/5.

Pop was totally hell-bent on revenge. He volunteered for every dangerous ambush or reconnaissance mission that was going out. He grabbed every opportunity to walk point, so he could have first shot at the enemy. He looked and acted like an older version of the Rambo character portrayed in the movies by Sylvester Stallone: he always carried the devastating light anti-tank weapons (LAW) rocket launcher snugly strapped to his back whenever they were available at re-supply.

The man was a manic aggressive, quickly growing to near all-out berserk levels. He was barely controllable and always a hair away from death because of his thirst for revenge.

Nobody had to ask, "Who was that?" when, on making contact with the enemy, Pop came bursting through the men in front of him like a loose cannon on a rolling deck. If his platoon was already the lead element in the line formation, he would already be walking in the point squad anyway. *He actually volunteered to walk point.*

No one wanted to go out on ambush with him anymore. Pop had become a liability to the unit. He had personalized the war, turning it into his own vendetta, and nobody wanted to become collateral damage because of his insatiable bloodlust.

Pop was wounded on many occasions. Sometimes, as a result of his own unsuccessful efforts at wildly hurling grenades through dense impenetrable tree lines at suspected bunker complex sites.

"Let me at those motherfuckers," he would grumble from deep within his expansive chest, and go crashing through the undergrowth, firing from the hip, yelling and hurling his grenades as he ran.

A sky trooper hunched behind a tree returning fire at an enemy position glanced up and shouted once as Pop bounded past him: "Jesus Christ, there he goes again. Man, that old fucker is crazy!"

Pop had dashed past the trooper frantically trying to unhook his grenades while simultaneously firing his weapon.

Some days later, in a sweltering jungle glade, Pop had been wounded again during an enemy engagement, primarily from his own acts of indiscrete hand grenade tossing.

Hands on broad hips, his face red, veins popping, he was arguing animatedly with the company commander, Captain Vowell, against the idea of his been sent in with the rest of the wounded men for medical treatment at a rear-area hospital facility.

Pop had sustained the perfect superficial, non-life-threatening wound known colloquially as "the million-dollar wound." It was the kind of injury that most people would love to get after spending just a few months out in the field: a ticket out from the bush for two weeks of recuperative nursing, and much needed succour in the rear.

But not for Pop Frag, oh no, he wouldn't have any of that shit.

"Send in some other weak-bowelled pussy to enjoy the creature comforts in there," he said, but not him. He was out there to fight a war, and we should all just relax and leave him alone to take care of it in his own way, he said sternly.

The CO said, "Sergeant Flagler, you are bleeding copiously, man."

"Sir, I'm telling you that it's only a scratch."

"Look, Flagler", Captain Vowell said, "I'm calling doc over, and if he says you're going in, guess what? You're going in."

"Come on, Six, give me a break," Pop continued to beg. "I only got back out here two weeks ago from my last hospital stint. I'm fine. Don't worry about me"

"Hey, doc." Captain Vowell called to me.

"Yes, sir," I replied.

"Take a look at the sergeant here for me. I know that we have three other people going in, and that we're left kind of short, manpower wise, but…."

"Sergeant Flagler, come here, man!" I yelled to Pop; not as a 20-year-old private first class, but as the senior corpsman in charge of an entire infantry line company of 100 men. It was sheer bravado, but it was also my domain.

"Roll up your pants leg Sarge, and let me take a look," I commanded. "Uhmmn. Ah. Uhmmn Oh oh, this doesn't look too good," I mumbled, shaking my head.

"Hmm Sarge, this injury is badly infected already, possible first stages of gangrene poisoning is setting in here. This wound needs immediate and urgent clinical attention at a proper medical facility."

Then I dropped the hammer. "Sorry Pop, but you're going in."

"Shit! Shit! Shit! Shit! Doc," Pop bellowed. "God damn it to hell. Christ! Just my fucking luck. Shit! I only just got back out here…."

Dispirited, Pop trudged off and crawled into the waiting medevac helicopter with the deportment of a man on his way to the gallows.

He shook his head from side to side all the while in aggrieved disappointment at being sent in to the rear area base hospital for treatment.

As the medevac helicopter lifted off with Pop and the other battlefield evacuees Captain Vowell sidled over to me, a gleam in his eyes. He whispered.

"About Sergeant Flagler, doc. How bad were his wounds?"

I looked around to make sure there were no eavesdroppers hovering, before responding.

"Wounds, Sir?" What wounds? Pop was right this time Sir. It was nothing, just a harmless little scratch."

Chapter 26

The Black Panther

We had a self-professed Black Panther in our unit who answered to the name of Jerome Whitlock in civilian life. One of the many non-military pastimes of this proponent of black pride and power was rechristening himself Astaphan something or the other. Whitlock, like me, was a combat medic in the First Battalion of the Fifth Air Cavalry division.

Another thing Whitlock loved to do, which I hated to participate in, was his daily, endless hand-slapping rituals. It was usually launched with a "Hey, bro, give me five" greeting that took a non-refundable 15 or so minutes out of your life each and every time you met him. But they were kind of mandatory, the practice of these rites, so as to avoid upsetting the constantly irritable private Jerome on too many occasions. He also had a tendency to behave violently at any given moment. So we all tried our best to pacify him.

Something he did regularly, which afforded me greater amusement, was threaten to blow Lieutenant Levy's "white ass" out of his underground bunker with a hand grenade. This threat increasingly became a disturbing possibility out there, though. It happened to officers, and it was called "fragging." As the name implied, it was the lobbing of a fragmentation grenade into a bunker that was occupied by an officer at the time, on most occasions killing him outright. Of course, this was an appalling thing, a wanton, indefensible act of murder. But because the fragging did not actually happen in our case, just the thought of Lieutenant Levy's world collapsing because of Jerome Whitlock always caused us to break down with laughter. Laughter always fortified us, at Quan Loi through very dismal times, and Jerome Whitlock was often the key player in these welcome episodes of comedic relief.

Whitlock was a short, stocky, "built like a brick shithouse" black guy from California who thought all white people were passé. Those he met, he said, he either had to get over or go around. He operated on a very short fuse and was also not partial to smiling very often unless lecturing all comers about the latest exploits of Huey Newton or H. Rap Brown.

The average combat medic would spend 10 or 11 months of his annual tour out in the bush with an infantry line company. But after just one month into his first assignment, Whitlock declared that he really did not care for jungle life and the resulting hostilities that came with it. He insisted that he had had enough (four weeks) of that shit for a lifetime. He sought a way out.

His first ploy was to succumb to every ailment indigenous to South East Asia. Later, he apparently became afflicted with other questionable illnesses not officially recorded in any of the medical journals on tropical diseases at the time. From many of the unit's doctors' mouths came the cry of amazement: "Jesus, Whitlock! My God, man, you on sick call AGAIN?"

Whitlock went down for the count to every possible disease available, and even invented some other unheard of maladies for good measure. But after these clever ruses got old with the increasingly unsympathetic military medical personnel, and stopped keeping him out of the bush, he decided to become a "conscientious objector" who would no longer willingly participate in the premeditated killing of people. He intimated forcefully to anyone foolish enough to be within earshot that, for this reason, he should be excused from the entire combat theatre by the powers that be, forthwith.

Unfortunately for Lieutenant Levy, as the man in charge he was the one who had to break the bad news to the belligerent Whitlock that he had to go back out to his unit each time he had recovered from his latest life- endangering tropical ailment. Whitlock did not like this at all; he just could not quite come to grips with the inconvenience of being shot at on a regular basis while doing the job the army had trained him to perform.

There was always a shortage of medics out in the field, as they got killed regularly in close order jungle combat, and this was exactly why Whitlock had decided to give up on the whole damn jungle experience in the first place.

"It's just too fucking dangerous," he moaned constantly. His point of view had been further substantiated when he heard Muhammad Ali's famous "I have no fight with those people" declaration on a bootleg tape recording. Whitlock promptly and loudly endorsed the view that neither did he! I myself loved Ali and did not know or care much about the politics of war.

"Hey, Byer, my man, look homes, listen up here now! I've had it, I'm gonna frag da muhfucker Levy's white ass this time for sure, yeah."

"Oh Lord," I moaned, "Whitlock's here."

"Come on, man, calm down. What's the problem?" I resigned myself to absorbing no more than ten minutes of bullshit before making a strategic exit out of there.

"You want to know wha' happen? I'll tell yah the whole thing. Da muhfucker Levy wanna send mah ass out to the boonies to join Delta Company, man. You hear dey been in some heavy shit out there today in some firefight? Dey got a medic daid in first platoon or some damn crap like dat. Muhfucker Levy wanna send mah ass out, today, on the very next resupply chopper as a replacement medic. He saying some bullshit about it's mah turn to go out, and it's mah duty to the battalion or some ole song and dance *espirit du corps* bullshit like dat. Everybody knows dat am a sick man. Imagine my poor ailing black ass, man, out theh now to get goddamn nailed like dah other medic? Sheeet...man, I cain't hack no field shit again, homes? I done MY time out dere. No way dey gonna send mah ass back out dere to no field.

"Look, Byer, doan be down in no bunker from now on wid dah piece o' shit Levy. I'm gonna frag his sorry white ass, I promise you dat ...and real soon, too.

"By the way Byer, you eat chow yet man?"

The problem with Whitlock, which would eventually work in his favour later, was that no company commander in the entire division wanted him in their unit as their medic. He had become the pariah of all combat medics. "No way, keep that lazy ass malingerer far away from us!" at least one captain declared when Lieutenant Levy had tried sheepishly to palm off Whitlock as a much needed replacement medic on some unwary unit operating with a new field commander at the helm.

No one wanted Whitlock to be *the medic* on the receiving end of the cry of MEDIC! during a critical firefight situation out in the bush, when the life that may be hanging by a thread was theirs.

A beleaguered Lieutenant Levy meanwhile kept praying that Whitlock would somehow get himself killed in combat, like other less threatening people had been doing from time to time. This would have relieved him of his worse life threatening worry of the war, or his life for that matter. Whitlock was a menace that had made Lt. Levy a stranger to a good night's sleep.

Having become universally undesirable, Whitlock spent a lot of his duty time at the Quan Loi base camp, safely removed from the hardships and hostilities of life out in the bush. He began to shrewdly run down his time left in-country by ensuring that he remained unwanted by every field unit commander in the entire area of the First Air Cavalry division's operations in the Republic of Vietnam, by just being himself.

Whitlock maintained the pressure on Lieutenant Levy on a daily basis; with promises of filling a prescription of life-shortening consequences for the lieutenant should he keep attempting to alter Whitlock's present address from the safer rear areas, by continuing to make plans that would send Whitlock out to a field unit.

As for Lieutenant Levy, because his heart was not into upsetting Whitlock unduly, he was unable to actually affect Whitlock's transfer. So the man was bizarrely covered on all sides and made it safely back home to California by simply sticking to his bullying ways.

I sometimes wonder, though, just how well Whitlock made out with the Los Angeles Police Department after he got back home. Never comfortable with authority, what scams did he attempt in civilian life to get over or around people, white or black? Or did he settle down, decide to behave himself and become a priest or something?

Should anyone run into a short, brooding, ill-tempered priest called Father Astaphan out there, look out!

Chapter 27

Village of the Dead

In the movie Omega Man, Charlton Heston portrayed the last surviving man on earth living among hostile mutants. As a result of this circumstance, each and every day of his life was a fight for survival. The movie was filmed in a major city in the U.S - Los Angeles - in 1971, and chillingly depicted the cold emptiness of buildings long vacated by living beings, and the creepy feeling the hero experienced of stepping on other peoples graves everywhere he strode.

This feeling of desolation and abandonment enveloped me as we stepped out of the somber jungle one morning onto a grassy plain basking in sunlight. As we settled down for our first break of the morning after a tedious foot patrol, we paused. We stood looking down at the view below us, transfixed, at what we realized with horror had once been a vibrant township, now a razed and smoke blackened victim of war.

The village had been bombed from the air by either US or our allied South Vietnamese aircraft. I did not know how many people had perished there or how many had survived the attack. I had no knowledge of whether the Vietcong or NVA forces had occupied the town earlier, before the attack, and if they had done so, whether they had fired anti-aircraft batteries provocatively at allied aircraft as they flew by, causing a subsequent retaliation on the village.

Maybe no one had died here, but I had the feeling that someone had. Because I could feel their presence reach out tentatively toward us as we looked down at the tableaux of almost beautiful ruins lying in somber repose below us. As I had discovered in previous experiences, there was always some form of beauty attached to tragedy. In war, it sometimes encouraged combatants to pull back from the very brink of hostilities, whenever an engagement was imminent.

This town must have been a beautiful place once. Situated on a gentle incline, the nearby jungle seemed to have retreated. Perhaps to allow the village more room to breathe and prosper. A nearby stream still gurgled along its meandering way, unperturbed by us, the transgressors trampling along her banks. Rays of sunlight still optimistically lanced through the area, and gentle breezes blew the untended grasslands with a mournful melancholy.

Even in their present skeletal state, the buildings retained some semblance of once proud and dignified forms. Their torn and gutted frames reached imploringly to the blue morning sky as if to say, "We are still here, outsiders. You have not succeeded in moving us from our rightful place. We are still here, and we will remain here."

The layout of the streets was well-thought out, by someone with a head for such things. All of the approaches led inevitably to a large village square where farmers would have once met to chat about the upcoming harvest season and hopefully good crop yields, while vendors bartered their wares in the colourful marketplace.

Where were the people of this once proud township today? If anyone had survived, would they ever return to rebuild here?

The voices of children playing in the park seemed barely recognizable. Maybe it was only the whistling of the wind in the trees that I actually heard?

Only the buildings, or what remained of them, knew what had happened here, but they would not speak to me. Not to outsiders whose uninvited arrival in the past always signaled discomfiture and a disruption of innocent livelihood.

Why should they acknowledge me? How could I convince them that I was different, that I cared about what had transpired here, when they had witnessed our treatment of their occupants before?

I was saddened by the plight of this ill-fated village, and not for the first time since arriving in Vietnam, I thought long and hard about my involvement in this war.

I had signed up for the Army on my own free will, but when I moved on from the village to continue my stint in the service, I did so with a heavy heart.

Chapter 28

Sick Call

Sick call was the military's version of a civilian's visit to the doctor.

It was a screening session held by the army's medical services for military personnel who were in need of care for a host of ailments that ran the gamut from ring worm and jungle-rot infections to diarrhea, from malarial diseases to regular battlefield wounds. All were addressed at sick call.

So the medics of Charlie Company were set up in a large tent on LZ Grant to hold sick call. The company, on temporary stand down from its normal search-and-destroy duties, was tasked with the LZs base defense duties for one week. So let the good times roll. Hot chow, ice cream, showers with running water, and mail from home. We almost felt like human beings again.

The medics on sick call duty, my buddy Steve Nordsworth and I, sat at the front of the tent's entrance. The doctor, a captain, was inside. We saw the patients first and provided diagnoses, using our discretion to treat the ailments we felt competent enough to deal with. Situations that were more serious, beyond the scope of our three months of medical training, we referred to the doctor.

Peter and Walter, two well-known troublemakers from second platoon, were our first patients of the day. Uncharacteristically, they were early, and they stood at the head of the line of men waiting to be seen on sick call. What was their problem now? we wondered as they fidgeted impatiently, shuffling about restlessly. Knowing these guys like we did, their downcast expressions and skittish behaviour gave us a hint as to what their problem might have been.

Eventually, one of them worked up the courage to blurt out, "Hey, doc, can you take a look at something here? I'm getting this awful burning sensation whenever I take a piss." At our prompting, they both unbuckled their belts and dropped their trousers to reveal to us what we had already suspected: they had both contracted a dose of the clap. We had the treatment available for this disease, but it was painful.

The guys had ventured into a nearby village, ostensibly to purchase fresh fruit to improve the company's dietary regimen. Apparently unable to liberate anything resembling an orange from the marketplace, they had instead returned to the base with a venereal disease procured from partaking in sexual activities without adequate protection.

Because our company was on base defense for only one week and would have to return to the field shortly with as large a complement of troops as possible in order to maintain full fighting strength, a rapid and definitive treatment protocol was necessary for treating cases of gonorrhea.

The treatment required was six injections of penicillin over a period of three days: two injections a day, administered to the buttocks, one in each cheek, using a large 14-guage needle for maximum effect.

This is what followed: On Day One, the first two shots were given to the troopers. Their response was usually something like "Ouch! Jesus, doc, that hurt like a bitch, man! What the hell are you people using on us here, elephant needles?" The men would then amble off to their bunkers, taking delicate steps, their backsides throbbing painfully.

On Day Two, already sore and stiffening up from Day One's shots, the guys walked back up to the tent, moving gingerly, taking small, measured steps as they made their reluctant approach towards us for shots three and four. They would slouch despondently over a bench when instructed to lean forward to receive their medicine.

They bore the pain in silence, but their eyes flickered wildly from the effect of a dull ache, and they shook their heads in despair as their assaulted backsides became completely inflamed because of the series of injections received so close together.

Now the guys were always firmly warned that if they broke the chain of treatment by missing just one injection, they would have to repeat the entire six-shot course from the beginning. So they never messed with this possibility, they always obeyed as ordered and reported for all their shots on schedule.

On Day Three, the two walking wounded returned, easing up the hill noticeably slower than they did on day Two. They mumbled to themselves about the unfairness of having to sleep on their stomachs all night long, and how they knew in their hearts that those holier-than-thou God- damned medics thought the whole damn episode was some kind of fucking joke.

It was hard not to feel sorry for those poor guys as we administered the final two shots to their swollen bottoms. They were so pain racked after having six needles, three on each side, prick them in an area of close proximity, that all they could muster was an almost inaudible groan of "Ugghh!" after the last shot was driven home.

We watched the two delinquent soldiers shuffle off down the slope from the treatment tent to look for some quiet place to lie on their stomachs and repent. They were bent over in agony and seemed to have aged five years in the past three days.

But we figured that they would no doubt think twice before their next assignations in a convenient village.

They may already be saved: by declaring themselves the latest poster-boy candidates for the army's COVER UP WHENEVER YOU USE IT health campaign. Anything to keep them off their backsides.

Chapter 29

Fire Support Base David
Cambodia June 1970

On April 30,1970, the armed forces of the United States of America invaded the country of Cambodia. And I had a front row pew. It was announced to the world at large that President Richard Nixon had authorized the immediate invasion of that country by US ground forces. One major significance of this military action was that it was not directed at Cambodia, its government or people, but at active combatants from another country who were seeking refuge and safe sanctuary within Cambodia's national borders.

It was, in fact, a response in accordance to the continuous pleas and complaints of US generals, who were clearly frustrated at Cambodia's providing safe haven for North Vietnamese infiltrators into South Vietnam. These soldiers constantly fled to safety and hiding across the border back inside Cambodia after openly striking at US forces operating on the other side in South Vietnam. The NVA would now be permanently routed out of their previous convenience by this invasion order. They would be caught with their pants down by this action. Or so the decision makers hoped.

The 1st Air Cavalry division, my division, was the obvious choice for the vanguard role in this operation. Cambodia's eastern border was also Vietnam's western border. You just walked across. The "First Cav" already operated in this area. It was our officially designated area of operations (AOP). It was our "hood".

We had all the helicopters necessary for the quick airlift and deployment required for an operation of this nature. We were also the best (based on our track record to date) US soldiers in Vietnam, ever. Why, then, use anyone else for this operation?

I remember well the late evening of the day the division air assault into Cambodia began. We had assembled apprehensively but also excitedly in large numbers in open areas, waiting for the fleet of helicopters assigned to airlift our units out. The large helicopter fleet would simultaneously airlift our entire battalion out to allocated drop-off zones. Out into the great unknown of another war, in yet another country.

We were going into a new country somewhat physically similar to Vietnam. The trees and the swamps would offer the same thrills. But the overriding, common concern here was the question of exactly what and who was out there waiting for us, and in what numbers. Nobody knew that answer, not even our military intelligence services. They could only guess at best.

Of course and as usual, they were not part of the action; they were not going into hostilities with us, only advising strategy about how to deal with it.

The atmosphere felt heavier than usual that evening. Preparing for battle was a unique experience; one's emotions ran the gamut of fear, intrigue, and apprehension mixed in with some genuine keenness at embarking on the adventure that lay ahead. The sprinkling of conversation that wafted through the pickup zone was delivered in hushed whispers.

When we eventually took off on our incursion, the sun was sinking towards the end of its working day in these parts, as we began ours.

My helicopter was a UH-1B, the dependable Huey. There were about seven other troopers on board besides myself, the two pilots and the two door gunners. As we lifted off, the sky was abuzz with helicopters of every imaginable shape. Hueys and Chinooks for troop transport, Cobra gunships for escort duty, followed by the large CH-54 heavy lifters, which were already bringing out artillery pieces and their support munitions for the sky troopers' immediate battlefield operational needs.

It was already dusk as our armada, airborne for a while, closed in on our designated LZ. This was located deep inside uncharted enemy territory. Our situation started to deteriorate from then on when we suddenly started to take ground fire! Our door gunners blazed away with their M-60 machine guns. I didn't know whether they could see what they were shooting at, but they dispensed Uncle Sam's ammunition freely into the tree line and surrounding areas.

All we could observe below us was the usual, never ending sea of green. "We're taking fire, we're taking fire!" A visibly shaken door gunner yelled. We knew. And the pilots too, because they would have been looking down directly at the green anti-aircraft tracer fire probing lazily upwards, its fingers reaching searchingly out to us as we got nearer to our LZ.

The whole area would be very hot tonight. They obviously knew that we were coming.

Our aircraft was suddenly hit! Shit, we'd taken some enemy rounds through the engine nacelle. The Huey shuddered then pitched forward sickeningly, lurching in a drunken swoon. The pilots maintained control of the craft as the rest of us tried desperately to hang on to something for dear life, but we had been severely crippled, and we all knew we were going down.

Acrid, oil-tainted black smoke belched from the engine compartment. Our situation was grim. We would have to auto rotate down to be saved, to a semi-crash landing, worryingly short of our planned LZ.

I believed we would make it down in one piece. There were patches of relatively flat and open areas of ground below us. *But we were going down* - that was for sure.

As the pilots fought for control, ground fire quickly became yesterday's concern. We had to go down in a controlled crash landing, one that was only possible in a rotary wing helicopter. It was called auto rotation. The Huey's wind- milling blades provided just enough lift to prevent us from falling out of the sky rapidly and uncontrollably like a dead weight. A feature, it must be stressed, only rotary wing (and thank you, dear God, for this) helicopters have and fixed wing aircraft do not.

Had we been flying in a plane, like the C-7A Caribou, as we regularly did sometimes…. Anyway, we made it down into an open field, more of a hard landing than an actual crash. Everyone was shaken, some minor cuts and bruises, but alive. The wind had been knocked out of us, but we considered ourselves very lucky to be still living as we sprinted for the relative safety and shelter of the forest's tree line.

Our valiant helicopter was now a dead pack animal, her battered carcass left behind at the crash site where she fell. But we were all very grateful to the aircraft, because she had brought us down alive, in one piece, without any serious casualties among us.

There was this great adrenaline-spiked feeling of elation at not being killed. It put back a spring in one's step, but there was no time to contemplate close shaves right then. We had to move out. We had to regroup, to find our unit, and most importantly, to find out exactly where the hell we were on the map.

Roman Browne was in charge. A competent black brother from Washington, DC. He was the squad leader, a SP-4, which was similar to enlisted corporal rank. He was outranked by the two warrant officers who flew the Huey, but we were on the ground, so he called the shots. We all looked to Roman with confidence. He'd been in-country for ten months. He was our man; we knew he'd somehow get us back to the main body of our unit.

We hunkered down together. We had moved away from the crash site, well past the tree line, and were heading further away from the downed helicopter. Enemy scouting parties would be all over the area real soon, ransacking the wreckage for salvageable equipment and endeavouring to make acquaintance with its most recent occupants. We had one working radio and tried desperately to raise our company command for help.

We soon gathered from radio chatter that we were not the only lambs gone astray. When we finally got through to our unit, we were told to stay together and stay put for the night, and be sure to be real quiet about it, too. It seemed that we had inadvertently landed quite close to a suspected, regiment-size, North Vietnamese force's base camp area.

The curtain of black night had by now descended upon us. It was an alien and inky dark one out here tonight. There was a persistent misty drizzle, to complement our miserable and gloomy surroundings, and it was cold and lonesome out here on our own.

The 12 of us stayed close for both moral support and bodily warmth. We established a duty rotation to man the radio in shifts during the expectedly long night ahead, and set up observation cover for all possible approaches to our small encampment.

We listened to the eerily distinctive crump crump of artillery shells impacting on their targets somewhere close by. There were also some clusters of illumination flares going off with a staggered regularity, as sporadic small-arms fire resonated throughout the area. Maybe caused by an ambush tripped off suddenly by somebody?

We didn't know what was going on or who was responsible for the night's activities. We only knew there was a war out there waiting for our participation as we sat and listened glumly to its ghostly echoes. We had since moved another kilometer away from the crash site. It was unlikely the enemy would pick up our trail tonight, but tomorrow we would have to move out early, and quickly.

At last we received the necessary coordinates from our company. At first light, we would hump about three klicks to rendezvous with them.

Mornings in the jungle were cool and somber as sunlight was usually held at bay by dense, overhanging foliage, garbled vines and clinging undergrowth. We got up, broke camp, and eagerly moved out to make contact with the rest of our company command.

Two hours later, we were home. Our humping had been incident free. Amid happy backslapping and friendly banter we greeted our buddies. "Can't read a compass, guys? Want to borrow a map? Maybe you should go back for the chopper." The friendly chatter heralded our reintegration with our company's main party. What a relief!

Our patrols inside Cambodia over the next week or so were routine: Small skirmishes, ambushing promising trails, and experiencing regular spotty firefights; dealing with the unit's necessary manpower replacements and helicopter resupply requirements. It was normal life in the bush for any infantry line unit.

We interdicted many unhappy, displaced, and fleeing NVA soldiers. Cambodia was no longer the safe haven they had treasured in the past. We had brought the conflict back to them, and they were not amused by this at all. We would stay on their asses until they were completely pushed out of Cambodia.

The other event of my Cambodian sojourn so far, was our discovery of a huge NVA cache of arms, munitions and supplies. It was among the largest such discoveries of the entire war, justifying one of our Cambodian campaign's major tactical aims, which was to deny the enemy sanctuaries and access to resupply facilities. This was a large munitions area buried unobtrusively within the dense jungle. We actually walked right up to it before seeing it; the area was so cleverly camouflaged.

It was huge, a veritable city of arms and supplies. Predictably, we named it *The City*. They had everything there: a hospital, trucks, food, uniforms, and a training school with a black board depicting how to shoot down helicopters. The latter, a kind of a chilling sight for some of us after recent experiences. They even had tanks, and weapons of every calibre, with the corresponding ammunition to go with them.

Our division commander, General George Casey, insisted that every individual in our unit be given a brand new Chinese-made SKS rifle--spoils of war. My own was still brand new and plastic wrapped in Cosmoline grease when I later sold it to a (low quarter) rear echelon cobra gunship pilot in Quan Loi. Guns were for taking to war, not for returning home with, and all I was thinking of more regularly then was of going home to a peaceful, relatively weaponless climate when my year was up over there.

* * * * *

We had just been ordered to assemble for extraction from the field. We were going into an LZ for base defense in Cambodia called Fire Support Base David. A FSB that was located in Cambodia's O Rang area. What they did not tell us was that David was an LZ situated some 115 miles north of Saigon and 36 miles north east of Song Be. This was four miles across the Cambodian border from Vietnam, deep into uncharted enemy territory, and, as we found out much, much later, it was the northernmost US outpost of the entire war campaign in Cambodia. But then why would the powers that be have wanted to upset us with that kind of detailed information then?

Every airlift out of the jungle produced a feeling of well-being for all. Getting out and going in. Leaving a hostile environment behind in exchange for the enjoyment of some well-deserved creature comforts like hot meals and clean clothes. An LZ provided all of these bonanzas, even though it was only for few days, before we headed back out to the damn sticks.

Approaching Fire Support Base David from the air, there was very little to presage what would shortly unfold here. On the contrary, it was one of the most beautiful places I'd ever seen. Situated on a vast sweeping range of meandering, rolling hillocks, it was surrounded by lush evergreen vistas and interlocking slopes of graceful elephant grass. The base's site commanded panoramic views to all points of the compass.

As we flew into the area, the gold-flecked and wind-tossed grass appeared to bow graciously toward our airborne flotilla in a welcoming dance. Beautiful scenery predominated here for as far as the eye could see.

David commanded the highest ground in the area, providing easy observation of all approaches from the base's lookouts. We got in on a Friday, replaced the outgoing base defense company, took up our perimeter guard responsibilities, and then settled in to defend this wonderfully sited base.

On Saturday afternoon, I requested a squad of security to accompany myself as medic on a med cap, or medical civic action program. When we flew in to David, I had seen a charming little Montagnard village located about two miles south of the base.

Medcap was a program where the medics, when available, went out to the villages to provide whatever help they could to the friendly "locals" of the area. We also gave the ever present children candy, and generally tried to foster goodwill among men.

It was a cool and wet Saturday afternoon, typical for the height of the monsoon season, when we trekked out from David in a southerly direction. After about one hour of moderate humping, we found the village I had spotted from the air.

The tribal settlement comprised a small group of thatched-roof huts, lean-tos, and log-hut structures huddled together in a somewhat haphazard fashion on one of the gentler sloping hills in the area. The fragile structures snuggled closely together, as if seeking comfort from their proximity. Each one balanced more precariously than the other on shaky- looking stilts built to keep them off the wet ground.

Situated prominently at the center of this commune was the most imposing of these structures. At the entrance, an aged, stooped Papa San--the village elder tribesman--greeted me effusively with something like "Gha ja kalthein whooo thiem woo, shuboh shuboh." I assumed this was a welcoming entreaty because of the expansive toothless grin that accompanied the words.

He invited me into his smoke-filled thatched-roofed hut, what we called a hootch. Together, we shared a large therapeutic water pipe that must have contained some highly questionable ingredients; because the effect of smoking the pipe left me feeling sort of dreamy, blissfully light-headed and very much at peace with the world at large.

These fiercely independent tribespeople wore loincloths and carried spears. They nonchalantly smoked hemp-stuffed pipes as they circulated freely and without guile around us. There was a definite feeling of having drifted back through space into another time. These people didn't care much for either the North or the South Vietnamese, but they always got along quite well with us.

The children were the same as carefree village children everywhere, running after us shrieking with the excitement of strangers among them. A few small, emaciated-looking dogs nipped at our heels, curious. I believed they sometimes involuntarily helped augment the protein diet of the villagers. I let them nip while they could.

The womenfolk giggled bashfully behind nervous smiles that could not quite camouflage their betel nut-stained teeth. Pungent smoke from communal cooking fires and the smell of burning charcoal cloyed at the damp afternoon air. It was another world, yes, yet a peaceful one.

We spent a pleasant and relaxing evening communicating by sign language with our grateful and easygoing new friends. These gentle villagers living on the periphery of modern-day society appeared to be quite contented with their lot (or little, to be more accurate). I treated some minor ailments, questionable maladies of the ringworm and jungle-rot type, and dispensed our food and candy offerings generously.

That afternoon, as we lay on a gently sloping hillside unwinding, I witnessed the very surreal (for wartime) ritual harvesting of rice in a flooded paddy field situated just below us, by local farmers, patiently driving their huge water buffalo before them. I also saw my first elephant that evening, stepping through a veil of mists into the open fields below us, striding gracefully and determinedly going somewhere.

Later, as we humped back to the base there was an electric vibration in the air. A sense of disquietude enveloped our small party. Although we saw no one along the trail, we felt that we were being observed or followed. This was very disconcerting. Our point man, Eric Bristow, looked over his shoulder at me and said, "Doc, I don't like it. I really feel as though someone is watching us."

Thunder pealed and lightning flashed on the distant horizon. The overcast atmosphere was getting gloomier by the minute. The afternoon's hint of a drizzle had graduated into a definitive downpour which began to fall steadily. Prescient doubts were screaming at us that something was not quite right, but what was it? The fairy-tale countryside that had embraced us earlier was turning the other half of its face towards us, the more ominous and menacing side.

We completed the rest of our journey looking over our shoulders. Most of us were by this time blooded combat veterans. We knew something was greatly amiss out there, we just couldn't say what.

When we arrived back at the base, we found the entire post on a Condition One Red Alert. Everyone was tense. Sketchy intelligence reports coming in from all points were warning of something very big and threatening building up around the camp. Nobody could confirm the size of the enemy units massing against our little outpost, only that they were doing so right now. Something was going on, it was in the air, and as soldiers we felt it in our guts.

We all had a bad feeling about it. Things weren't looking too good for us out here tonight on our isolated base. Radios were buzzing, and people were moving about purposefully.

They were about to send somebody out to look for us when we arrived back. They had started to think the worst.

"Hey, you guys, wait up for me. Hold up, for Christ's sake. Oh God, they're all around us, they're out there in numbers and they're coming in! Jesus, they're all over the place."

Right behind us, as we entered the perimeter, scampering for his life was one of our long range reconnaissance patrol soldiers. In actuality, he was a sniper. LRRPs went out in four-man teams to scout, and to try to shoot enemy officers and to disrupt the enemy unit's operations. Similar to what the VC tried to do to us whenever opportune.

The LRRPs belonged to the army's elite Ranger Special Forces units. They were the toughest of the infantry units and were tasked with highly dangerous missions. But this shadow of a soldier was dirty, disheveled, wide- eyed desperate, and near to complete mental and physical collapse. He had been on the run for the entire day, evading and hiding from numerous enemy scouting parties—the same pursuers who apparently were now tightening the vice around our lightly defended base.

The last enemy unit he had barely evaded, he said, *was concealed to the south about two miles away, close to the old Montagnard village*. He tried to catch his breath while pointing with unerring accuracy in the direction of the village, my village, the same place we had just returned from spending an entire afternoon at.

"Shit!" I started, suddenly more interested in what the LLRP had to say, "close to where....?" He told us he was the sole survivor of his scout team. The three other members would not be coming in, but the enemy, he assured us, would be, tonight.

"We have beaucoup movement," he then said. These were chilling words. Words infantry soldiers in our combat environment never ever wanted to hear at any time under any circumstances.

Perimeter security had started popping flares. The curtain of rain was down. No air support would be available to us; the weather ceiling was 200 feet. Too low to fly missions of any kind. We were "socked in" by heavy ground fog, so we were on our own.

Lookouts scanning the darkness surrounding the base now reported that they saw something moving around out there. Moving and closing in on all sides of our camp.

We sat huddled in ponchos, shivering in the rain and waiting. We all had our guard duty shift rotations down on the perimeter defensive line. We popped an abundance of illumination flares, looking through our rifle's star light scopes at an eerie green landscape of deep tree lined gullies shimmering with ghostly visages. We were hemmed in by both the weather, and the gathering enemy. To a man, we would have rather been somewhere else that night.

A spectral, green glow emitted from the starlight scopes on top of our weapons. Through the scopes we could see vivid shapes moving about out there in the dark. Our overall situation was bleak. A hell of a battle was upon us, we could feel it in our bones. We steadied ourselves as best as we could and made ready to face whatever the darkness would deliver. Stoic apprehension and resigned fatalism set in.

There would be no external assistance for us. FSB David and her defenders would have to see the long night through with every shred of guts and determination at our disposal.

Then it began.

At 0250 hours on Sunday morning, a reinforced company of North Vietnamese infantry launched a sudden and all-out ground attack on FSB David. In the gloomy drizzle and thick ground fog they had crept up on to our heavily guarded fortifications like avenging, black-clad wraiths from hell. They came up and into the heavily mined perimeter wire with determination, and we responded with all the massed firepower at our disposal.

They attacked from the north and east simultaneously, backed by batteries of 122-mm rocket and 82-mm mortar fire that were already "walking" rounds inexorably up the slopes and into the base. They blew bugles to confuse and terrorize us.

We repeatedly locked and loaded our weapons to counter their deadly assault. Black pajama-clad suicide bombers we called sappers had breached the outer fences and were setting off satchel charges to blow openings through the inner concertina barbed wire defenses that led into the inner camp. Some of them were making it through, even with our withering grazing fire from our crew-served M-60 and .50 caliber heavy machine gun emplacements blasting directly into their charging vanguard.

"Jesus," someone shouted, just how many of them bastards are out there, anyway?"

"Look out. Shit, they're coming at us from two sides!" another cried out. The noise of the gunfire and rockets blasts reverberated in our ears. They kept on coming and had somehow managed to overwhelm the secondary defensive wire and infiltrate further into the base.

They crouched low as they ran up the hill through the rain towards us, their AK-47s, AK-50s, and B-40 rocket propelled grenade launchers spitting death at us. We responded with our own .50 calibres, M-60s, massed M-16s on full automatic—selected to rock 'n' roll and our M-79 grenade launchers and hand-held LAW light anti-tank weapons. We threw everything we had at them. We had to.

I was down in the aid station bunker helping with the more seriously wounded. It was raining hard. Lightning flashes mixed with bursts of small-arms fire. I was underground. The battle raged above my head like a fully fledged hurricane. I had experienced one hurricane called Janet hitting my island, Grenada, when I was five years old. The similarities were palpable in the sounds, gunfire for thunder, the flashes - muzzle blasts for lightning, and the gripping fear, the threat of the unknown that enveloped everyone.

We - the medics, would have to make periodic trips to the perimeter to bring wounded back to the aid station. That was our main task during a major ground attack assault.

The excessively loud stutter of an AK-47 startled us. It sounded unbelievably close! It sounded like it came from right on top of the aid station, directly above our heads. Could this be?

"Jesus Christ, what the –?!"

An NVA sapper had gotten into the heart of the compound, and *he was on the aid station's roof* firing his weapon at our perimeter forces from behind them. Somebody in the bunker urgently extinguished our lamps.

"Shhhhhhhhh! Quiet, everybody, for God's sake, he's right above us!"

Someone pointed frantically at the bunker's roof. We were trapped.

The infiltrator was just two feet above us. We could hear him clearly, moving about and reloading his weapon and firing over and over. We could hear his excited, heavy, rasping breathing. He was so close to our heads that we could have easily reached up and touched him. But for some reason, maybe due to the heady distraction of the ongoing firefight, he was disoriented and unaware of our proximity to him, easy prey, literally trapped beneath his scuffling feet.

He may not have known he was positioned on top of an occupied bunker. He may have thought he was just standing on a built-up sandbag area. If he had known exactly where he was, he could have and surely would have bent over and slipped us a pin-less grenade or a satchel charge. There were 16 of us in the bunker. Not many of us would have survived the resulting blast in that enclosed underground space.

"It was related in First Air Cavalry Division lore, and recorded in the army's official account of the battle, in the *Stars and Stripes* newspaper, what happened when a SkyTrooper looked back from his perimeter position. He later told a reporter: "I could not believe my eyes when I saw this gook on the roof of the aid station randomly shooting up everything all over the camp. I paused, thought about it, but only briefly, then blew his ass off the aid station roof by emptying a full magazine from my M-16 rifle into his sorry ass."

We were still down in the bunker aid station when a frantic radio call came in from the eastern perimeter berm (fortifications), where the ground assault was the fiercest. They needed a medic down there urgently, as they'd been taking multiple casualties on the outer-defensive line.

Tuffy, our base sergeant said, "We have to send out somebody, but they're saying they don't know how we would get down there because the firing on the perimeter was so intense. But they had a 'stretcher case', someone who was badly shot up, possibly bleeding to death they believed." Tuffy looked around at the group of us. He didn't want to send any of us out there into the firestorm, but somebody had to go, and go soon, because it was our job to retrieve the wounded.

"The heck with it, I'll go", I said, and stepped forward. After the joker on the roof, I was feeling a bit claustrophobic. I would take my chances outside. No more being cooped up for me. If I had to get it, let me get it out in the open. Another medic, Tommy Johnson, a quiet, thoughtful young man, said, "I'll go with Roge. We'll need two pairs of hands to carry the stretcher anyway."

In a situation like that, you don't ever give yourself a chance to reflect. So we just went, quickly.

Keeping very low and praying really hard, we dashed out and up from the bunker. We grabbed an available stretcher leaning outside the bunker and ran directly past the dead body of the NVA insurgent sprawled on the aid station's blood-soaked roof. "Screw you and the horse that you rode in on," I mumbled.

This guy had only recently scared the shit out of me. I could not bring myself to commiserate his passing in a more dignified manner. Someone had already removed his weapon, so he was no longer a threat.

Our footing was slippery, but flashes of lightning, incoming rocket and mortar explosions, and illumination flares helped guide us through the maze of structures on the blacked out base. They also exposed us to enemy fire, not good.

We worked our way down the slope. As we ran to the perimeter, sliding in the wet mud, we kept falling down behind sand bags, glad sometimes to take much needed cover for a while, and to catch our ragged breaths.

The noise of the firefight was deafening. Claymore mines going off in the wire. B-40 enemy rockets and mortars landing inside the base. The enemy AK-47 assault rifle's recognizable crack. Everywhere noise. Bedlam.

We made it down to the wounded guys eventually. One was bad, looked like a sucking chest wound. We had to get him back up to the aid station. Up there, out of the rain, we had more room to work, and could set up an intravenous drip and get some plasma into him.

The firing on the line was intense. Our heavy .50 calibre machine guns and M-60's harmonized with an unbroken cadence pouring out an incessant firestorm of hot lead. We bandaged up and gave some morphine shots to the wounded on the perimeter then steadied ourselves for the return dash uphill.

Back up the slippery slope, with a critically wounded man on a stretcher, with all of us fully exposed to incoming fire. Crouched over, ready to run, I told Tommy, "Look, when there is a lull in the fighting, we go." Waste of time, there was no lull coming, so we just went anyway.

Small arms fire, incoming mortar, and rocket rounds engulfed us again. We didn't stop to think. Couldn't stop to think. Crouched low, flinching at every impact or at any burst of incoming fire, we scrambled back up the hill, desperately trying not to die in the process. We experienced difficulty breathing, straining like fish out of water from the exertion and ever present anxiety. We were almost spent, but somehow we dug deep and we kept going with our patient.

The stretcher weighed a ton. We were trying to slide up hill in the damn mud, as if that were possible, and doing everything in our power to make it under our crippling load. It would have been comical if the situation hadn't been so dire.

With each desperate misstep, our ungrateful patient groaned. But we held on somehow and made it up to the aid station with the stretcher case still alive. We passed the lifeless sapper still lying in the same place we left him on the way out. His circumstance remained the same.

"Alright, Jesus, they made it," someone yelled.

Tommy and I hugged each other, trembling with relief. Wet, cold, mud slicked, and shot at. Shit, I needed a drink of something.

Tommy and I made *that* stretcher trip. Other medics in the unit made similar trips throughout the night all over the compound. *Every* medic on David put their lives at risk to carry out the job they were trained to do. They were all outstanding in the performance of their duties, each and every one of them. The urgent cry of MEDIC! was responded to throughout the long night - it was our job and we did it to the best of our ability.

But those fuckers were still blowing their bugles out there. Jesus. It was wave after wave of attack from these (as we learned later in the morning) dope-inspired fiends. They kept on coming. They never buckled under our onslaught. They just kept on coming in.

It was just as eerily disturbing to hear the enemy hurling verbal abuse at us like rocket fire. Unseen, disembodied voices shouted, "Chieu Hoi, Chieu Hoi, no fucking Chieu Hoi," repeatedly. *"All Yankees will die in Cambodia and go back home to America in body bag."* "Chieu Hoi, Chieu Hoi? No fucking Chieu Hoi tonight for American GI. Only dead American in green stinking body bag."

Chieu Hoi (open arms) referred to an amnesty program offered to all VC and NVA personnel who surrendered to the US or their South Vietnamese allies. The ones who came over were welcomed with a job and a fresh start at a new life in the South: To help build a democratic South Vietnam.

The NVA's aggressive taunts, throwing the amnesty back at us, was a grim reminder that we were up against a non-repentant, battle-hardened and purpose-driven foe.

Our gunners maintained their firing steadily into the early morning hours, trying to somehow stem the surging tide, the repetitive attempts by the NVA to breach our defensive line. The heavy machine gun fire we laid down had not eased, but settled into an urgent, rhythmic pulse of its own.

I went back down to the sandbagged perimeter a few times, with the other medics, always in a low crouch, to do our jobs, tending to the wounded. The M-60 machine guns manned by our gun crews on the dangerously exposed defensive line that encircled the entire base's perimeter kept on firing throughout the long night. Doing their job.

We had to constantly pop illumination flares, to try to see through heavy ground fog to identify the enemy emerging from the mists, coming up straight at us.

The low-weather ceiling combined with the monsoon downpour cut ground visibility to almost zero. Our flares lit up glaringly against the white overcast sky, producing a blinding, incandescent white-out effect. Our arching, red, tracer-fired outgoing rounds intermingled with green, incoming, enemy-fired tracer rounds. It was a virtual light show of deathly madness. And the noise continued.

Black-clad shadows slipped out of the shrouded tree line in small groups, dispersed, then melted into the gullies surrounding the base. "Shift your fire to the left. I just saw one of them duck down there," someone shouted.

A loud blast rent the air, the concussion ringing our eardrums. Dust, debris, and who knows what else rained down on us as a sapper-fired B-40 rocket-propelled grenade slammed into our fortifications. The sandbags absorbed most of the blast, but it was a near miss all the same that left us momentarily stunned.

The effort to launch the rocket exposed the sapper just long enough for an alert machine gunner to cut him into shredded meat and bone matter. The pulverized NVA folded into himself slackly.

We thought we saw two more mysterious shapes. But we couldn't be sure just what we saw or didn't see in the appalling weather.

"Pop some flares to the left again." An urgent request. "We have a lot of movement. We need reinforcements up here, now!"

"Somebody try to get through to the TOC on the radio." The tactical operations command. "They're coming up on us heavily on this side now. They just keep on coming!"

The voices were shrill and excited, tinged with growing apprehension, a lot of fatigue, and an increasingly urgent need for permanent relief from it all.

Our firing only subsided long enough for the machine gun crews to change a spent belt of ammunition for a fresh one on the overheated guns. Weary, pain-numbed, cold fingers carried out this transfer for the millionth time for the night, or so it seemed. Brain to fingers, fingers to brain, then all over again.

Above our heads, up at the main base, we heard the slow, comforting cadence of our large .50 calibre machine guns. Their distinctive *bup, bup, bup bup, bup, bup* reassured us down on the lonely line that we were not alone. They were putting down long, sweeping swaths of heavy fire. Mowing bullets directly into the forever advancing enemy forces.

But this couldn't go on. Something had to give. Either their bodies or our ammunition supply. Maybe both.

Then at long last the intense firing had checked, an insistent round had popped off here and there sporadically, but that too petered out somewhat reluctantly, then it had all stopped as suddenly as it had begun. Silence prevailed.

It would be another two and a half hours before the liquid morning light seeped weakly through the lifting mists, so that we could first register then start to digest the full magnitude of the brutal encounter that had materialized here.

The heavy rain had stopped and the curtain of mist had risen as if to say look! Daylight's stark reality of what had ensued here overnight was sobering. As we emerged slowly from shell impacted bunkers, stumbling around like zombies, we were grateful to be alive, considering the state of the base.

We stood awestruck at what we saw before us.

Ruined gun emplacements and shredded sandbag fighting positions. Small fires burning all over the place. The damp air reeked of cordite from spent munitions.

Oily black smoke drifted lazily from a cluster of unrecognizable structures that once comprised our artillery fire direction command centre. Everything was dank and wet.

Ruptured and collapsed base fortifications blended with the cratered red dirt of the hillside. Innumerable quantities of expended shell casings of a variety of calibres littered the landscape like confetti.

Down on the base's helicopter pad located at the foot of the hill, just outside of the perimeter, two weather grounded helicopters had been transformed into smouldering hulks by enemy B-40 rocket fire during the night. And that other scent, the by then all too familiar and repugnant odour of weapons violated corpses, assaulted our senses.

The mist retreating slowly down sodden slopes, encouraged by an early morning zephyr, revealed the startling tranquility of a still beautiful, but now battle-scarred countryside.

Lying tangled in our wire defenses and spread sporadically in and around the base's environs were the bodies of 29 NVA frontline soldiers. All dead. Our casualties totalled 26 wounded, and most unbelievably, none dead.

Some of our attackers had been literally cut in half by our machine gun fire. Others had been pulped into unrecognizable lumps, with shards of bone sticking pathetically out of torn uniforms.

They were all well outfitted and fully equipped with sophisticated, high-powered weapons. Most significantly, large quantities of narcotics and hallucinogenic drugs were found stashed on every corpse.

Even with the discovery of the drugs, there was still a disciplined and military look about these North Vietnamese Army soldiers. This was no ragtag group of Vietcong part timers we had faced off with, but a finely honed unit of professionals.

They had come here with a plan, to kill or die, if necessary, while accomplishing that task. Albeit they may not have bargained for an opponent as irrepressible as the troopers of the first air cavalry division.

I discovered later that my two-man sleeping quarters was rubble. It had taken a direct hit from a 122-mm rocket during the battle.

If I had not been down in the aid station bunker but asleep in my quarters during the attack…. Life was quite full of ifs, what-ifs, and suppose-I-had. I moved on.

The ground fog was dissipating rapidly. We heard the sound of approaching helicopters in the distance. The rear area generals and opportunistic photographers were coming out to decorate, photograph and pester us, no doubt. A sense of "normalcy" was already beginning to return to our little corner of the war.

It was all so stunning and surreal. Death and destruction on a beautiful hillside in Cambodia. Later, some four-star general, incongruously outfitted in neat, heavily starched fatigues and shining boots, mumbled something about duty, honour, and country, as he pinned two pieces of coloured ribbon (representative of the Bronze Star and Purple Heart medals that I would receive later for this battle) on an intact portion of my torn and filthy tunic.

For heroism in ground combat and wounds received, he told me. "Thank you, sir," I had responded respectfully.

Some of us got medals, but as far as I was concerned, everyone on the base was a hero that night.

I'd been wounded on my waist by rocket shrapnel, not serious. Probably hit on my trip down to the berm or on the way back up with the stretcher case. It was only after someone pointed out the blood to me that I started to feel some pain.

The truth was that we couldn't wait for the ceremonies to conclude to get at the more satisfying reward of hot, helicopter-borne chow. Our bellies were growling. When did we last eat?

And my mind was reeling from something else. I could not shake off the two bits of information we had just garnered from inside of our battalion intelligence operations unit.

The first was gleaned from documents taken from the NVA soldier's corpses. The assault and hopeful overrunning of FSB David was a very important assignment for both propaganda purposes and face-saving reasons. Their mission was to storm and completely wipe out the most remote and lightly defended US outpost in Cambodia.

It would have been a major and humiliating defeat for the entire US military's Cambodia campaign. The troops sent to carry out this task were therefore the best the NVA had. A crack and seasoned veteran NVA ranger assault task force.

The second realization, more the product of hindsight but nonetheless confirmed, was the chilling fact, that when our small and vulnerable party had ventured out from the base that afternoon on our medcap detail, we were intentionally allowed to walk unchallenged to and from the village by the concealed enemy strike force, so as not to compromise the element of surprise for their greater plan.

We were part of the enemy's menu for the night, but fortunately for us we were not the main course.

We would never question that old feeling of foreboding again, because our soldier's instincts had been right all along, when we had felt that something was very wrong that afternoon, as we made our way back to Fire Support Base David from our trip to the Montagnard village.

Chapter 30

The Old Lady and the Bracelet

A few days after the ground attack on Fire Support Base David our Company was back out on patrol. Our task was to flush out any enemy support units or remnants of the forces that had recently staged the assault on the base, by carrying out a protracted search and destroy operation that blanketed the entire area.

As we humped, the monsoon rain's consistent damp conditions kept us in a state of abject misery.

At the foothills of the O Rang district mountains we came upon yet another Montagnard village. This one situated to the North of the base. We stopped for a break at the village, and dispensed the usual candy bars to the children and C rations to the adults. We normally used these opportunities to also offer medical assistance to ailing and infirm villagers.

I always loved the Montagnard people because they were so uncomplicated.

A young boy approached me directly and took my hand, as these people would affectionately do. Using re-assuring gestures he led me to a ramshackle lean-to. Pointing into the smoky interior, he called out an unpronounceable name to someone within.

I peered into the haze and eventually made out the form of what appeared to be an old woman languishing in a hammock. Her face was dark brown in colour and her skin had a leathery parchment-like texture. Her body was frail from indiscriminate exposure to the elements and the passage of too many moons.

She sucked doggedly on a misshapen pipe and moaned continuously "Oahwee ohhh, oahwee ohhh, oahwee ohhh."

My nostrils bristled at the rank odour emanating from the lean-to, a musty smell akin to that of spoilt fish or soured milk that put paid to any thoughts I may have previously entertained about entering the hovel.

The woman inside could have been 40 or just as well 75 years old. Difficult to pinpoint, because the Montagnards lived hard and precariously on the fringes of all measurable and established societal norms.

The Mama san and the boy then started babbling and gesticulating in an excited and exaggerated manner. Both of them pointed at her forehead. Accompanied by a variety of hand signals they chanted a sing song chorus of, "ban amawsgrehji, alrefhytoo, ooh, ooh, argh, argh, alrefhytoo, arrgh, arrgh!" Observing from some distance outside, I listened attentively to all of these descriptions of the mystery affliction, but found myself clueless as to anything that was said. I even tried scratching my head for elucidation – but nothing.

So how then would I recognize and treat the articulated malady? How could I put my training manuals from Fort Sam Houston to use? I had to stand back and look contemplatively at the suffering lady. I wished that some form of divine intervention would have made a much needed appearance.

Then the simple solution I was looking for perhaps too deeply hit me: It was a headache - just give her some aspirin!

With the assistance of the boy, I gave her two of the white healing discs. She gulped them down with a swallow of tepid water from a bowl. I then sat nearby, to anxiously observe my ground-breaking medical diagnosis take effect, while entertaining visions of my name being mentioned in the next edition of the *Physicians' Desk Reference*.

What a magical sunrise, that which followed, as the sheer, unexpected relief from chronic headache pain eased the permanent scowl previously etched on this long suffering innocent's brow.

The old lady smiled a countenance-transforming smile of relief and joy. How long had it been since she was last free of pain? Could she even remember a time when she was not racked with discomfort?

She presented me with a copper bracelet made from old shell casings as a small token of her gratitude for my assistance. The toothless grin that accompanied the gift said it all.

I wore the bracelet for many years, initially at a time when it was not yet fashionable back home in Grenada for men to wear bracelets in public.

Not that I particularly cared, but who would have appreciated the story of its origin anyway, even if I had felt inclined to explain to curious people where it had come from?

A small thatched hut in a little hamlet way up in the mist shrouded foothills of the Cambodian highlands, one wet afternoon as I was....

Chapter 31

The Jungle - Don't Ever Trust Her

The jungle was a selfish all-encompassing colossus that began everywhere but ended nowhere. So it seemed to us after spending the last eleven months of our lives patrolling deep inside of her threatening and haunting environment.

She was a massive and sometimes oh-so-deceptively peaceful entity. Yet she had the ready ability to spawn a host of life-threatening surprises. Ruses that at first ensnared and then securely enmeshed the unwary in the many mazes of her wondrous but deadly defiles.

If you ever trusted her cool, welcoming, early morning sunrises filled with chirping crickets and singing birdsong, you would fall victim daily to her craftily spun tricks.

It was deadly dangerous to be flattered into such complacency.

Made arrogant by the fact that she would outlive us all, she rustled her floral skirts at the offensive license taken by humankind, who sometimes, while scurrying and floundering around on her forest floor, negligently riddled her tree things with the instruments of war - ricocheting bullets and misdirected shrapnel.

But just as quickly as she took offence, she simmered down and shrugged off these delinquent actions.

She used her vast reservoirs of power to revitalize herself and medicate gaping wounds—abrasions to bark skin—with plentiful sap. Medicated, the resultant scar tissue that formed over the affected areas would be as strong and resistant to outside influences as the old skin ever was.

Her evergreen minions would be all healed and rejuvenated well before next spring's growing season.

She may have welcomed us into her calm and alluring recesses. But once in, she never wanted us to leave her realm again.

Her moods and faces were legendary and misleading as she changed from a crisp early morning distraction to a stifling midday heat.

Then, while your over-tasked senses worked overtime to make the required adjustments, she had already skipped ahead, as good schemers do, to prepare sudden and violent heavy afternoon monsoon showers.

This could and often would be followed by rapid late-evening cooling. Eerie, deafening silences would prevail thereafter.

Fickle in her every action she would sometimes sit alone and brood whilst jealously guarding her inviolable command of all who dared to venture into and or traverse through her haunting pathways.

That was who the jungle was. I had lived within her deceitful grasp for almost a year and I knew her for what she was. So I reminded myself not to trust her, ever, because she was nothing but a Trojan Horse.

Chapter 32

Doc, Get Your Shit Together – You're Going In

I had been a survivor for almost a full year of deadly hostilities, fighting tooth and nail against determined VC and NVA forces. I had managed to overcome ambushes, poisonous snakes, blood-sucking leeches, and hungry disease bearing mosquitoes for months on end. I had learned to live with the fear of dying, a sensation that can be likened to having your personal precursor of doom shadowing you, everywhere you went.

I had shrugged off torrential rains, swamps, and viscous mud while sleeping in treacherous jungle environs. I had had my share of dangerous helicopter insertions and extractions under enemy fire, none of them were routine, and experienced several mortar and rocket attacks on bases that I'd been serving on when they were besieged. But at last I was short. It seemed to have happened overnight.

I was poised to take that first, long-awaited step on my return journey home to civilian sanity and welfare, to where I belonged. Only, I was not a hundred percent sure when the end of my humping would occur because my replacement had not come out to the field to relieve me as yet. So I woke up unaware whether this would be the last time I would fold up my poncho and air mattress from my final jungle floor camp site.

I was cognizant of the fact it would happen sometime soon, but that was not the same as "it's today." Whenever I left, I would never return to this place. There would be nothing and nobody left to come back to. I would never again live so closely to and with so many brothers. All of us dependent on each other, operating every day with one mind, 100 men thinking alike. Each and every one of us focused on the same objectives, sharing the same yearnings, dreams and desires, enjoying together the exact same relief when assigned to a base defense mission on an available LZ or FSB.

In what future circumstance would I ever so hopefully and so drunkenly sing with a group of comrades, "We gotta get out of this place?" Most importantly, we all wanted the same opportunity out of life, namely, the chance to be able to keep breathing a little longer.

We were getting ready to begin our daily humping through the jungle for the day. The radio had just squawked, there was a resupply helicopter inbound. We had supplies coming in, so we waited for them before pushing off. Smoke was popped as the beating blades of the Huey grew louder and louder. I could see the familiar outline of the resupply bird as she settled into the small clearing we had recently hacked out from the un-cooperative woods.

As the chopper's spiralling blades ground to a halt, a squad of men was dispatched out to her to pick up the incoming food, mail, and necessary ammunition supplies.

I hoped that we would get some ice cream on this trip. I also yearned for something else. As I scanned the helicopter, my probing and hopeful gaze homed in on the lone deplaning passenger: A young guy, who stepped uncertainly off the helicopter.

He looked around, exhibiting that frazzled where-am-I-what-am-I-doing-out-here-am-I-about-to-die-right-now look that only a terrified and disoriented FNG could display without the aid of a professional acting coach.

His uniform was crisply starched and very green. Everything about him screamed newness ...and he was carrying a medical aid bag.

My God. The guy was a medic! A sweet, wonderful, mint condition *new* medic. My heart started thumping.

I started to choke up, momentarily forgetting how to speak, how to breathe. My eyes burned. Part of me thought, this can't be happening right now, even though another part of me had been praying so long for this very thing to happen.

There was a shout from the NCO in charge of the helicopter movements, Sergeant Bill Musgrave, "Doc, get your shit together, you're going in. Your replacement is here!"

I tried to gather my thoughts. I would never forget hearing similar words hurled at me, but in the reverse "Byer, get your shit together you're going out!" But I knew what I heard now, and I'd take the "in" over the "out" any day of the year. I immediately scrambled to gather my things and dash to the waiting bird to get out of there pronto. But, settling my fevered mind, I paused; I realized that I had some important farewells to make first.

The perplexities of life were sometimes puzzling and overwhelming. How could I have suddenly felt as wistful as I did then? At long last I had been granted the reprieve that I had been yearning for. Then, in sight of that wish being realized I had paused. But I had to.

There were some people out there I'd grown attached to, and I could not just turn my back on them like that. But I had to leave them all, and I was sad about that, because it was unlikely any of us would ever meet again. In this lifetime anyway.

I took a look around me one last time. As if drawn by some malevolent force, I locked eyes with my old nemesis the jungle, that evergreen verdant conspirator of so many of my friends' misfortunes. The jungle was impassive and remained as silent as a graveyard. It could have been my own. I hated the place, and since I was very very short at this point in time, I mocked the tree line with glee.

"To hell with you, jungle," I yelled hysterically, giving it the finger. It was, of course, unmoved. "You tried your hardest, beast, but you didn't get ME! You can kiss my butt, choke on your constipated creepers and rot out here in lonesome perpetuity for all I care."

I knew it wanted me to remain entwined out there in its myriad paths for all time, to fall victim to its mantraps forever. The jungle had its chances. No more, not with me. I was finished. I was going home at last.

Goosebumps rose like welts on my arms. Staring at the jungle, I was saturated with bittersweet memories that would haunt me for the rest of my life. Names, places, events, and happenings that ran the gamut from hilarity to sheer gut-wrenching horror. Death and valor, heroism and cowardice, happy hour and available whores, jokes and unparalleled human comradeship.

Ice cream, warm beer and mail from home. Body bags, both empty and occupied. Incoming fire, smells of burning wood. Rotting vegetation mixed with incense from Buddhist shrines. Montagnard tribespeople smoking hemp pipes, betel nut rotting their teeth. Monsoon rains that started six months ago, and I really couldn't remember a dry crotch out there. My mind was on fire.

I huddled with the guys one last time. Congratulatory backslapping (because I had won my bid to live).

Some warm hugs, high fives, and empty promises to keep in touch back in the world. Plenty of bawdy jokes about all the willing women lining up and waiting impatiently to service me back in Saigon.

The last man I talk to was Six, Captain Vowell, my company commander. For the past eleven months, he'd been a few other little things to me as well, like father, confidant, and most importantly, friend.

"Six, I've got to go in now," I mumbled. My throat was tight; my frigging eyes were burning me.

"Yes, Doc, you have to go, don't you?" he said soberly. "I want you to know that we all think that you're a hell of a guy, a great medic, and a damn brave soldier, too. We'll all miss you tremendously out here." He paused.

"You've done a fantastic job for us, you know, all the men think so. It will be hard out here without you… But, boy, we had some great days together, didn't we?" A faltering smile made a very shaky and temporary appearance on his lips: "You deserve a full and rich life, so go with God's speed, son."

A surprisingly large group of guys had by then gathered around. Some bowed heads, some awkward shuffling of feet. Mixed emotions of envy and regret jostled around for positions of prominence in weary homesick minds.

"Thanks, Six" I said. "I have to tell you … that you are the best company commander that I could have ever had the privilege to serve under, bar none. You brought a lot of us single-handedly through all of this shit on your broad back, sir". There were a couple of hear, hears.

"I will never forget you, sir, and thanks again for everything you have taught me." I then straightened up and knocked off the best frigging salute even I didn't believe I still had lingering inside of me. There was a last round of backslapping and bear hugging with the guys that was rudely intruded upon.

"Hey, soldier, let's go, let's go, man!" This came from the door gunner on the waiting helicopter who was flapping his arms, impatiently waving me onboard. "Hurry up, man, hurry the fuck up, we have to get out of here *now*," he screamed, stabbing his watch and pointing meaningfully at the rain-threatening sky. What was it with those freaking door gunners?

I was not surprised that he would have been totally oblivious to the significance of my final departure from my mates. Well, fuck him, I thought. *His* ass would have to wait on me this time. Maybe this was my opportunity to tell one of his kind where to jump off.

As I walked out to the waiting bird, I could not bring myself to look back at the guys I was leaving behind. On my way at last, I grunted a clipped hello and goodbye in the same breath to my replacement, George somebody, as I hurried past him. Not really fair to him, but the other medics would have to clue him in. My future was calling me. I had completed my mission. I was not responsible for him. I was going home. I had to go.

But then I stopped. The door gunner was apoplectic, but I didn't give a shit. I had to say something to the frightened FNG before I went in. I owed it to myself. Had it been only 11 months since I was him? It seemed like ages.

I turned to the young FNG wearing a spanking new uniform. I took both of his trembling hands in mine, held them firmly to my chest, and inhaled deeply. I looked him squarely in the eyes, and served him up three rapid-fire contradictions that originated from the bottom of my heart.

"Listen, guy, everything is going to be OK. It's not as bad as it looks out here, and the experienced guys will take good care of you," I lied.

I gave him all that I could give him - hope. Let him survive, poor guy, to pass on the same message to his replacement someday ....

Finally I boarded the waiting helicopter, ignoring the seething door gunner. He was no threat to me and he knew it, because the M-16 rifle clasped in my right hand was a used one. Dutifully, I performed our standard grunt field-leaving ritual, with the "black power" clenched-fist salute delivered with my left hand, my M-16 thrust upward and outward with my right.

I balanced precariously without a handhold on the rising helicopter's swaying skids, baying at the open sky. "Ooargh! Ooargh! Ooargh! Ooargh!" It was a ceremonial thing, a system cleansing. We just had to howl when we left the jungle; it really made you feel so much better.

I looked out at the guys of Charlie company, my brothers in arms, my family for almost a year of slogging through swamp and bush, for one last time. I settled on the floor of the helicopter with my back resting uncomfortably against empty ammunition crates and my mud-encrusted boots dangling over the sides.

I'd left the field just as I came in, physically, but inside my head I was a much changed human being: a veteran of a terrible fighting war, an observer of too much pain and loss.

But I had to go, to "di di mau" out of there.

Captain Vowell stood on the chopper pad, somewhat apart from the other guys who had assembled to see me off from the field. He stood, his mind at rigid attention even as his body swayed in the prop wash, his head cocked, and his face turned upward as the Huey rose steadily, slowly banked over the surrounding tree tops, then quickly faded away from the pickup zone.

Chapter 33

Low Quarter: Under the Floorboards

So, at last I had become a low-quarter, rear-echelon motherfucker -- more cordially referred to as a REMF. Great. Hip, hip, hooray for me! Having spent 11 trauma-filled months in the sweltering jungle, I had secured my short-timer's job at last. And I was heading home in a month's time, God willing. I'd made it out of the field, and that was what counted for everything.

Our unit's medical doctor, Captain Vaughan, who had taken over from the survived-and-made-it-back-to-the-USA-Lieutenant Levy, had wanted someone experienced, reliable and short to put in charge of battalion medical resupply. This was necessary for the weekly refurbishment of our unit's operational needs out in the boonies.

Guess who was now short enough and thus eligible for this plum of an assignment of medical resupply coordinator for the battalion? Specialist fifth class (SP-5) Byer. The job was all mine, lock, stock and every oh-so-deserving barrel of it.

A "low quarter" was really a soldier's black dress uniform shoes. It was also the derogatory term used to refer to the substantial number of military men serving in

Vietnam who spent the entire war living in unabashed luxury in the rear areas.

Totally removed from the back-breaking, soul-destroying labours of the actual shooting war, they were paid the same salary as we the worker bees were to eat, sleep, and fornicate in comfort "in here", whilst others were getting their asses shot off "out there." We worker bees, understandably, didn't like the low quarter REMFs too much. Now, since I've become one myself, I loved it all.

My new job, really a pilot program, introduced recently by our Division with yours truly at the helm, was based not at our brigade headquarters in Quan Loi, but at the large military base at Bien Hoa, just outside of Saigon.

Saigon was the seductive, alluring capital city of South Vietnam. It was a buzzing metropolis of fun, dripping with sex, and degenerate women, and it was situated literally right down the road, a stone's throw away from my new work station.

I was just past my twentieth birthday, and recent job openings had given me encouraging hope that I'd see my twenty-first landmark also. The 11 pay cheques I had earned were all languishing in the currency of MPC, the military pay script we used over there, forgotten and unspent. What would I have splurged it on in the jungle, anyway? But then to be assigned to a place where everything imaginable, and some deliciously not so imaginable, went on but a short jeep ride down the road from my new sleeping quarters every day and every night of the week, was wonderful!

What was a poor guy to do? Stay in the barracks and play monopoly with the fellas? And I'd been assigned my own jeep. A necessary perk of my resupply job. Ha ha.

As I yawned and stretched lazily on my new bunk, and appraised my cozy surroundings again, I wondered at the gross incongruity of it all. I made a promise to myself there and then, and I really meant to keep it: if and when I arrived back in the U.S there happened to be another low-quarter, rear-echelon motherfucker on my flight who, having spent his entire year in the lap of luxury, declared to his welcoming party, "I've just spent a year fighting in the Vietnam war," I would haul off and deck the sucker right on the spot. I wasn't a violent man by nature, but I did try to be an honest one.

My barracks had about six cots in it, and we all had new mosquito netting. Large ceiling fans kept us cool. A small desk provided for our radio/tape deck musical interludes and letter-writing leisure. Not that anyone was writing home with any frequency by then. Saigon beckoned, on too many occasions.

We had an old Papa San who came by every day to clean out the area and make up our bunks with *fresh linen*. The several mess halls were all opened to us. Anywhere we wanted to eat at anytime was OK, the food was really good, and it came in the usual gargantuan American portions.

The gas pumping facilities? First and most likely last time in my life that I would be able to drive a vehicle up to any available pump, fill her up then drive off without having to reach into my pocket for money to pay the tab. I intended to enjoy my time on base while I could.

The base at Bien Hoa was a massive, sprawling resupply facility. There was a large airfield located there for military aircraft of all types. Both attack jet aircraft and transport planes took off and landed around the clock, without let up.

All the individual services had rear areas there, like the military police, vast ammunition dumps, grave registration, medical supplies, red caps riggers/fitters, and military vehicle maintenance of all types. Military assistance command Vietnam (MACV) headquarters was located there. They were the biggest of the big fish among the U.S war planners. The war was fed and managed from the base at Bien Hoa.

But anywhere in the US military that large groups of men were forced to congregate, quickly spawned the necessary type of entertainment and fun establishments all healthy young soldiers required to unwind. This was apparent in the number and variety of bars, whorehouses, bars, dancehalls, bars, nightclubs, bars, restaurants, bars, massage parlors, bars, movie houses, and bars.

American GI's spent money fast, and the wider world had found out about this readily available source of income from past war- time experiences. So all of the necessary enticements and inducements to remove a soldier's money from his pockets were often found around any large American military facility.

The Bien Hoa base was no exception to this rule, and entertainment was provided in a big way. We gave the locals every opportunity and fully supported their tireless efforts to relieve us of all our hard-earned pay cheques. We were begging to be fleeced.

Lieutenant Mike MacCallum was an infantry First Louie who was short and on the way home like me. He had exactly one month left, again like me. He was about 5'11" tall, had black hair he kept combed straight back a la Kirk Douglas, wore a pencil-thin moustache, and, as he reminded anyone interested enough to listen, he sported a California tan just beneath his prevailing Vietnamese tan. MacCallum was proudly from The Golden State of California. This guy was a bullshit artist par excellence and also my new found friend.

An energetic, fun-loving, son of a bitch, Mac, along with Steve Nordsworth, became my last best friends in Vietnam. Mac was one of those very rare people who was truly unpretentious about his own good looks. He did not make you feel aggrieved by the fact that he was so handsome. That in itself was a fantastic accomplishment in the very man's world we occupied at the time. A sworn disciple of Bacchus, he was a good-time guy. A natural wit and an avid storyteller, Mac was an unrepentant rake who simply loved *all* women. He loved to love them, too. I had no doubt they all loved him in return. He had a wily, devil-may-care smile and lost-boy-lost-without-you approach that make women feel warm and weak-kneed and suddenly desirous of cuddling him.

Men, to their own chagrin, bitterly regretted they, too, couldn't help but like Mac. We couldn't begrudge him his success with all the available women on the blasted planet. This was the guy who befriended me in the rear area and wanted me to join him in spending each and every one of my waking, off-duty hours sampling the incredible fare of the entire greater Saigon area brothel establishment--right up until the very last hour before we boarded our respective "freedom birds" to journey back to our civilian worlds forever.

Mac was not interested in anything except having fun and getting laid every day. This attitude did not always go down well with the "higher ups."

As a commissioned officer, he was expected to behave better than that, and to maintain a certain level of deportment and gentlemanly decorum. He was always in trouble with his superiors, which severely dampened his prospects for promotion. He really didn't care and frequently reminded his bosses that he was going to engineering school when he got back home.

Although it was not common practice for officers and enlisted men to fraternize, all of this was taking place well away from the office. And he provided us with a convenient passport into and out of Saigon after curfew.

The MPs were a bit more reasonable and understanding when dealing with rule-breaking officers. But they would have dumped the whole jeep-load, enlisted men lot of us in the brig if we were ever caught out-of-bounds without Mac's being in the mix.

My other partner in rear-echelon shenanigans was a fellow medic who was short too, Steve Nordsworth. Steve also hailed from California. He had been wounded in the ground attack on Fire Support Base David. He was decorated for gallantry and now walked with a very pronounced limp from the grievous leg wound he sustained in that battle while doing his job saving troopers' lives.

Steve was actually one of the people in the aid station with me on that terrible Sunday morning in Cambodia, when that enemy insurgent was shooting from the roof, right above our heads. But we were nearly home, and we had to have some fun before we left. We owed it to ourselves.

Steve was a stocky, 5'5" dose of stubborn and determined working-class temper. A lovely guy if you were a friend with whom he had fought together with on the same side, but a rough-and-ready brawler with most other humans, especially when inebriated.

Steve was a nasty drunk when he had had too much beer, which he attempted to do at every available opportunity. He tried to drink everybody under the table, including himself. He usually succeeded with the challenge, one away or the other. Another thing about Steve worth mentioning: he wore his blackness on his shoulders like a badge of honour.

"Hey, doc, get your ass in gear, man. We're going in to Saigon tonight," Mac would shout as he broke into a jig. More often than not, I was fully up to it. I was just as corrupted by pleasure as my friends were. We were allowed into Saigon, just down the road, once we behaved and left town at 1800 hours. Fat chance of either. We were all in our twenties and full of bluster. So who on earth would have gone into Saigon to behave unless it was badly?

We always left the compound with at least two jeep loads with about four or six other guys from our company's neighbouring units joining our party. It was better for us to go out in secure numbers in case we met those jackass U.S Marines, who always wanted to fight with us whenever we all ended up drunk together in the same watering hole. A circumstance that happened on a nightly basis.

Those guys always got offended just because we insisted on reminding them at every God-given opportunity that we were sick and tired of being sent out into harm's way to rescue their sorry asses whenever they got stuck high up on some mountainside, which occurred quite often, whenever they attempted to scale those hilltop fortifications using their outdated and inappropriate World War II beach-landing tactics.

They got even more upset with us for reminding them in detail of these acts of military incompetence while in the presence of or within earshot of the bar women. I never understood why they were so thin-skinned. Anyway, superior numbers were necessary to try to jump them first, before they got the jump on us.

Saigon was the capital of South Vietnam. It was a smorgasbord of sexual depravity, alcohol, drugs, and other delights. It provided every temptation imaginable to young soldiers with a couple of dollars in their pockets and an increasingly confident feeling they had made it through the worst of a really bad time, and were only a few days away from going home again.

Entering Saigon as you crossed the river, the sight of the masses of humanity riding rickshaws, every describable type of cycle, buzzing motor scooters with two or four people on them, or small, zippy ugly little French cars driving through a mess of unconcerned jay walkers, was in itself a mesmerizing welcome.

The city was a mixture of beautiful old French-colonial buildings and gaudy new-age structures. Statuesque cathedrals, small parks, with restaurants and bars everywhere. Commerce throbbed industriously in the middle of a bloody war. Saigon's Chinatown, the Cholon district, looked pretty much like other Chinatowns do. Garlands and lamps hung all over the place, and garish pictures of fierce-looking dragons greeted one and all at sundry eating establishments.

Young Buddhist monks in their bright saffron robes mixed with ARVN troops, South Vietnam Army soldiers, and sweating, rickshaw-pulling coolies. Military police, both indigenous and U.S, swaggered around as military police do everywhere in the world.

Most interesting, and not surprisingly so to us, were the sweet young things who glided by, gracefully wearing their tailored ao dais, or loose-fitting, pajama-type outfits. All fitting them ever so well as they floated alluringly along the overpopulated sidewalks.

We passed the famous Tu Do Street, headquarters of drugs and illicit sex in Saigon. But already, at this stage of the war, it carried a reputation for being a little too risky, grubby, and disease-riddled for us.

The Miramar and Continental hotels were both a bit too elegant for our desires. We were looking for a middle-of-the-road establishment. Mac knew what we wanted and had been honing in on such an establishment. He was driving, of course. After a while, though, we thought the fucker might be lost.

I kept seeing the river on my same side every time we went around a corner. "Mac, you know where we are?"

"Shit, doc, I'm looking for that special outstanding place

that I told you guys I had found last week, man. Just be cool."

The other jeep impatiently peeled away from us. Probably back to Tu Do Street to do hard drugs. Good riddance, I thought. We half-heartedly planned to meet up with them at the Green Lantern club later, to bait any available marines. We all expected to be pretty drunk by then.

It was Mac, Steve, a cook friend of ours named Robin Higgins, and me, and I was convinced then that we were certainly lost. We turned down a blind alley and didn't have a clue where we were and it was getting quite dark.

"Where the fuck you going, Mac?"

All of a sudden, there was an urgent scampering of sandaled feet. What looked like a gang of young boys confronted us in the stark beams of the jeep's headlights. It took me a while to focus. When I did, I realized that we were being held up at gunpoint by a ten-year-old kid with an M-1 carbine rifle. Our veteran eyes quickly confirmed two disturbing facts. The weapon was loaded with a full clip and the safety lever was off.

The boy was hopping up and down, shouting, "Fucking give money, or I shoot fucking GI's now!" The arrogant little bandit peered up at us from under the brim of a New York Mets baseball cap that was two sizes too big for him.

Unfortunately for us, or maybe fortunately so, Steve was sitting in the front seat with Mac. Robin and I were in the back of the jeep. The aggressive bantam was now up in Steve's face. "Gimme watch now, or I shoot all damn fucking American GI." He pointed to Steve's shiny new gold Rolex oyster watch, which to buy he had put aside money for six months and purchased a week ago while he was on his R and R stint in Bangkok.

Steve then said to the agitated boy pointing the loaded gun directly at his head.

"Fuck you, you filthy little pint-sized slope headed piece of dog shit!"

Mac and I were alarmed, and fidgeted in our seats. "Give him the fucking watch, man," we both shouted. After all the crap we had been through, and all of us so very close to going home, what was a damn watch? I can't die this way—that was all I was thinking at that moment. It was too ridiculous to even contemplate. After surviving the jungle, all those battles and everything else, to get it in a piss-reeking alley from a kid? Uh uh, no way.

"Give the little fucker the watch, Steve!" I said. "Here, take mine." I scrambled to give the boy the one off my wrist.

"No, give him mine," Mac said.

Then Steve tells the gun-toting kid: "You want this watch? Then come and take it! No? Well, then go ahead, shoot me if you have to, you little dink bastard, but don't miss. Because if you do, I'm coming for your scrawny ass little neck, and I'm going to wring it slowly off your dirty, diseased-riddled body." A stare down ensues.

The kid's nerve wavers and finally breaks first. He bolts, disappearing silently and empty-handed down an adjacent alley. Accompanied by his friends, they all effortlessly melt into the same shadows they had so casually materialized from earlier.

We hurried to back the jeep onto the main thoroughfare. That fucking crazy man Steve was highly amused by it all, laughing his head off loudly. "That little, slimy fucker wasn't taking *my* watch, no way," he said. "Not Mr. Nordsworth's watch, uh uh, not today, Jose."

What could you say or do about a stubborn asshole like Steve? Probably nothing. The rest of us were relieved it was all over without anyone getting their heads blown off. But you couldn't help but love the guy, Steve, anyway.

We headed for the closest open bar to obtain alcoholic refuge. This we accomplished with calculated urgency. We left the jeep un-parked on the side of the road, and walk into the nearest available watering hole.

Thankfully, there were no marines around. It was really too early to get into a fight, and we had to be drunk to deal effectively with them anyway. The oasis we chose to grace was called, incredibly The Old New York Tavern Club. The people in Vietnam could both adapt, and adopt, amazingly so.

We proceeded without further delay or distraction towards a warm and safe alcoholic buzz. We very much needed at that moment to reach a plateau where our confused and disjointed thoughts didn't always have to make sense to anybody, including ourselves.

Our table in that small, incense-scented and gaudily lit adult fun palace was filled fast with an alarming number of overflowing pitchers of lukewarm beer. The long bar was being both held up and overwhelmed by droves of slobbering, slouching, drunken servicemen. People having a good time were jammed into every available space in the low-ceilinged room.

The modest, elevated stage was occupied by a local group who sang an out-of-key version of Jimi Hendrix's "Hey Joe." Or so we thought. It was close enough for us to kind of recognize it as something along the lines of a badly interpreted version of the classic rock song. But that was all right because the group also had a cute, half-naked Vietnamese girl with them onstage, sensuously gyrating and stripping off every shred of her clothing to the suddenly forgettable beat of the music. We had few complaints.

The place was chock a block with GI's from every service organization imaginable and bar girls who could provide every pleasurable service in existence. So we were all servers of one kind or the other, serving happily together.

Across the table from me, crazy Steve shouted, "Doc, your turn to get the next pitcher. What the fuck are you daydreaming about, man?"

Later, when I'm ancient or have the urge to recollect or want to teach my children something about life, I'll tell this tale, I was thinking to myself. I didn't know exactly when or why, I just knew I would have to. Sometimes I would drift off, the record button on in my head. "OK, Steve," I said. "I'll get it. Chill out, dude, cold beer coming up."

The few unattended bar girls glanced invitingly our way now. Mac, of all people, admonished us to resist their charms, to have patience, because he still had that very special place to take us to later. "We're spending the night there," he said without any trace of a smile. Still, I wondered if he was joking .

"Shit, Mac. We're still recuperating from that last 'special place' you had our sphincters squeezed into recently. Do you remember a certain alley?" I said. "I owe it to myself never to go anywhere with you crazy California assholes again." Anyway, we stumbled out or were thrown out of the good old "Tavern," very likely the latter, at about 0130 hours the next day.

It was Steve who threatened to smash the cocky bandleader's guitar amplifier if he dared to launch into yet another off-key version of "Hey Joe".

The bandleader, claiming arrogantly that he was a Vietnamese citizen and would not be spoken to like that in his own country, locked eyes with Steve, who was by then dangerously reeling. The bandleader was acting like a marine in need of hill-assault training.

Steve hauled off and slapped the poor drummer, who had been sitting quietly on his stool minding his own business. This set him off. He too claimed to be from the same Vietnam as his band mate was, and was also not partial to being slapped around, especially not by a fucking drunk GI. So he took an almighty swing at Mac, who like the offended drummer had himself been just standing around minding his own business.

"Watch out, doc!" Somebody I couldn't see jumped on my back, long fingers trying to yank as much hair from my scalp as they could. I figured it must be a woman. I twisted and turned drunkenly to heave the body off me, but I only succeeded in causing both of us to collapse on top of a table fully loaded with glasses and bottles. We crashed to the floor. Stunned, breath knocked out of me, embroiled in a mess of spastic arms and legs, only half of them mine, I let the stripper slip through my fingers. She had scraped her lovely shins in the melee.

Some official- looking, burly, swaggering, local types with pomade-slicked hair and wrap- around dark glasses descended on our group.

With our hands twisted into the small of our backs, accompanied by some shoving and a lot of kicking, we were ejected from the "tavern" and told never to come back.

We dusted ourselves off, swore, tried to get out bearings straight and went in search of the jeep.

A vehicle skidded around a corner. The other guys from the Tu Do Street dope dens were back.

"Where the fuck you guys been?" they bluster. "We've been waiting for your sorry asses down at the Green Lantern all night long."

Waiting my ass. More probably they had just finished getting totally fucked up mainlining heroin or something. Later for them, we said. We were simple juicers, that was all.

"OK, Mac, let's see what you got for us while we can still stand," I said.

Mac briskly commandeered our jeep through a middle-class neighborhood. For the first time that night, he drove like someone who actually recognized where he was going. An encouraging sign .

We pulled up to a large gabled house backed by some smaller buildings. There was no wastage of living space. Every building touched its neighbour. The better buildings spread out, depreciating into shanties eventually at the lower end of the societal scale. Claustrophobic structures densely packed with humanity. Even through our alcohol- and drug-hazed minds, we were well aware that we were crossing a line and delving into a serious violation of our curfew laws here.

We were military men who lived by rules that in the main kept us alive, once adhered to. Ignored rules were usually bad omens for soldiers. But here we were, breaking them all, big time.

We bundled out of the jeeps, which we had parked well camouflaged behind the houses and away from the prying eyes of the main street patrolling MP party-poopers.

The main reason for the curfew was to protect us from ourselves. The dangers posed to us in places like the ones we had entered were not imagined but real, and they were too often ignored. Easily recognizable foreign soldiers, we stuck out like amputated limbs. We were in an environment where everyone else looked alike, in a city where the Vietcong also lived, and didn't wear or need identifying uniforms in order to kill us at any given opportunity, anywhere at any time.

In reality, we were a long way from home, lonely, stubborn, drunk, and barely twenty years young. We knew better, but what we chose to do was not sensible at the moment. Up the steps we bounded, two at a time, led by a rejuvenated Mac.

We entered a cool, regal parlor on the ground floor of the large house. Here, tables and comfortable settees ringed a pleasant but heavily curtained boudoir reeking of incense.

An elegantly coiffed, heavily powdered, mascara-painted but smartly dressed Mama San appeared from behind a low screen partition. She was short and portly, matronly and middle aged, and bowed real low while smiling ingratiatingly. She glided over to greet Mac.

Taking his already extended hands, she clasped them to her ample breasts and coos, "Oh *trung–uy* Mac." She knew his rank—lieutenant. We were obviously in the right place.

After a brief welcome, we were all pointed towards some large, comfortable chairs and reclining sofas, and told to sit and relax. Some young girls then materialized, silently and mysteriously from behind beaded floor-length curtains, bearing trays of scotch with coke chasers, ice, and cold tiger piss beer. None of these girls were stunning beauties, but they were young females who were pliable and willing.

We were young, horny, and very partial to sampling the fare, as most soldiers on liberty tended to do when on the town. Mac had already negotiated price and bedding arrangements on the group's behalf with Mama San. She must have driven her usual hard bargain with the soft spendthrift American, because she was all smiles.

We retired enthusiastically to the upper rooms of the house.

My chosen partner for the night's shindigs was a shapely dark-haired, almond-eyed girl named Mai. I hoped she was at least eighteen.

To be honest, I wondered about this only briefly. I was no saint, only an energetic young soldier looking for some fun.

The sex that followed in a sprawling feather-mattress bed was raw, torrid, and tension alleviating. No love was gained or lost here, only the satiation of lust. But no one was asking for anything else, and should not. An arrangement had been made, and it proved to be gratifying and relatively harmless in the scheme of things. If you could enjoy it and just leave it like that, you should enjoy it and just leave it like that. And so we always did.

So far, the night could hardly have been termed dull. Being held up at gunpoint, thrown out of a nightclub, and then that brothel experience.

Mac, who shared the room with me and our respective bedmates, was reclining contentedly on his own large, feather-stuffed mattress bed. He sat up, eyes gleaming. He leered at me and said, "Hey doc, let's hide from the MP patrols, and stay here for the entire night with these nice girls."

I said "Mac, you know we have to get back to base. We're already in deep shit here —!"

"Simmer down, man, you worry too much!" he replied.

Yes, I was worried. The tone more so than the words sounded too familiar. What the hell was I doing associating with this guy? I could have been safely back at the Bien Hoa bowling alley, or at the enlisted men's club on base playing bingo jackpot with other sober-minded men, or writing letters home to my mother. But no...I found myself joined at the hip with Mr. Push It To The Limit.

If the MPs caught us here, we risked jail, loss of rank, and most terrifying of all to me, the loss of my plum of a job, which could have necessitated my ass going back out to the field... I'd tasted the sweet fruits of low-quarter life; I really couldn't risk losing it all just because I had not mastered the art of choosing proper friends.

The other jeep had apparently left. Everyone had gone back and left me alone to deal with Mac. Even crazy Steve had deserted me and gone back to base. It was possible he had been carried out on his back, but if I found out later that he had intentionally left me alone to deal with Mac all by myself….

Suddenly there was a loud knock on the front door downstairs. Mama San came running into our room. Her face was grey and noticeably paler than during monetary negotiations earlier on. She was shaking. The frigging MPs were here. We'd been caught in the act. Oh shit!

She would have to let them in. She had no choice. She didn't want to make enemies of them. I was also sure that they were occasional customers, too.

Mac calmly said to me, "Mama San is going to hide us under the floorboards doc."

"Under the what?" I nearly shouted.

"No time to dress or anything, just as you are," he said. "Let's go, man, quickly now for fucks sake."

Naked, we were spirited from our rooms by the two girls down a narrow flight of steps at the back of the house leading to the ground floor but well away from the front of the house. The only thing that I was wearing as I pounded fretfully down the steps was a scowl. The only thing that I was carrying in my mind was a list of all the bad things I could possibly do to Mac and get away with. Meanwhile, Mama San had returned to the front door to stall the MPs until we were safely out of sight...

In the large kitchen, a trapdoor concealed under a threadbare carpet was hastily sprung back to reveal a dark, and dank-looking underground chamber of some kind. A decrepit looking wooden ladder extended down the hole.

Seething with rebellion I spat out "Mac, who the fuck do you think is going down in that hole?"

"Come on, doc, simmer down," Mac purred. "Remember military police, capture, back out to the field for you…?"

"OK, OK," I mumbled in submission. I relented meekly. Mac was always convincing. Maybe that's why HE was an officer. And there was fear. I descended into the hole.

We climbed down about ten feet to step into some brackish water with mysterious things floating around in it. As we huddled naked underground, we heard the disturbing sound of something big and heavy being dragged into place across the trap door's entrance. Great. Now we were virtually entombed in a Saigon whorehouse's basement crypt.

Down in the hole it was cold and dark. Some feeble light squeezed through the wall's cracks. Just enough for us to be able to examine each other's greenish faces. Sweat dripped down our panicked mugs onto our bare chests. My stomach was twisting itself into seaman's knots.

"What the fuck are we going to do now?" I whispered. "Mac, YOU are responsible for all of this shit, you know that, eh? I told you we should have left earlier. But no…"

Above us, we heard the drone of murmuring voices. We couldn't decipher who was talking up there because the sound only got to us at the indistinct murmur level. Was it the Vietcong or U.S personnel? Was there a way out of this situation that wouldn't cost us our naked skins? Or had we stuck it big time to ourselves?

There was heavy tramping above us, back and forth above our heads. The voices became argumentative. Mac's face grew concerned. Good, he should suffer too.

This was déjà vu for me. Shades of Fire Support Base David. I was mentally transported back there, down in the cramped aid station again. There's a gook on the roof shooting up the base. Somebody says, "Shhhh, quiet everybody, for God's sake, he's right above us."

Fuck, I was hallucinating. I couldn't breathe in the dark, tomb-like trap we had desperately climbed into. Everything was closing in on me.

Mac flicked on a flashlight. His colt .45 automatic in his other hand.

"What the fuck—?" I said. "Where did you get that shit from?"

"You know that I'm an officer, doc, and that they issue officers with handguns." -----"Arrghh!" Sometimes I felt like strangling that smarmy bastard. It was about 0430 hours. Tomorrow already.

It felt like a decade and a half had passed. I made full use of the time to think about and regret every action in my life that had led me down the pathway to my present circumstances. I promised every deity I could think of absolute fealty should I ever be released from this dungeon alive. Eventually we heard something being moved above our heads. The trapdoor groaned. Then it popped open, letting in a little light. Prayers answered?

Mai stuck her pretty head into the hole. "OK, boys, it's safe to come up now."

Mac and I crawled upstairs and headed straight for our clothes. Mama San's face had closed in on itself. A picture of oriental inscrutability. She wanted us to go. We understood. Mai and the other girls couldn't stop giggling. Maybe it was the pathetic sight of our shriveled scrotums. I wasn't as tickled by the situation.

As we drove onto the base, a young MP on guard duty saluted us. "Took an early morning drive, sir?" he said. It was 0530 hours.

Mac replied in his gruff, made-for-military voice, "Yes, son, that we did. You have a nice day now," and pulled off an academy-crisp return salute to the sentry.

I shook my head. Before I could start up again on brother Mac, I remembered two old people's sayings, as we called them back home in Grenada.

One was "Birds of a feather flock together." The other, "Show me your friends, and I'll tell you who you are." At that moment, I had to accept the full meaning of both.

I turned to Mac, and said, "Hey, let's check up on that crazy fucker Steve before we crash." I wanted to make sure that my little buddy-deserting pal had in fact made it back to the base from Mama San's safely with the dopers.

I subsequently found out that Steve apparently owed me one, because he had left with the dopers on his own two feet, hence willingly so.

Later, we also found out that it was in fact the M.Ps who were looking for us at Mama San's place, and not the Vietcong. Either way, we were lucky—not to get caught.

Chapter 34

ARVN and General Giap

If I had to point my finger at any group of people to blame for the fall of South Vietnam and the eventual 1975 reunification of that country as Communist Vietnam, it would most certainly be the ARVN – The South Vietnamese Armed forces.

This is a militaristic, not a political perspective. As for the fact that the country had since reunified: More power to them. I genuinely hoped that they continued to make steady progress with their nation-building efforts. America and other Western countries' investments were already making a positive impact on the country's economy. So my viewpoint was not about politics.

My experiences with the ARVN had not been favorable. Yes, they did fight in some battles, as all armies were expected to do from time to time. The problem, especially if you fatefully found yourself on a joint operation with them, was that their fecklessness was legendary. In the middle of a heated firefight with the NVA, or Vietcong, they would suddenly remember that they had something else they would prefer to be doing some hundred or so miles away.

They would hastily withdraw, pull back their forces, or just up and leave, not caring that our asses would be glaringly exposed by their retreat. They loved wearing their uniforms, but did not extend that love to fighting for their country with the same fervour.

Their easy access to overwhelming military equipment in the form of US-supplied armaments and the finest training available was in reality no match for the enemy's resilience. They lacked fortitude, therefore their purpose as a fighting unit was forever compromised.

The Americans went into to South Vietnam to assist that government in maintaining its democracy: To forestall, and hopefully reverse, the Communist-inspired "domino theory" in South East Asia: The fear that if you successfully infiltrated one country, all its neighbours would eventually fall.

The ARVN were always too ready to walk away from a fight, even before it actually began. Their ass-backwards attitude was always that they were reluctantly helping *us* to defend *their* country, and we were always asking too much of them in this regard.

Pit this attitude against that of the Vietminh, the predecessor liberation forces that evolved into the Vietcong National liberation front - the VC. They were the ones who dragged heavy artillery pieces by hand up sheer mountainsides in 1954 to launch a successful surprise attack against those other occupying aggressors of the time, the French Foreign Legion, at the battle of Dien Bien Phu.

In the same spirit, the Vietcong dug, built, and maintained kilometers of underground tunnels at Cu Chi, containing hospitals and supply depots, and operated large manpower and resupply facilities right there, literally under the American fighting force's feet for years, while carrying on their war efforts.

This explained why the capital of South Vietnam was changed from Saigon to Ho Chi Minh City. Ho was the freedom fighter, motivator and father of Vietnamese Communism. The NVA and VC fought for what they *believed* in, with determination and courage. This paid off for them eventually when they won the war in 1975.

In the latter years of the war, and especially after the Kent State University incident (where demonstrating students were fatally shot by the National Guard), the US home front began to increasingly and understandably question the very rationale for the continuation of American troop involvement in Vietnam.

Nagging questions started creeping into young soldiers' minds. We read the newspapers, too, whenever they were available. Why were we dying, being dismembered, and shedding our blood out here for people who didn't seem to want to even try a little harder to succeed in their own stated cause?

As a soldier, you could fight an opponent with every means in your power. There would be blood, death, and no quarter given. You didn't have to really understand him, and it was probably better if you didn't like him, but you could still respect him at the end of the day.

Throughout the war, I always felt a grudging respect for the NVA and the VC. I could never say the same about our "allies" the ARVN. I never felt a shred of respect for them, because they had never earned it.

Incredibly, it was the same general, Vo Nguyen Giap, who defeated the French in a very bold and unorthodox attack at Dien Bien Phu in 1954, whose military genius would eventually lead to the Communist victory of 1975 in Saigon.

I considered General Giap one of the unprecedented tactical geniuses of modern twentieth-century warfare. He didn't have much to work with, manpower-wise, and he had overwhelming material odds stacked against him, in the form of American firepower, but he was able to twice defeat the superior military might of world superpowers like the USA and France. And all within the space of 20 years. It was an incredible achievement for any military man to have on his curriculum vitae.

As a lesson to be learned from history, the next time that we take on an adversary in his own back yard, and there will be 'next times'. We must realize that we would be disadvantaged from the outset because we would be confronting a force with obvious home-field advantage. We would be challenging him in the same neighbourhood where he once played hopscotch as a child.

Mission success under these circumstances was probably unachievable well before it was even undertaken.

The outcome preordained.

Add to that a lack of attention paid to history lessons on our behalf, and it was not so surprising to see how and why a general like Vo Nguyen Giap was so successful in his military campaigns against us.

Chapter 35

Looking Forward at Myself

One of the most compelling idiosyncrasies of the Vietnam conflict comes to pass due to the military structured, exact, one (1) year tour of duty that a US armed forces serviceman spent 'in country'.

If he made it through his tour, he normally left Vietnam exactly one year after he arrived there. He arrived, he stayed a year, and he left thereafter. Providing, of course, he had not crossed over "the big pond" before the year took its bloody time rolling around.

This arrangement enabled the serviceman to see his other self twice.

The first time, when he arrived in-country, he glimpsed an image of his future self leaving; the second time, when he was departing, he got to see what he looked like when he first arrived. It goes like this.

When I first stepped off the aircraft on my arrival in Vietnam, I was immediately transfixed by the sight of the old young men waiting to take my flight in- country outbound, to return home from their war. The same plane I arrived on would be transformed into the welcomed Freedom Bird to take those deserving veterans out, back to the US of A, albeit in a very different kind of mood.

I watched them waiting impatiently, standing in a state of eager anticipation, but doing so in an eerily contemplative manner. They all wore that familiar thousand-mile stare. They had witnessed too much in too short a space of time for their young brains to adequately process and make sense of.

Green uniforms stained from red mud and jungle rot that never washed out. Moustaches defying army regulations. They were in fact what I would not only look like, but become, by the end of my tour.

A year later, when I left Vietnam, I would be waiting as impatiently as they had, surveying the new arrivals stepping off MY Freedom Bird.

I would muse... what were they, Cannon fodder? FNGs freshly trimmed and neatly adorned in starched green uniforms, staring blandly like proverbial fawns caught transfixed in headlight beams on some highway, blessedly unaware of for whom amongst them the bell would toll.

A distraught group on the verge of spiraling down into the depths of an all- encompassing terror. Is that what I looked like a year ago? Poor bastards.

Anyway, I had my boarding pass. I'd done my time, and I was going home.

Chapter 36

Leaving on a Jet Plane

My orders were cut. I was no longer just an enviable short-timer; I was finished with my tour of duty. Having survived the ruthless jungles and battles alike, I was on my way. Going home at long last. I was about to leave the Republic of Vietnam, forever.

I had to travel by bus from the Bien Hoa Replacement Center to Tan Son Nhut airport. This was after getting through a comprehensive country-leaving inspection. "No snakes, shrunken-head souvenirs, or weapons of any kind in that duffle bag, boys," drawled the phlegmatic staff sergeant on clearance duty at the centre. Nothing was ever simple in a war zone. It just never was.

The bus had heavy mesh wire covering all its windows. In the past, along the same route, "unfriendly" elements used to lob farewell gifts at the departing GI's in the form of hand grenades through the then more accommodatingly opened bus windows.

The mesh was lesson #4167, learned from the Vietnam experience. It was part of a widely read chapter in an official army manual on Dos and Don'ts in the Republic of

Vietnam. Mandatory reading for all newly arrived in-country personnel.

As my bus exited the compound and joined the airport main road, something amazing happened. I glanced down from my window seat and looked directly into the eyes of a fellow Grenadian, Ronald Lewis, who was inexplicably standing on the sidewalk as my bus sped past.

Ronald was a schoolmate from my old primary school, the St. George's Anglican Junior School – "Hindsey School". As boys we had fished together for 'grunts' and 'long gars' on the Carenage waterfront in the town of St. George.

I knew immediately that it was Ronald, because of the cocky way he held audience with a group of GI's on the roadside, exhibiting that same air of confident persuasion that he had used to separate me from my marble stocks in the school yard, many moons ago.

I was stunned and confused, and my mind froze stationary as the bus sped away. Was it a hallucination? It was certainly a shock to encounter someone else from a small country like mine with a population of less than 100,000 people, in Vietnam.

Especially when that person was somebody you had last seen when you were about ten years old, and you were exchanging fisticuffs with him over a game of marbles in a dusty school yard! But good old Ronald it was.

Years later, after the war had ended, I met Ronald back in Grenada, both of us in mufti again. I told him that I had seen him in Bien Hoa in 1970 on the day I was leaving Nam. He confirmed that it must have been him because he was indeed in Bien Hoa on the date in question. After some 'in country' talk about where were you and what unit were you with, he had smiled coyly and told me what I should have suspected all along.

Apparently he had experienced far less discomfort than I had encountered in Vietnam. He admitted that he had been a low-quarter, and had spent his tour comfortably ensconced at the secure Bien-Hoa base working in re-supply; hence he was never exposed to the shooting war.

I believed him and wanted to strangle him for his good fortune. But then again, what did I expect from Ronald?

This was the same wheeler-dealer I had known from my schoolyard days, long before I had graduated to the stage of wearing long pants.

Anyway, the bus driver drove real fast, madly careening through villages, as cycles of every description, motor scooters with passengers clinging to the backs of their riders, pedestrians, mini-cyclos, little box-type French cars, goods-laden ox carts, various animals, and droves of ever present children, all scattered for their lives. No time for highway etiquette, as we rapidly made it through all of these obstacles to the airport, intact.

Once there, we settled into the perennial army hurry-up-and-wait syndrome. All we could do was suck it in and bear it. I could see a large shiny blue and red civilian airliner parked on the ramp. The sight of it caused my heart to gallop. I was sure it was our Freedom Bird. New replacement arrivals streamed off the aircraft, wearing their spotless uniforms and confused looks with equal discomfort.

"What the hell were they staring at us for?" we growled irritably.

There was a loud but very garbled announcement from somewhere nearby.

"Are we ready for boarding yet?" someone asked excitedly. "Is that us? Is that us?"

What else could it be? The announcement of a winning bid at Sotheby's auction house in London?

The sanctimonious "movements" personnel then tell us, inexplicably, to relax, and that we should all take our time when we walked out to board the waiting aircraft. The aircraft that would spirit us safely away forever from our year's exposure to ambushes, rocket and mortar attacks, suicidal sappers, chronic diseases, poisonous snakes and booby traps. Take our time and relax, eh?

They tell us also that there is no need to run out to the plane. Apparently, there were ample seats on board for everyone.

Being obedient soldiers, we started to walk out to the plane soberly, but we all, to a man, ended up breaking into a wild dash. Officers and enlisted men alike, all ran. You would have had to be a really cool, pulse dead, ice-water-running-in-your-veins cucumber to just walk out from that passenger ramp, good soldier or not.

We boarded the flight in a slightly more respectful and subdued manner, and proceeded with some dispatch to our seats. Then everything slid into a slow motion mode of inactivity, as we sat and stewed.

Jesus! They were taking a year to complete the loading of the baggage. The conveyor belt must be stuck. The agent's paperwork for the pilot seemed to be wrong or something, so they were arguing instead of flying. The refueling tanker's hose was still attached to the plane's wing...and I knew we could not take off with it firmly clamped to the damn aircraft.

The ground crewmen moved around on the ramp in a listless dream state. Maybe because they were sleeping back here tonight anyway. What was that loud noise? Was that incoming? Or a friendly outgoing artillery fire mission? How close was the impact, about two klicks? Another noise?

The engine's finally started. We were taxiing. Thank God for small mercies. We were finally moving, but we taxied at a snail's pace. I wondered whether one or more of the plane's tires were flat? Sabotage? I hoped the airfield's perimeter was a secure one. Were they shelled last week? Someone said...I couldn't remember....

Then something happened inside the airplane's cabin. Everybody was glancing around at each other. People actually recognized faces that looked kind of familiar, from our flight in together a distant year ago. Although everyone was a lot leaner, quite darker, and wired taut from their experience, we recognized each other.

"Hey, my man, how's it been buddy, remember me?" A faintly familiar face said to me.

"Oh, yeah." I responded listlessly. "Where were you stationed?" I asked politely through gritted teeth.

"Up in Pleiku, seen some hot shit up there, man. What about you?"

"In the III Corps area, you know the parrots' beak?"

"Yeah, I heard that down there was some pretty tight crap, too. But we made it, my man, we made it, yeah! And we are all gonna di di mau out of this fucking place, like right about now, too. Oh, Yeah, Sireeee!"

At least someone was having fun. I tried to remain by myself, alone with my thoughts for a while, but those guys would not stop talking.

"Remember that tall guy that sat somewhere in front of us last year coming in? I don't remember his name, but he chatted a lot."

I contemplate hissing, "Yeah, like some people in present company."

He was from Texas, I believe."

"Heard that he got hit real bad, a mine, he was down in the Delta area, he didn't make it. Anyway...."

I tuned out as much as I could. The truth was that I didn't fucking want to hear any more of it. They were talking about people we had been on a plane ride together with a year ago. The fact that some of those guys weren't on the return trip with us said enough.

I really wanted to leave all of that baggage behind me, right where it belonged, in Vietnam. I couldn't take any of that shit home with me, and I could not understand why they wouldn't leave it the hell alone. I just wanted to go home.

I did not necessarily regret my participation in the Vietnam War but it was an experience that I had had my fill of, and one that I would rather not reminisce about before it was completely over with!

The plane reached the end of the taxiway, and the guys finally fell silent. I bet Marco Polo could have easily carried out all of his adventures and explorations with some time to spare, too, since we started taxiing.

At long last, we were lined up on the runway and ready for the takeoff.

My palms were wet. Swollen rivers of sweat streamed down my nose cascading down from my forehead and into my eyes, blinding me. In the claustrophobic silence a host of angels passed by. Their flyby goes unacknowledged. It was as silent as a tomb... bad reference, maybe that thought should be - a library reading room.

We were in limbo, a crippling kind of stasis conjured by our keyed up minds. The takeoff roll began its reluctant creep. The large aircraft moved forward but with a punishing nonchalance.

But the plane was being willed forward, upwards and away, by the combined minds of 200 uniformed survival wannabes. You could feel the energy. A force that insisted: We will get off the ground. A low, vibrating chant was felt more than heard inside the tense cabin.

I found out later from a talkative flight attendant that it was always the same on every Freedom Bird flight she had operated out of Vietnam. The very same scenario always unfolded on each flight.

As if the whole performance had been choreographed beforehand by all of the players involved. But how could that ever be? It was mumbled slowly and softly at first then repeated increasingly louder, in rhythm with the aircraft's forward speed, as the aircraft's ground roll and forward movement increased.

Go! Go! Go! *Go! GO! GO!*

Just as the aircraft's wheels broke ground, we broke seats and jumped up in elation. The aircraft had finally rotated, irreversibly breaking her earthbound shackles.

We were off the ground and airborne and we were leaving the Republic of Vietnam at last, headed for home.

Hysterical laughter, clapping, sputtering, backslapping, incomprehensible pseudo-psychobabble overcame everyone. "We made it! We made it! Oh God, we really made it!"

After a while I collapsed back onto my seat. I closed my eyes and heaved a sigh of relief. For the first time in what felt like forever, I exhaled completely.

Eventually, I looked out of my cabin window and down at a rapidly receding Vietnam.

The view was that of a country spiraling away rapidly, blurring away into my past.

But so was Six, Chief, F/O, Thanh, Quan Loi, John who was known as John, Lieutenant Levy, the Mad Minute, Mr. Deathwish door gunner, Mike Vickery, John Rice, Cam Rhan bay, Cobra gunship (Blue Max), incoming mortars, FSB David, night ambush, Montagnards, I smell Asia... chief lend me some dry socks... you did well today son... you can't hear yourself think out here... monsoon rains... good luck-- jump... you're now the senior aid man...

I'm going into the trees too... dead gooks in the wire... tiger piss beer... claustrophobic rubber trees... we got beaucoup movement... bodies cut in half... fire for effect... get your shit together you're going out... doc, your replacement is here – you're going in... bugles blowing... pop smoke... di di mau, papa san... Medic!... FNG... death... village of the dead... number one... number ten... laughter... hot food... cold beers... gimmee the watch... tears... red mud... you got mail... cocoa mix in a package... I'm short!... we gotta get outta this place... lock and load... he's right on top of our heads... smoking a water pipe... just hold your finger there... winch him up...

No Xmas '69 for us... under the floorboards... pop frag... two wild pigs... something big and something bad... base defense... mama san... doc, should we call in the medevac chopper tonight?... snake in the hole... they're dead... we got step ons... we got line ones... Mac... Steve... and Mai... give her two aspirins... who's walking point?... doc, some chocolate man... Plunkett tripped... there's a gook on the roof...

Fence Post 7... General Motors 65... what's your sitrep... fire in the hole... I'm gonna frag tha muh-fucker... Thanh, I am so sorry... Chief, please don't go... goodbye, Six....

I pressed the palms of my hands against the cabin window, silently mouthing their individual names, calling out to my rapidly fading friends. I could not connect with them, I was unable to reach them or touch them. They had all drifted back, to remain in that very same past that I was so determined to leave behind me.

"Wha's it?" Someone was gently shaking me, informing me that we had begun descending into the Oakland area. Landing at last, back in the US of A.

I must have slept the entire flight, because I could not remember eating anything, or whether the cute flight attendant had sat in my lap or offered me her hand in marriage during the long trip over the pacific ocean. When we landed in California it was under such sunny skies, that I wondered for a moment if the whole damn thing wasn't just a bad dream.

As I stepped off the aircraft and walked into the arrivals area, I heard a Beach Boys song playing in the lobby. It was the one with the lyrics that go *"Round round get around I get around."*

But as we entered the terminal building the iron curtain of de-processing descended on us with a vengeance. The long arm of military officialdom was waiting for us to dampen our spirits as usual.

Some idle masochist had come up with the brilliant idea of organizing a *returnee delaying* "Welcome home" steak dinner for us followed by a "Welcome back" debriefing session.

"A debriefing what?" We groaned en masse. We gritted our teeth but weren't about to bear it.

"Shit, man! Give me a break!" I mumbled too loudly to the bespectacled, neatly dressed duty sergeant, who no doubt lived close by with *his* family in comfortable base housing.

"WE WANT TO GO HOME" we all insisted.

I only had a measly month off to depressurize and catch myself before I had to take up my reassignment duties at the 595th Medical Company at Fort Devens, Massachusetts, in the guaranteed-to-be-freezing winter month of December.

I was 21 years old. I came from a small, warm, Caribbean island that had been calling out to me and summoning me back home every night for the past year.

I had the remnants of a year's pay and overseas duty bonus in Uncle Sam's currency in my wallet waiting for dispensation, and they wanted me to stop here to eat a piece of beef and talk about America's future prospects in Vietnam?

Eventually, they left us alone. We never had those two unimaginably unnecessary pit stops to endure. It was the only time I recalled refusing a steak dinner though.

"This freaking army delaying shit," I grumbled, heading for the exit with the others. "You people better get to fu..."

"Hey, soldier, hey, hey!" The officious little NCO martinet jumped up from his chair blocking my path. He stood arms akimbo bristling in response to my insubordination. "You saying something to me, trooper?" he demanded threateningly.

Not taking chances with my reinstated freedom, now that the scents of my mother's cooking and the sea spray on Grand Anse beach were getting stronger, I replied, "Yeah Sarge, I was just saying how great it was to be back!"

Chapter 37

Fort Devens: Di Di Mau – Time to go Home

I landed at Logan airport in Massachusetts on an Eastern Airlines shuttle service from La Guardia Airport in New-York. It was December 1970, and it was alarmingly cold. Earlier, I had flown into JFK from Barbados, where I had made my connecting flight on a British West Indian Airways Boeing (B-707) jet. I had come into Barbados from Grenada on a much smaller LIAT inter-island turboprop aircraft that day, the last of my leave.

All of this because Grenada did not have an airport of the size capable of handling long-haul jet aircraft at the time. The route I took was the least complicated in those days, to get to the United States.

Actually, there was an occasion when I had travelled back to the U.S from a stint of leave at home, in an even more unconventional manner than described here. I had gone home to Grenada on a one-way ticket and had decided to hitch a ride back to mainland USA on a military flight out of Barbados.

The U.S Air-force operated a C-130 cargo freighter service out of Puerto-Rico that performed equipment maintenance and flight check duties for some of the islands like Barbados that had radar facilities.

Once I got to PR it would have been simple for me to make a commercial connection onwards to the mainland travelling military standby/ youth fare – costing a monetary pittance. Anything else was beyond my means. Eleventh hour frugality was necessary back then as I had customarily depleted my entire pay package on alcohol consumption and party activities whilst at home.

Nursing a two week long hangover I had not bothered myself with the details of my flight route back to the USA. Especially as the trip was free of charge.

So after making a lengthy stop at Coolidge airport in Antigua we had progressed on to yet another stop on my island hopping trek Northbound. Being a cargo flight with a paucity of creature comforts, there was no PA system to announce where we were landing. So that when I disembarked to take a stretch, my first awareness that I had landed on 'Papa Docs' territory was the faded terminal sign that proclaimed welcome to "Aeroport International De Francois Duvalier". Aha, so we were in Haiti. Hmnn.

The impression of Haiti that held sway in my mind was not the exploits of Toussaint L' Ouverture or even Henri Christophe (a fellow Grenadian), but that gripping 1967 movie adaption of Graham Greene's book "The Comedians", that starred movie luminaries Richard Burton and Elizabeth Taylor. The film had introduced me to the existence of the sun glasses sporting violence prone Haitian secret police called the Tonton Macoutes. Papa Doc's private army of swaggering bullies who regularly beat up or killed anyone who was opposed to any dictate of Duvalier's rule. 'So what me worry?'

Maybe plenty, due to my attire. Because as I descended from the aircraft to the tarmac, the first thing I saw was a group of swaggering chain-smoking young men wearing wrap-around sun glasses. Shambolic in looks they nevertheless oozed evil. They had honed in on me, or maybe I should say my uniform, like a swarm of bees to a honeycomb. They appeared to be ready to pounce.

The vibes they emitted were an unspoken threat that declared that they were loitering objectively - with a purpose, and that purpose was to cause harm.

Walking around the terminal environs wearing my potentially threatening US Army dress greens uniform was probably not a good idea.

When I made a bathroom pit stop or purchased some munchies from the restaurant, I kept bumping into this same group of humourless men who looked too much like the Tonton Macoutes in the movie Comedians' to be anything else but Tonton Macoutes. But this was not cinema.

They seemed to be stalking me in the sobering reality of the Caribbean sunshine. *You know something?* I had mused. *I better wait for my departure on board the plane.* So I had done so without further ado.

Back in the USA, an airport taxi from Logan airport to the Trailways bus terminal in Boston, and I was promptly on a bus headed to my next posting at Fort Devens.

Fort Devens was situated just outside of the cute little mill town of Ayer, Massachusetts. It was a small township about nine square miles in size in Middlesex County. Ayer was popular as a terminal junction for north-south and east-west railway connecting points. It was just 34 miles, or approximately 45 minutes, from the city of Boston by highway.

I was assigned to the 595th Medical Company, where I'd spend the final year of my three-year enlistment in the US Army. I was Specialist Five (SP-5), having been promoted in October just before leaving Vietnam. This was the equivalent of a Sergeant E-5 hard rank. I had returned from Vietnam only a month ago and had wasted no time heading home.

Back in Grenada, my close friends were very happy to help me spend my accumulated pay on parties and beach picnics, as fast as I could fork it out. The fact was, most of them were still in or barely out of school, with little pocket money. We all had a real good time feting together.

I would declare to my best friend, "Psycho," Chris, Tony Harford, Terrence, Selloe, Gerald, Arnold, and the three Cherman boys--Andre, Richie and Tony. "Come on, boys we're all going down to the BBC club tonight." Pool playing, beer drinking, and whatever else came up.

We would pile into my parents' car and go careening down the island's narrow roads, flying around the many hairpin bends in search of alcoholic fun and other forms of adult entertainment.

I couldn't get enough of anything. I was alive. I had survived. I would stop my parents speeding car, packed full of the guys, on the roadside. (By this stage, no one wanted to sit in the front seat next to me in any car I was driving). I would stop the car, lean over the drain and puke forcefully so as to make room for more alcohol consumption later.

Crazy, yes, but I felt as if I had been given a second chance, a reprieve, and therefore entitled to enjoy some of it as I saw fit before sorting out my life and moving on.

The greatest treat for my friends during my holiday home occurred whenever a car backfired nearby: I would dive headlong for cover, usually into the closest gutter. Great hilarity for them. For me, not so funny. It was clear it would take a little while for that residual fear and the necessary self-protection mechanism that had carried me through combat for a year, to relax its control over me.

But it was so good to be home. I avoided speaking about Vietnam, ingested the atmosphere of the island, ate some good food, like my favourite, Grenada's national dish "oil down", fish broth and curried conch. I drank and partied too much, but everyone understood and took good care of the homecoming boy who had ventured so far away and yet came back home alive.

My mother cried again, but with joy this time, as she told me the pain that she and my Aunty Olga went through each and every time they heard a news report about a helicopter being shot down in Vietnam.

I was invited back to my old school, the Grenada Boys Secondary School and I spoke to the boys in the assembly hall one morning. I couldn't tell you today what I may have told them then, but they had applauded warmly at the end of my speech.

Back at Fort Devens, I shared a room in the barracks with the company clerk, who was an SP-4, one rank below me, but the holder of a key job in the unit. He was a guy from Maine, called Leide. He was one of those people whose smile just could not ever seem to complete the trip from his lips to his eyes without first faltering hopelessly somewhere along that short route. Maybe he was just prejudiced about something. I spared few thoughts on what it could possibly be.

It was no more open barracks for me. I was a non-commissioned officer (NCO). The living accommodations were quite comfortable. I bought a small TV, and a hotplate to counteract the boredom of the mess hall meals. Some days, I ate in my room. Choices again.

Quartered next door to me was another SP-5 by the name of John Coleman. His was a sad story. John was from the Washington DC ghettoes, an area located curiously close to the seat of the greatest economic and military power in the Western world. His family had lived in poverty right there in the shadow of the oval office. He had to look after his five younger siblings at an early age because of an alcoholic father.

The army was his only way out of a life of disillusionment. But his earlier struggles had already taken their toll on him when I met him. John, at the young age of 25, was already himself completely lost to the vodka bottle. A very gentle and amusing guy when sober, he was a handful when not. He became one of my best friends during my posting at Fort Devens.

Later, when Leide (thankfully) sought and secured alternative accommodation, Don Costa, a Portuguese-American fellow medic, moved into my quarters and became my roommate. Stocky in build, Don had the same short fuse as my old Vietnam buddy, crazy Steve from California.

I spent many warm, family-oriented, fun-filled weekends with him and his pregnant wife, Cindy, at their home in Fall River, where I was introduced and became addicted to anchovy-garnished pizza and chorizo, a spicy, sausage-type condiment.

During this period at Devens, whenever I was off duty, I flew up to Toronto, Canada to spend my liberty weekends with some friends from Grenada--Georgie, Roger, Ronny, and Christopher, who had themselves just recently migrated to Canada. It cost me next to nothing, as my fare was military standby. Probably about as much as one would pay to ride a bus nowadays on the same route.

One night, or should I say early one morning, about 0300 hours, I was commuting between La Guardia and Logan airports on my way back to the base from Toronto. I was sitting in a small waiting room between flights. I was travelling on the Eastern Airlines' shuttle. My gaze kept returning to this tall familiar figure wearing a long trench coat. I didn't habitually stare at men, but there was something really familiar about this guy. He came off the connecting plane first, by himself, and boarded the shuttle first, a VIP.

He looked around at me sitting in the sparsely populated waiting room and noticed I'd been trying much too hard not to stare at him. He gave me a knowing smile that he must have dished out a thousand times before in similar circumstances. It was Burt Lancaster, the legendary tough guy actor of movie fame.

Most people of my generation agreed that, apart from maybe Kirk Douglas, Lancaster was probably the most versatile and enduring leading man of any age of cinema.

Three days later, on March 8, 1971, in the expectant company of my pals John Coleman and Don Costa, I made the reverent trek to the Boston arena to see on close circuit, big screen television another great man of the day known as Muhammad Ali take on Smoking Joe Frazier at Madison Square Garden for the undisputed World Heavyweight Boxing championship title. As we settled into our seats, the ringside announcer introduced the "guest" master of ceremonies for the night, "Mr. Burt Lancaster." That explained where he was going the other night.

I turned excitedly to my friends. "You know, guys, I met Burt the other night." They both looked at me and said, "Yeah, sure, Roge." I left it like that, because we had other pressing problems. Our hero, Ali, was regrettably and uncharacteristically losing the damn fight to a determined Smoking Joe. Joe was himself on a mission towards spoiling somebody's party with an upset decision.

Ali's three-year suspension by the boxing authorities because of his refusal to be drafted into the Army was simply too long (I was sure old Whitlock would have had a lengthy opinion on this too). It had taken the edge off the master's craft. He would be back, though, of this we had no doubt.

We left the Boston arena emotionally drained. There were feelings of loss and frustration running through our disappointed and heart-broken minds. This was 1971. This was Ali - Muhammad Ali was nothing short of a sporting God figure. WE all loved him. He was a flamboyant fighter who was built like an Adonis.

And he had successfully defied the mighty US of A by his refusal to submit himself to the military draft board. This bold stance appealed to all young people of the time, *whether they were in uniform or not.*

Joe Frazier had won; probably the best fight Ali or anyone had ever fought. Joe went directly from the ring, stretcher borne to an area hospital to be treated for excessive fatigue and a concussion. Ali, after giving post-fight interviews to his adoring fans, visited "the winner" later that day at the hospital to congratulate him and to mess with his head a little bit.

It was the weekend back on post, and most of us were off duty. It was early enough in the month so that we weren't all entirely broke just yet, only almost. But we were having a party. To be honest, a "drink up."

There was an old apartment complex located across some rusty old railroad tracks in a section of town that had definitely seen better times. Some of the guys from the base had apartments in this ramshackle building, which could not pass any serious inspection of any kind. There were also some older, harder prostitutes living there. But we stayed far away from them for obvious health reasons. The rent was cheap, so one or two of the guys had girlfriends staying there. What the apartments really provided for us was a convenient party venue.

We were all gathered in Pegher's apartment. He was our new company clerk. Pegher was a compact, fastidious guy who took over the job from my former roommate, Leide. Leide did not like the fact that I drank and smoked, or that all of the guys would end up in our room watching TV and singing until ungodly hours of the morning on most nights. Leide was a goodly, quiet Christian boy, or so he claimed. My friends and I were admittedly not, at that point in time.

The group at Pegher's comprised my friend John Coleman, who was already well plastered even before the party began, Don Costa, Randy Squires a tall, lanky redneck from Tennessee and his downtrodden wife, Alice. Randy was yet another booze affected soldier. He suffered the same affliction as John did. Unfortunately, he drank as many beers as he could get his hands on, every day.

Tony Alfonco, an Italian-American with dark, disheveled good looks, was also there. Tony was fated to become a mafia goodfella when he returned to his Boston home after the army. He spoke in undertones and never fucked around. He wanted me to come and stay with him for a while after we both got out of the service in a few months…

By the way, my name was Roger again, known as Roge to all. I was no longer called "Doc," and never would be again unless I applied to medical school. We were all medics anyway, though only two of us were Vietnam vets, Don and I.

It was a cold winter's night, and we lay sprawled in the old, crumbling, under-heated apartment getting drunk and watching the New York Yankees beat up on the Seattle Mariners. Although not exactly out of the blue, because he had been growing ever more belligerent and baiting everyone for the past hour or so, Randy announced very loudly, enough so anyone in the neighboring counties could hear, "I hate niggers, and I hate all spicks. Fuck all niggers and all spicks, too, for that matter present company included!"

We were soldiers, and we tended to play rough. Some of us had only recently returned from a shooting war, and we were all drunk. So our mental fuses were a bit short, and we didn't take too much shit from anyone under most circumstances.

Tony and Don moved first. Tables, chairs, bottles, and glasses overturned in the mad scramble for Randy's redneck ass.

Just as Tony's quick fingers encircled Randy's throat, poor Alice, his wife, made the mistake of telling her alcohol-demented husband, "Please don't say those awful things, Randy. Please behave."

He gave her a back-handed slap that sent her up and over the couch she was sitting on.

No one in the room was fond of woman beaters. It was an unwritten "no no" within our group. Randy was in for it. He was one of those "brave" men who frequently fought with women, and won, but was always hesitant to duke it out with another man.

"Oh God! Randy, don't!" Alice shrieked.

"Let me at that motherfucker," Don yelled. Don was fast, and he threw Randy onto the ground. He then jumped on before pounding his head into the carpet.

Pegher was aghast, jumping up, too, scared and yelling, "Don! Watch it with his head. I can't afford to get blood on the new carpet, the landlord will kill me."

Somebody was pounding on the ceiling from the apartment below in perfect time with the thud, thud, thud of Randy's head striking the landlord's new carpet covered floor.

John sprang up, awakened by the double pounding. He stumbled out the door and yelled down the steps.

"If you people want to join the party, bring beer and ice. If not, then shut the fuck up with your rude pounding. You're disturbing us up here. I was trying to get some sleep."

John had slept through the entire earlier assault. He hadn't noticed Randy, blue in the face, having his head pounded in.

Alice was shrieking. "You all are going to kill him; you're going to kill my husband." The rest of us sitting on the couch chuckled – "we hope so!" We sure as fuck hoped so!

Women arghh! It never ceased to amaze me. Here was a physically and mentally abused woman witnessing her tormentor getting his comeuppance. So what did she do? She pleaded her head off in fear for his lousy life.

Randy was now begging for Don to stop. We reluctantly pulled Don off. That piece-of-shit redneck was simply not worth it. And Don's wife was pregnant, after all.

* * * * *

A few days later, I left with Don to spend the weekend with him and Cindy in Fall River. Their place was about a two and a half hour drive to the south. Don and I got a ride with another Fall River native, agreeing to help pay for gas. The car erupted with laughter as I explained to our driver where "John the juicer" was sleeping while Don was choking Randy at this crazy party.

Since all the chairs and couches in the old apartment had been overturned during the rumpus, John was actually snoozing on the large dining room table, dead to the world, until the double hammering began.

The table was apparently the only piece of furniture that had managed to remain upright and stable. We were also still trying to figure out just who the hell had invited redneck Randy to the weekend party in the first place.

At any rate, we got to Fall River in good time. Don and Cindy had an apartment on the top floor of a building in the town itself. Quite cosy and comfortably furnished. Don's father-in-law, Fernando, was a bartender at the neighborhood bar. A really jovial and kind man who was also very gay. My view was always that people's sexual orientation was theirs to choose, so for me it was not the issue it might have been with others I knew from the Caribbean.

Fernando plied Don and me with extraordinary amounts of free beer. We were generally quite happy and feeling no pain when we got back to the apartment to enjoy Cindy's delicious non-military home cooking.

Don and Cindy had been high-school sweethearts and were, as far as I could tell, happily married. She was a demur, petite woman with dark hair and brown eyes. He, as I mentioned before, was a rough and tumble kind of guy. They made a wonderful couple, maybe because they were kind of opposites.

Cindy and I got along really well, and Don always got me to talk to her on his behalf when he was in the doghouse. When he went home alone, he complained about having to lug loads of food back to the base for me from his wife. Just who the hell was the husband here? He'd mutter to himself on the long drive. Cindy, of course, was always trying to set me up with a nice girl.

I was eventually paired off with Cindy's friend Donna, a nice girl of about 20 years of age from the neighbourhood. Donna and I hit it off pretty well, and we all went out to an amusement park and had a good time on the rides. When we got back to Don and Cindy's place, we had my favourite chorizo or chourico sausage and a large anchovy-laden pizza, by now ritual food when I was with them.

Donna and I retired to the couch after Don and Cindy went to bed, to get better acquainted. This aim we managed to accomplish to our mutual satisfaction until about 0300 in the morning. I then walked her home. She lived only a couple blocks away.

I had to be careful not to lock myself out of the apartment again, which I somehow did on previous occasions after being out with Donna or another girl I had dated.

Next day, Don, Cindy, Donna, and I visited the World War II battleship *USS Massachusetts*. The ship, berthed at Fall River, was a historical museum sight and popular tourist attraction. It was a massive and impressive wonder.

When you went below decks and entered a compartment, prerecorded tapes of shouting sailors getting ready for high-sea battles echoed realistically throughout the area. This brought back warm and familiar childhood memories of the days when I ran down the hillside in St. George's with my friends to greet British naval vessels that came into the inner harbour to dock. This had been the beginning of my infatuation with the military.

My Fall River weekends usually revolved around drinking too much beer at Fernando's bar, eating too much of Cindy's delicious spicy food, and spending some good times on the couch with the charming Donna on evenings. It was not a bad life at all, while it lasted.

We normally left Fall River at about 0330 hours for the drive back to Fort Devens, to get back in time for reveille at 0600.

I had been made responsible for a squad of men because of my E-5, or sergeant, rank. I had to get back in time to get their lazy asses up for formation. We were still in the army.

The end of my enlistment was in sight for me now, but my life was beginning to unravel a bit too fast. I had always been a conscientious and disciplined soldier. But lately I had been falling down on the job. I had been hanging out with and was being influenced too much by the would-be Mafioso, Alfonco.

The other night at the post cinema, (movie theatre on base) we sat through the playing of the national anthem while everyone else was standing at attention, hands over hearts, of course. We were promptly arrested by the post MPs and dragged off in cuffs to the brig.

Our company commander, Captain Grimsby, who knew me in Vietnam, had to come for us to secure our release. He told me personally afterwards that I was drowning in bad company, which I knew to be true. He also warned me that I was beginning to wear thin my exemplary status in the unit as a decorated war veteran. I had to cool it, he said.

A couple of days before, Alfonco and I had walked past a group of officers and did not salute them. We were not arrested on that occasion but pointedly told to shape up. Could be I was tired of being responsible, the guy you could always depend on when the chips were down? Fuck it! Let somebody else carry the weight.

We had endless barrack parties almost every night. There were weekend trips into Boston, where we headed straight to the newly opened Playboy club. My pay cheque would be spent in one night. I was waking up in some dangerous parts of the city that I could not remember going to sleep in, too often, with barely enough money left for bus fare to get back on post in time for reveille. And I was a squad leader in charge of a whole squad of men, subordinates who expected a much better example from me than what I was showing them.

I was rapidly evolving into someone I didn't admire or even recognized anymore. One day I found myself behind the orderly room sparring in a ring encircled by a group of jeering men. Why was I fighting John Coleman, one of my best friends? The guy was a drunk. What were we fighting for? Even if I knew then, I wouldn't remember later.

I let my hands fall limply to my sides and walked dejectedly away from the fight, which felt more like an organized brawl. I was disgusted with myself. How could I ever think of hitting John, of all people? I was suffocating. It was time for me to go home, and soon too.

Knowing the end was near was not all that bad, and eventually over a period of weeks of soul-searching I managed to rally, to pull myself up by the boot straps, and put a check on my runaway partying. I also put some distance between John Coleman, Alfonco the Mafioso and myself.

Those two were going to get me killed if I wasn't more careful. I realized this fact, though it took some time. I put in the same effort to pull up my socks that I put in during basic training to max the PCPT test. I did this by completely altering my life style.

Subsequently, on most evenings, my new routine consisted of Pegher, the company clerk with the blood-splotched living room carpet, my roommate Don and me going into Ayer to play a game of pool in a quiet and comfortable neighborhood bar.

We listened to soothing James Taylor and Gordon Lightfoot songs while we drank cold brews and snacked on pickled eggs and pizza. At last I could boast that I had found something that I could write home to tell my Mum about that did not require prolific censorship.

There was also a shop in Ayer that made the best submarine sandwiches anywhere. When you opened the door and stepped in from the winter cold into the warm, well-lit interior, the smell that assailed your senses was simply wonderful. Their roast beef, tuna with melted cheese, ham and cheese and meatballs sandwiches, were all delightful in taste and large in size.

I was becoming a really good pool player, though one would never have guessed from my win-loss record. Both Pegher and Don had worked in pool halls in their pre-army civilian lives. They normally ran the table unless they were distracted by a pretty girl entering the bar just as they broke the rack. In which case, they would then smartly wrap up the game in two or three more shots.

Because I always lost to them, I never realized how good I was until I racked up with mere mortals like myself when I got back home.

I was appointed the re-enlistment NCO, and I had my own fine office at the company administrative department, but I was not about to win any prizes for successful retention rates. The fact that I was not staying in myself made it a bit awkward to encourage others to re-up. I'd only re-enlisted one lifer so far, who was going to stay in the service on his own accord anyway.

I tried to discourage Pegher and some of my other friends who I liked a lot from volunteering for Vietnam duty. I saw that familiar glint in their eyes when they looked at my medals. I knew the respect and the awe with which they sometimes referred to me as a battle-experienced veteran and survivor of *the war*.

They thought of me as a war hero, because telling a few war stories was inevitable. I remembered that there was no stopping me when I wanted to go, so I understood. But I still advised them not to do it. They were my friends and I did not want them to spill their blood over there-for what?

They would never understand blood death and occupied body bags unless they were part of it. By then, it would be too late for some of them to reconsider volunteering. Maybe the war would end before they got shipped over there. I really hoped so.

Then, on a chilly day in November of 1971 the hour glass emptied. The time for me to go home had arrived. My three year enlistment in the U.S Army was up.

It had been a fantastic ride. As a soldier, I'd had my war, and I had seen another world. It was time for me to di di mau, to get off my three year roller coaster ride, intact.

But as I prepared to leave the United States Army for good, little did I know that the Army was not about to leave me, completely. Not just yet.

Chapter 38

Full Circle: Operation Urgent Fury (1983)

At 0500 hours on the morning of October 25, 1983, the United States' armed forces invaded the Caribbean island of Grenada. An attack upon my homeland, the country of my birth was underway. This was home, the place I had returned to, to live again, after spending three years as a soldier in this very same invading force's army.

Six days earlier, on October 19, Grenada's popular Marxist Prime Minister, Maurice Bishop, was overthrown in a bloody coup. He was mercilessly executed along with some of his loyal cabinet ministers after being deposed by hardcore left-wing elements in his own political party who had earlier taken control of the island's armed forces.

American President Ronald Reagan, a long-time opponent of the Bishop administration because of its close ties to Cuba, seized this opportunity to divert a flotilla of ships and manpower already at sea. They had been steaming towards Lebanon in the wake of a suicide bombing of a U.S marine barracks there that had claimed the lives of 242 U.S marines.

This task force was re-directed to Grenada to urgently "rescue" approximately 1000 mainly American students attending an American offshore medical school, The St. George's University School of Medicine.

U.S paratroopers landed at the uncompleted Point Salines International airport. U.S marines came ashore on landing craft, hitting the white sand beaches on the island's western side. The horizon was obliterated by a huge task force of naval vessels of every description that ringed the entire island's coastline.

At the airport construction site, armed Cuban construction workers put up a fierce resistance against the numerically superior invading forces. The Cubans had been building the airport for the Grenadian government.

Since the Grenada revolution of March 13th 1979, Cuba and Fidel Castro in particular had been a big supporter of the new government, providing both material and requisite manpower for the ambitious dream of the construction of an international airport on the island.

I had left Grenada 15 years before to join the US Army to fight in the distant reaches of Vietnam and Cambodia. It was some 12 years after I had hung up my army dress greens uniform in my bedroom closet. Naturally, I experienced a potpourri of conflicting emotions concerning the invasion of my country.

How had my life evolved after I left Fort Devens in November of 1971? I was now a commercial pilot. I took the opportunity to go to flying school on the GI Bill and had obtained a commercial pilot's license with a multi-engine and an instrument rating at Embry Riddle Aeronautical University in Daytona Beach, Florida.

I returned home to the Caribbean after qualifying and flew for a charter company called Tropicair for a while, flying celebrities like Mick Jagger, Elton John and her Royal Highness Princess Margaret of Great Britain between

Barbados and the exclusive tropical hideaway of the rich and famous - the island of Mustique in the Grenadines. I joined LIAT, the inter-island airline, sometime after, and flew with that company until 1980.

After the Grenada revolution, Prime Minister Maurice Bishop, whom I had known personally and shared certain family ties with (as is normal in small island life), offered me a job to fly his private turbo prop executive aircraft, a gift from his friend Fidel. At the time I was flying for LIAT and based in Barbados where I had been recently transferred from LIAT's Antigua base.

I jumped at this opportunity. I was not very happy at LIAT, and more importantly I was looking for an opportunity to leave and to return home anyway. Here was my chance, so I did not hesitate.

During this period of my life, three very important and profound things happened to me. I was fortunate to meet a special woman from my own country and sensibly married her. We had two daughters, both of whom were as precious to me as life itself. Finally, we were able to purchase our own home, which is located on the sun-blessed and breezy side of a mountain called Morne Jaloux (Jealous Mountain). The property has a breathtaking view of both the Atlantic ocean and the Caribbean Sea.

A couple days after the sad events of October 19th which culminated in our Prime Minister's brutal death, I had been relaxing, having some beers with the guys in Batson's shop, a popular 'watering hole' in my neighborhood. It was a few days after the U.S forces had generally secured the island.

The Prime Minister of the country and a few other Ministers had been brutally executed. Some of them were my friends. In the main, they were good people. Most of the country was still in a state of shock at their sudden and savage demise. It was a small community, and their losses were heartfelt and personal. Not to everyone, obviously, but to many including myself.

Because of Grenada's dependence on tourism, the international airport project was by far the largest capital undertaking in the country's history.

Its completion and eventual operation was likened to the effect of the railroads on the settling and expansion of the US' western territories.

The government of the day also had ambitious education and welfare programs in the works. I supported all of this when the Prime Minister was alive. With his sudden death, it was all over. The wind had been driven out of the sails of Grenada's revolutionary experiment.

Three U.S military personnel entered Batson's shop for some refreshments. They struck up a relaxed and easy conversation with the people in the establishment. I was speaking to the officer in charge, a major, when his radio squawked.

His RTO took the message, then passed the handset to the major. Something was discussed heatedly. The major seemed eventually to concede some point to the caller. He then turned towards me and said, "Are you the same Roger Byer who was Prime Minister Bishop's personal pilot?"

"Yes, I am." I replied.

The major shrugged. He was a soldier, and he apparently had orders. Orders that involved me.

"Roger Byer, I have to take you in for questioning," he then said to me. "Your name is on a special list, as you were the Prime Minister's personal pilot. I tried to tell headquarters that I'd spoken to you and that I was convinced that you were not involved in any resistance activities, but they wouldn't budge. I'm sorry."

I sent a hurried message up the hill to my wife by some of the local guys. I didn't even know where they were taking me, or for what reason.

So I am arrested at home by the same people that had awarded me the Purple Heart and Bronze Star medals just a few years before; now I was to be interrogated by them?

I had to drive my own car. The major sat in front with me, and two soldiers with M-16 automatic rifles (my old weapon that I still had fond memories of) sat in the back seat, covering me no doubt. I felt captured and helpless.

We drove down to the Point Saline's airport construction site, where the friendly major formally handed me over to the military intelligence unit for interrogation. They had built in a not surprisingly fast time a penal-type camp that was heavily strung with barbed wire, severely enclosed and impressively re-enforced.

The major made sure, subtly, that the detention people were aware I was a Vietnam veteran. He then reassured me that I should be released promptly once the necessary paperwork had been sorted out. It was beginning to get dark. Somehow, I doubted I'd be home in time for supper.

The major reluctantly handed me over to the large military policeman on duty, who seemed to want to hit someone. I was handcuffed, a formality, they claimed, but another first for me. The situation was deteriorating.

I was directed to a bench to sit and wait for my interrogator to arrive. But I was not unduly uncomfortable at this stage, because I had not committed any offence and had nothing to hide.

The only disturbing matter, as I looked around me with some trepidation, was the presence of a long row of about

40 small, wooden, cage-like structures. Coming from inside of them was loud, frenzied banging, hysterical shouts, and streams of swearing.

I realized with some discomfort that they were keeping prisoners inside of those boxes, which looked like outhouses. An uptight military intelligence major, very unlike the one from earlier, arrived to question me. No rough stuff, but after wasting my time by asking for and listening patiently to my entire story, the intelligence officer started quizzing me with a series of probing questions, like what part of Libya did I train in -throwing out sprats to catch whales, as we would say locally.

When your only story was the truth, it was easy to stick to it. I held to the simple uncomplicated reality that I was the government's pilot, and that when I was not flying the government's plane I also worked at the local civil aviation office on the Carenage, where I spent my days seeking opportunities for young Grenadians to train abroad as air traffic controllers and meteorological officers to man the new (yet to be completed) Point Salines airport. So sorry, but I had no military secrets about the island's defenses to reveal.

About eight hours later, after plenty of phone calls (and, I was sure, positive reassurances), the clarification of questions asked and answers given, the major said gruffly, "OK, Mr. Byer, you check out all right. Everything is fine. You may go now."

It was good not to be considered a threat by the army you once served loyally, but it was also 0200 hours, so I replied, "if it's alright with you, sir, I would rather just sit here quietly, and wait until daylight to depart."

The reason for my strange refusal to accept the offer of immediate freedom was based on experience. I was a veteran, so I understood where I was. We were in the middle of a tense war-zone situation, at two o'clock on a dark and seemingly unfriendly morning.

The whole area was dug up with trenches and fox holes for the defensively emplaced and hunkered down soldiers. There were no landmarks or road signs anywhere. The troopers out here would be young, jumpy and scared. I definitely knew that.

There was still some sporadic small-arms firing around the area, most likely triggered off by those same young, jumpy and scared sentries. No other vehicles were moving in the entire area at that hour, and he wanted me to go out there all alone, driving a civilian vehicle, exposing myself like a drone target?

I had lived through similar circumstances before in faraway places. There was a curfew on for civilians, and illumination flares were being popped repeatedly all over the place to spot any out-of-bounds civilian, like me: To shoot dead first, then answer awkward questions from my grieving relatives about my regrettable demise later, if at all.

So I refused to leave. That was until the major unclipped his .45 pistol from its holster, and indicated to me through gritted teeth that he had had a very long day. He further declared: "I told you to leave this facility, and I mean fucking now!" He yelled, "Get your ass out of here Mr. Byer, right now!"

Put that way, I carefully reconsidered my options. They were scant. Maybe I'd better go. "Ok, I'm off your compound, sir," I limply replied. I'd been there before. I'd take my chances out there again. My past seemed to be in dog step with me. It was déjà vu time.

Shades of the bunker on FSB David with the stretcher case or that stinking alley in Saigon, 13 long years ago, with

Steve Mac and the brazen kid. A little piss ass threatening our lives for a watch.

If those guys could see me in this situation, *at home,* what would they think? "Doc, how could you find yourself in that shit again?" They'd probably laugh their heads off at my circumstances.

Illumination flares were going off all over the area as I exited the compound scrunched down low in my car seat. I drove around disoriented in the dark in ever widening circles. There was no discernible roadway or guiding signs to tell one how to get out of that place.

I was promptly halted by nervous, stressed out, belligerent, and sleep-deprived soldiers stationed too far away from home. The scenario was not a good one for me.

I tried to recall how I would have felt—did feel—in their situation, but I was too damn tired for all that mind shit.

"What the fuck are you doing out here at this hour? Get out of that fucking car and down on the ground now."

"Spread 'em, hold your hands out where we can see them!"

"Are you crazy or suicidal?"

"Man, what the fuck are you doing driving around by yourself at this time of the morning?"

I respond "but I've just been released…"

I was stopped about eight times.

The soldiers yelled at me in a concerted babble of excited voices. But I understood what was going down. I just wished I didn't have to carry out my end of the discussion spread-eagled on the wet and filthy ground under wavering gun muzzles controlled by itchy trigger fingers. I showed them my detention release papers. They let me up and advised me to get going, again. The very thing they had been preventing me from doing for the past half-hour. Christ!

I reached my mother-in-law's home later that morning, emotionally drained and physically spent. My wife, Ermine, and my daughters, Mandy and Stacey greeted me warmly and anxiously. Everything was okay again, if only because they were still securely in my life, just waiting for me to come home to them.

* * * * *

Two days later, Eddie, my niece Andrea's boyfriend and later husband, agreed to take the chance to go with me to check on our house at Morne Jaloux. We'd been all--my whole extended family--hunkered down at my mother's house in Belmont, which was located about two miles from our own property, about a ten-minute drive away.

Eddie and I took about two hours to get up to the house. We were stopped about twelve times by patrolling U.S forces along the way, sometimes roughed up a bit: Made to lie face down on the hot asphalt by the surly troopers because they thought we were Cubans.

We were both relatively light skinned in complexion, especially me. Faulty US intelligence had told their soldiers to look out specifically for lighter skinned people who would in most cases be marauding Cuban renegades.

When we got close to my house, a squad of US Army soldiers were carrying out routine house-to-house searches in the neighborhood. Things were a bit tenser than usual up there because the Cuban embassy that was still occupied, was located just around the corner from where I lived, about 200 metres away from my house.

Tattooed Memories

I let the soldiers into my house with my keys to forestall them opening my front door with their boots. As they made their routine checks, I began to examine the damage done to my verandah's screened glass sliding door.

Our house was situated high on a hill. When U.S navy jets operating from the offshore aircraft carriers made their bombing runs at the nearby local army base, Camp Fedon—located at Calivigny just to the south of my home, they had all lined up over our house for their final target runs. The resultant vibrations from their repeated low overhead passes had forcefully torn the verandah's sliding door up and out of its metal tracks, breaking the large pane of glass in the process.

I recalled other U.S jets over another hill, this one a battle ravaged hill in Tay Ninh province. Jet fighters making long, sweeping bombing runs on a misleadingly beautiful January day as we hastily retreated down bloody slopes after a costly firefight.

"Hey Sarge!" An excited shout came from inside of the house, jerking me out of my reverie. "Jesus, Sergeant, come and see this!"

What now, I thought, as we scurried inside in the direction of the alarmed voice.

Standing in my bedroom in front of an open closet, was a private first class. He was gingerly holding up my U.S Army full dress greens uniform jacket with its four and a half rows of assorted medals and decorations, overseas bars and unit citations ostentatiously displayed on it.

He seemed completely enthralled by his discovery, examining the jacket as if he had stumbled across Jason's Golden Fleece or the Holy Grail.

The insignias worn on the uniforms of the soldiers milling around my bedroom, were identical to the ones that stood out boldly on my uniform jacket's sleeves. The platoon sergeant's eyes blazed and his nostrils flared, his head swiveled around threateningly, reminding me of the snake on LZ Prudence. He barked to the room's occupants at large, "Just who the fuck does this jacket belong to?"

I paused before answering, sensing that the tide was about to turn in my favour here. I looked over at the sergeant and calmly replied, "it's mine."

The day immediately brightened. Soldiers inspecting adjoining properties were immediately called over. "Come and take a look at this," their buddies said to them.

"You won't believe what we found here, in a house on a hill on a Caribbean island." It didn't always feel that way, but, yes, it was a small world after all.

When we were ready to leave, the sergeant who was in a far more cooperative mood now, suggested, "take that jacket with you, it will save you some hassles on the way back." This turned out to be good advice, because as we passed the same twelve check points on the way back down, I drove while Eddie held my uniform jacket out of the car window. We did not have to stop, not once.

All those guys from my past adventures, my military family, their presence was suddenly very tangible, front and centre in my thoughts.

I embraced the memories as they fluttered through my mind, but I had come full circle here, and I could now put my military adventures to bed for good.

But Six, Mac, or crazy Steve, where were they in the world today? "Any of you guys interested in going out for a cold brew tonight?" I would ask if I was lucky to see any of them again one day, say, walking along the Carenage in St. George's after disembarking from a visiting cruise ship.

Because I had known them so well, I expected that the reply to my invitation would be "Sure, doc, but where are we going out to misbehave?" Without missing a beat, I would respond "What do you guys mean by *where*? Down to the Old New York Tavern Club, that's WHERE!"

It would have to be the good old New York Tavern Club for our reunion to be meaningful. Although, in retrospect, chances were slim that we would have been welcomed back at the tavern club. Because on most of the nights that we patronized that establishment, for some unfathomable reason, the owners always threw us out, well before closing time.

*

POSTSCRIPT

Some forty two years after the experiences I related in this book occurred, I succeeded in getting in touch with my former Company Commander William Vowell, now a Colonel US Army (Ret).

He was able to give me some wonderful news. He told me that my good friend Francis "Chief" Billy had fortuitously survived the NVA ground attack on LZ Illingworth, the Firebase he had been transferred to from our Company in 1970.

The enemy assault on LZ Illingworth had claimed the lives of our compatriots Lieutenant Cleve Bridgman (F/O) and SP4 Bob Layne. "Chief", who was previously reported as KIA, along with Bridgman and Layne, had in fact survived the enemy incursion, and had made it safely back home from the war.

I also learned that some of the guys from our unit, Charlie Company, led by Lieutenant Dan Barlow, had visited Chief in Navajo country Arizona some years ago, and that they had found him to be of sound mind and body.

RB. (Aug 2012)

*

GLOSSARY

Aid Station – Small medical treatment facility.
AIT – Advanced individual training.
AK-47 – Russian/Chinese assault rifle.
AOP – Area of operations.
APC – Armored personnel carrier.
ARVN – Army of the Republic of Vietnam.
Arc-Light – Heavy aerial bombardment.
Basic – Mandatory initial training for all soldiers.
B-40 – Rocket-propelled grenade launcher.
Beaucoup – Many.
Bird – Aircraft, but especially helicopters.
Blue Max – Helicopter attack gunship.
Boondocks – Jungle/Forest.
C-130 – Type of troop-carrier aircraft.
C-4 – Plastic explosive.
Cs or C-Rations – Army food in cans.
Charlie – NVA, or Vietcong.
Chinook – Type of transport helicopter.
Chopper – Helicopter.
Claymore – Anti-personnel mine.
Cobra – Heavily armed helicopter gunship.
Contact – Sudden Enemy engagement.
CO – Commanding officer.
CP – Command post.
CQ – Charge of quarters.
DI – Drill instructor.
Di di mau – Let's go, or get away!
Dustoff – Medical evacuation helicopter.
Fire mission – Artillery or naval fire called in to support ground troops.

FNG – Fucking new guy.
F/O – Forward Observer
Frag - Fragmentation hand grenade.
FSB – Fire support base.
GI – Government issue, but refers primarily to an American soldier.
Gook – Derogatory name for a Vietnamese.
Ground Attack – Massed Infantry attack on an Installation.
Grunt – American foot soldier.
Hootch – Native building.
Huey – UH-1 series helicopter.
Hump – Route march.
Incoming – Enemy bombardment coming into a targeted base.
In-country – In Vietnam.
KIA – Killed in action.
Klick – Kilometre.
KP – Kitchen police.
LAW – Light anti- tank weapon.
Lifer – Career soldier.
Line One – U.S casualty
Low Quarter – Dress uniform shoes; Personnel living in comfort in the rear areas.
LRRPs – Long-range reconnaissance patrols.
LZ – landing zone.
Mama san – Older Vietnamese woman.
Medevac – Medical evacuation helicopter.
Mess hall – Army eating facility.
Montagnard – Cambodian tribespeople, now known as the Hmong.
MOS – Military Occupational Specialty.
Movement – Signal that enemy is physically close by.
MP – Military Police.
M-16 – US automatic assault rifle.

M-14 – US assault rifle with bolt action.
M-60 – Belt fed U.S assault machinegun.
No.1 – Vietnamese slang for good.
No.10 – Vietnamese slang for bad.
NVA – North Vietnamese Army.
Papa san – Older Vietnamese man.
PCPT – Physical Combat Proficiency Test.
PFC – Private First Class.
Point Man – Soldier walking at the front of a unit on patrol.
PRC-25 – A field radio.
REMF – Rear-echelon motherfucker.
RPG – Rifle-propelled grenade.
R&R – Rest and Recuperation liberty.
RTO – Radio telephone operator.
Sapper – Base penetrator, satchel charge bearing attacker.
Short – Little time left on tour of duty.
SITREP – Situation report.
Step on – Enemy casualty.
Sticks – Jungle.
TOC – Tactical operations command.
Top – First Sergeant.
VC – Vietcong.
World – Anywhere outside of Vietnam.

Vietnam War Combat Deaths

U.S Forces   -   58,159.
A.R.V.N   -   223,748.
N.V.A / VC   -   1,100,000.

About the Author

Roger Byer was born on the Caribbean island of Grenada. For a number of years he was recognized as one of Grenada's best competition cyclists. In 1968, after graduating from secondary (high school), he enlisted in the US Army.

One year after his enlistment he was deployed overseas where he experienced combat in both the Vietnam and Cambodian wars. He spent his one year stint in South East Asia serving as a combat medic with an infantry line company of the First Air Cavalry Division.

After completing his military service, he attended Embry Riddle Aeronautical University in the U.S, compliments of the GI bill education program, and obtained the required certification to qualify as a commercial pilot.

He worked as a pilot in the Caribbean for about seven years, first with a charter company, Tropical Air Services, then with the regional airline LIAT, before returning to Grenada in 1980 to fly Prime Minister Maurice Bishop's personal executive aircraft.

Roger is married and has two grown daughters. He still lives on his island home of Grenada, where he works in the field of real estate when not practicing his writing skills.

Made in the USA
Columbia, SC
13 February 2022